'This is the "masters and apprentices" book of compliance – practical insights for the professional and lay person alike.'
Christopher Wright, Head of Compliance, LafargeHolcim

'The authors of this book succeeded in explaining precisely, pleasantly and in an easily understandable way what everybody should know and practice in compliance and ethics. Nobody may say any more: "I didn't know how to do it".'
François Vincke, Member of the Brussels Bar, Vice-chair, ICC Commission on Corporate Responsibility and Anti-corruption, and former General Counsel, Petrofina

'The engaging style of this book will take its audience beyond the word "compliance" – seen as so negative by so many. In coupling it with ethics, and recommending the head of function should be called the Chief Ethics and Compliance Officer (CECO), it demonstrates how to win over hearts and minds. The stories are a useful and practical way to make the learning more memorable and therefore effective. The authors are to be commended for their approach in delivering a must read for every CECO.'
Philippa Foster Back CBE, Director, Institute of Business Ethics

'The authors have created a book that is as valuable as any to date in explaining how to create a successful and effective compliance programme. Just as importantly, the book provides the right balance between ethics and values on the one hand and compliance programme elements on the other in discussing what works and what hasn't. Brilliantly written and easy to understand, it provides meaningful insight for both the experienced compliance professional and newcomers to the field. It masterfully weaves real stories and anecdotes into the materials in an entertaining way, bringing the discussion to life. Destined to become a classic in the compliance literature, it is required reading for anyone on the compliance journey.'

Keith M Korenchuk, VP and Chief Compliance Officer, Diagnostic Platform, Danaher Corporation/Beckman Coulter Inc., and former partner, Arnold & Porter LLP

The Business Guide to Effective Compliance and Ethics

*Why Compliance isn't working –
and how to fix it*

Andrew Hayward
Tony Osborn

KoganPage

Publisher's note

Every possible effort has been made to ensure that the information contained in this book is accurate at the time of going to press, and the publishers and authors cannot accept responsibility for any errors or omissions, however caused. No responsibility for loss or damage occasioned to any person acting, or refraining from action, as a result of the material in this publication can be accepted by the editor, the publisher or the authors.

First published in Great Britain and the United States in 2019 by Kogan Page Limited

2nd Floor, 45 Gee Street	122 W 27th St, 10th Floor	4737/23 Ansari Road
London	New York, NY 10001	Daryaganj
EC1V 3RS	USA	New Delhi 110002
United Kingdom		India

www.koganpage.com

ISBNs

Hardback	978 0 7494 8780 5
Paperback	978 0 7494 8297 8
Ebook	978 0 7494 8298 5

British Library Cataloguing-in-Publication Data

A CIP record for this book is available from the British Library.

Library of Congress Cataloging-in-Publication Number

2019022460

Typeset by Integra Software Services, Pondicherry
Print production managed by Jellyfish
Printed and bound by CPI Group (UK) Ltd, Croydon, CR0 4YY

CONTENTS

List of figures and tables xii
Preface xiii
About the authors xvii
Acknowledgements xix
How to use this book xxi

PART ONE

01 Why compliance isn't working 5

Fatal flaws and collateral damage 5
Culture 7
How to be ineffective 7
'Defensible compliance' 9
Compliance as impediment: doing the legal minimum 10
The Age of Damage 11
Making compliance effective 12
What creates effective compliance? 13
Zero harm 14
Compliance, culture and ethics 14
In a nutshell 15
10 reasons why compliance fails 17
Note 20

02 The meaning, origins and role of compliance and ethics 21

Why have compliance? 21
Compliance: a short history 22
What is 'compliance'? 29
What are 'ethics'? 30
What about 'business ethics'? 32

What is 'integrity'? 34
Compliance and ethics in practice 35
So, what is a 'compliance and ethics programme'? 37
The consequences of failure 38
The rewards of success 39
Notes 39

03 Barriers to success 41

'Here be dragons' 41
The dragon of doubt 42
Three attitudes: the sceptic, the champion and the
    in-betweener 43
So... who is responsible for compliance? 45
Psychology and human nature 45
Nudge theory 45
Danger? What danger? Burning platforms 47
Silence 48
Incentives 50
Culture 51
Resources: 'The cuckoo in the nest' 56
Management time and attention 58
Poor skills, bad approaches 59
Short-termism 59
Notes 60

04 Looking for answers 61

Mission impossible? 61
So is it all about culture? 63
The art of persuasion 64
One size doesn't fit all 65
Personal versus business values 66
Simplicity 68
Storytelling 69
Hire the right people 71
Compliance: with us, not against us 72

Bureaucracy can be good! 73
Integrated compliance and ethics 74
A culture of responsible accountability 75
Incentivizing accountability 76
What's in it for me? 77
A little nudge can deliver big change... 78
Technology: friend or foe? 78
What if doing the 'right thing' *ethically* looks like the 'wrong thing' *commercially*? 79
In it for the long term 81
Stop saying 'compliance'! 81
Keep it alive 81
Notes 82

PART TWO

05 The anatomy of a compliance and ethics programme 87

The road to compliance 87
Starting points 88
What about small and medium-sized enterprises? 88
Key programme components 90
The nine components used in this book 91
The role of Compliance and Ethics Committees 100
'Hanging in the balance' 101
Useful sources of guidance 102
Across the minefield: compliance and ethics meets real life 108
Notes 109

06 Top-level commitment 111

Introduction 111
Tone at the top... 112
... and everywhere else 112
What senior leadership commitment looks like 113
Looking for champions – and working with them 121
What makes top-level commitment? 122

Why 126
Top-level commitment as an 'enabler' 127
Top-level commitment through 'enforcement' 130
In conclusion 131
Across the minefield: compliance and ethics meets real life 131
Note 133

07 Risk assessment and due diligence 135

Before we begin 135
The psychology of risk 136
The problem with assessing risk 137
Why risk assess? 138
What is 'reasonable risk management'? 139
When to risk assess? 140
Risk assessment in compliance and ethics programme planning
    and design 142
Third parties' compliance programmes 156
In summary 160
Across the minefield: compliance and ethics meets real life 162
Notes 163

08 Code of conduct and policies 165

We the people 165
What is a code – and what is it for? 167
The beginning, not the end 169
How to create an effective code of conduct 171
Corporate policies 175
How much detail should a code provide? 176
'Never mind the supplier's own code – make them comply
    with ours' 178
Some common but problematic policy areas 180
When there's a conflict between your minimum standards and
    local culture or laws 199
Across the minefield: compliance and ethics meets real life 200
Notes 201

09 Communication, education and training 203

La grande illusion 203
Communication versus education and training 205
Creating awareness 205
Training versus education 206
Making training land with your audience 206
Making e-learning more effective 215
Communication 216
Collective action – including communication with
      governments, ministries, local communities, NGOs,
      embassies 220
Always remember... 223
Across the minefield: compliance and ethics meets real life 223
Notes 225

10 Whistle-blowing hotline and speak-up culture 227

The importance of whistle-blowing 227
The problem with whistle-blowing 228
The importance of creating a process people can trust 230
Regional and cultural differences 231
Anonymity 233
Investigation and remediation of whistle-blowing cases 236
What types of cases should be regarded or treated as 'whistle-
      blowing'? 237
Why use an external whistle-blowing helpline? 238
Making it live and work 240
Branding 240
The importance of communicating success 241
The characteristics of a speak-up culture 244
Across the minefield: compliance and ethics meets real life 245
Notes 246

11 Procedures and controls 247

What are 'procedures and controls', and what are they for? 247
Identifying where procedures are necessary 248

How procedures can help 249
Types of procedure and controls 251
The dreaded compliance clause 254
Some key procedures and controls specific to compliance
    and ethics 257
Across the minefield: compliance and ethics meets real life 261
Notes 263

12   Investigations, remediation and enforcement 265

When the need for an investigation arises 265
The importance of enforcement 266
Being fair, consistent and even-handed 269
Having the right skills and guidance 270
Managing investigations: some good practice guidance 271
The investigator's perspective and the pitfalls to beware 282
Across the minefield: compliance and ethics meets real life 286
Note 287

13   Assurance and continuous improvement 289

The need for assurance 289
Monitoring and auditing 290
Implementing a compliance and ethics assurance
    framework 291
Quantitative versus qualitative assurance 299
An independent compliance monitor 302
Measurement and reporting 303
The road to continuous improvement 305
Across the minefield: compliance and ethics meets real life 308

**14   Implementation: The Compliance and Ethics function –
and everyone else** 311

Hammers and nails 311
The position of the Compliance and Ethics function in the
    organization 312
Structuring the Compliance and Ethics function 313

Examples of how compliance and ethics might be structured 321

Centralized versus decentralized Compliance and Ethics function 324

Centralized versus decentralized compliance and ethics programme 325

Implementing a compliance programme in JVs, fiercely autonomous subsidiaries and conglomerates 326

Deploying the right skills and resources 328

The (very) ideal model of a chief ethics and compliance officer 329

Role description for a chief ethics and compliance officer 332

'Mind the gap' 334

Other specialist functional responsibilities 335

The role of management 338

The role of employees 338

So in the end, who is responsible for effective compliance? 339

Across the minefield: compliance and ethics meets real life 339

Note 341

A final word: So what's the future of compliance and ethics? 343

Index 347

LIST OF FIGURES AND TABLES

FIGURES

Figure 2.1   The continuous evolution of compliance and ethics: the journey from voluntary to mandatory 36

Figure 2.2   A compliance and ethics programme 37

Figure 4.1   An effective compliance and ethics programme is holistic and multi-dimensional 65

Figure 5.1   The nine components of a compliance and ethics programme 92

Figure 10.1   One bad apple 242

Figure 14.1   Compliance responsibilities assumed by other functions 336

Figure 14.2   An integrated global compliance and ethics programme 337

TABLES

Table 11.1   Gift and hospitality approval thresholds 258

Table 13.1   Compliance and ethics programme assurance framework 292

PREFACE

Since stories are going to play a big part in this book, let's start with one...

THE NORTH WIND AND THE SUN

Once the North Wind and the Sun were having a furious argument. Like many arguments, it was essentially about who's best.

Then along the mountain path just below them came a lonely traveller wearing a cloak. Seeing him, the North Wind and the Sun agreed to a challenge: whoever could make this traveller remove his cloak would win the argument.

The North Wind went first. He blew and he blew with all his might. But the more he blew, the tighter the traveller wrapped his cloak around him. And in the end, his cheeks cracked, gasping and spent, the North Wind gave up.

Then it was the Sun's turn. He stepped out from behind a cloud... and smiled. And in the sudden brilliant warmth of that smile, the traveller took off his cloak.

Aesop's fable is, of course, about the art of persuasion. And put at its simplest, that's what any really effective compliance programme is all about – how to get everyone always to do what you want them to do.

The problem lies with those two words: '*everyone*' and '*always*'.

Which is why compliance programmes lay out a bunch of rules, try to ensure everyone understands them, and warn people in chilly terms of the consequences if they do not comply.

But is that then 'job done'?

The snag – as Aesop's fable makes clear – is that instead of opening hearts and minds, this kind of persuasion can lead to people closing their cloaks ever more tightly around them. The moral? If a compliance programme is just a wind-bag of statutes and warnings written in lifeless legalese, not much is likely to get through.

We believe compliance can – and should – be something very different. Not one of the biggest turn-off words in the language, but a living story that is all about how a group of people agree they want to behave, and the ways in which they act together to uphold the principles and values of that agreement from day to day. And while precision of language will always be required to tell this story, that does not mean it needs to be written in a language few want to read and no one speaks.

Employees increasingly expect and demand that the organization they work for has a higher purpose they can believe in. Compliance isn't just about aligning with that purpose – it is a way of bringing it to life and ensuring the organisation fulfils it.

People are far more likely to do the right thing, *and actively defend it*, not because the organization they work for tells them to, but because they want to – because the world clearly illuminated by the programme is the world they want to live in. Its sunlit landscape reflects who they are and what they believe, *and* they feel confident that in standing up to maintain it they have the support of their community and their leadership.

But *'far more likely'* is still not the answer to *'everyone'* and *'always'*.

Sometimes some people will do things that go directly against what they know and believe to be right, and sometimes they will act in haste or under pressure – or just carelessly. For sectors and situations where the details and minutiae of the rules must be maintained, even a small lapse can be catastrophic.

This book sets out to examine what makes compliance most effective. That often means simplifying the rules. But it also means they must be mapped – and agreed, owned, lived, followed and enforced by the community whose values and interests they represent. That requires organizations to re-imagine what compliance can be – not simply an enforcing mechanism, but a way of positively setting the tone, climate, shared culture, personality and purpose of an organization, and articulating the things its members, and its leadership, cherish together.

Really effective compliance is the voice of the community it belongs to and can only be achieved when the Sun and the Wind are working together.

Andrew Hayward
Tony Osborn

ABOUT THE AUTHORS

Andrew Hayward

Andrew Hayward is Head of Compliance and Ethics at Subsea 7, which is listed on the Oslo Stock Exchange and provides engineering and construction services to the offshore energy industry.

From 1999 to 2009 Andrew worked for AstraZeneca Pharmaceuticals, where he became Chief Counsel, Global Compliance in 2008. From 2009 to 2014 Andrew was Head of Ethics and Compliance at Balfour Beatty plc, a UK-headquartered infrastructure services company. He worked closely with the independent compliance monitor appointed following the company's 2008 civil settlement with the UK Serious Fraud Office. He also worked with the British Standards Institute on the first anti-bribery standard (BS10500) and was part of the UK delegation on the development of the International Anti-Bribery Standard (BS ISO 37001:2016).

Tony Osborn

Tony Osborn is an award-winning writer, creative consultant and content developer. He has worked with the UK government, with leading corporations around the world, and one to one with many different leaders as they seek to find and tell their stories and connect with their stakeholders.

He's helped to create events of national memory and importance, such as the Falklands 25 ceremony and the Fromelles First World War reinternment ceremony. He was also one of the creative directors delivering the opening and closing ceremonies for the 2014 Commonwealth Games, held in Glasgow, and a creative associate in the recent opening ceremonies for the 2018 Commonwealth Games in Australia. He has written extensively for television, with some 50 scripts broadcast to date.

Last but not least, he collaborated with Andrew on the award-winning Balfour Beatty Code of Conduct.

ACKNOWLEDGEMENTS

Andrew would like to extend the customary thanks to his wife for her tireless proofreading and insightful comments. But since the book is about compliance, her reaction was like many when they hear that word: 'I suppose I will have to read it eventually.'

Tony is still negotiating the reader's fee with his wife.

However, a number of people did read drafts of this book, and we would like to thank them for their time, care, thoughtfulness and insights. Our two formal reviewers: François Vincke, Member of the Brussels Bar, Vice-Chair ICC Commission Corporate Responsibility and Anti-Corruption, and Former General Counsel Petrofina; and Christopher Wright, Head of Compliance, LafargeHolcim, and himself an author (under a pseudonym).

Their extensive comments and wisdom helped us to improve many aspects of the text. All remaining errors are ours entirely.

Two others reviewed the near-final manuscript and were kind enough to provide positive endorsements: Philippa Foster Back CBE, Director, Institute of Business Ethics; and Keith M. Korenchuk, Vice President and Chief Compliance Officer, Diagnostic Platform, Danaher Corporation/Beckman Coulter Inc, and former Partner, Arnold & Porter LLP.

We should also like to thank the team at Kogan Page for commissioning the book in the first place, sticking with us through some unanticipated challenges and delays, and then guiding us through the editorial and production phase: Rebecca Bush, Melody Dawes, Carly Linghorn, Katherine Hartle, Amy Minshull, Adam Cox, and all those whose names we never had the good fortune to learn about.

Last but not least, we would like to acknowledge the significant contributions made by Tom Hickey, who travelled with us on the first part of the journey and helped us to set our course.

HOW TO USE THIS BOOK

We have set out to write a book that re-imagines compliance and its role in helping to develop a culture of ownership and engagement, and a trusted business that is better equipped to succeed in the market place. Plenty of other thoughtful observers and practitioners see things the way we do. We are not claiming to be unique or the first, but we are all swimming against a strengthening tide.

Compliance and ethics is a critical part of what makes business support the world we all want to live in. So the key mission for us has been to make the reasons for why compliance fails, and the things that, when working together, will make it succeed, clear to everyone – not just compliance officers.

We've designed this book to be accessible and easy for anyone to use. As well as detailed discussion, written in a friendly style, you will find plenty of practical examples, stories and illustrations that bring the issues to life.

- Discussion follows a clear and logical path, and each chapter starts with a brief summary of its contents to help you navigate the book.
- You will also find an extensive index with cross-references to all the important words, phrases and subjects discussed, so you can easily track a single issue right across the book.

Part One

Part One provides a wide-ranging view of the origins of compliance, the many reasons why it fails in so many different kinds of organization, and the critical new role compliance and ethics must play in helping businesses to thrive amidst the challenges of today's – and tomorrow's – world.

- In just four chapters we survey the broad landscape and cover the key issues, ideas and 'philosophical' debate that surround compliance.

- At the same time, we present the fundamentals of a better approach to achieving effective compliance and ethics. This offers a different way of thinking about how compliance can be part of defining the purpose of an organization, and of bringing that purpose to life for employees, consumers and stakeholders alike.

Part Two

Part Two rolls up its sleeves and gets down to the basics of how to design and build a best practice, modern compliance and ethics programme that also reaches deeply and broadly into the culture of the organization.

- We outline nine key components, and then take a step-by-step approach, focusing on each one in turn.

- Finally, in Chapter 14 we look at how everyone is involved in implementing compliance and ethics, and what each person's role is.

While Part Two is intended to be a hands-on guide, we also make it clear that there is no 'magic formula' – every organization must find its own best path, and what works for one will not necessarily work for another.

What about SMEs?

This book is also intended for small and medium-sized enterprises (SMEs). We say this because we are conscious that most companies are SMEs, whose owners, managers and employees will be keen to see if this book is relevant to them, and indeed if the best practice expectations and recommendations of regulators and practitioners, including the authors, are realistic and workable for SMEs.

In our experience, many such readers tend to view compliance (though, to be fair, not usually ethics as well) as an unaffordable burden, something that is too difficult and therefore surely not for their organization. So while for convenience and simplicity in our examples and models throughout this book we normally envisage a relatively large, commercial company that is privately owned or listed on a public stock exchange, we frequently pause to consider the case of SMEs, and everything we say applies to organizations of every size and type, in every sector and geography.

'Across the minefield'

It's easy to forget that, when it comes down to it, compliance is mostly a series of challenges in which real people are tested by real dilemmas every day, and must make and take what are sometimes problematic decisions and actions.

Compliance officers and senior managers in turn need to be able to 'solve' and provide guidance on these dilemmas and adapt the compliance and ethics programme, policies and training accordingly to help ensure it is fit for purpose to help the organization and its people face these challenges and make good decisions.

- So at the end of every chapter in Part Two we put away theory and discussion, and enter life's arena, presenting a series of illustrations and dilemmas that highlight the kinds of issues people living and working together within an organization will face day to day.

- These short 'real life' sections are designed to help anyone thinking about how to bring compliance to life through training, education and conversation. We hope they'll also remind you that compliance is deeply enmeshed not just in the real world of business – but of life.

A word about terminology

The landscape we'll be walking across is littered with jargon and terminology. We've tried to clear some of that litter along the way. There are two specific terms that we use which are worth clarifying at the outset:

- The chief compliance officer or head of ethics and compliance is usually the person officially responsible for compliance in an organization. For reasons that will become clear we prefer the term chief ethics and compliance officer (CECO), and we use that term to describe the head of the compliance function, regardless of the title actually used or whether an organization only has one full-time or even a part-time person performing that role.

- For similar reasons, we often use the term 'Compliance and Ethics function' instead of simply 'Compliance function'.

PART ONE

May you live in interesting times.

Today capitalism and globalization are under increasing scrutiny. New and searching questions are being asked about the role of businesses in our societies.

What is their purpose? How are they benefitting us? What role are they playing in issues like sustainable development that are more and more on the minds of employees, customers and stakeholders? Is what businesses say they do actually what they do? And do they actually do it in the way they say they do it? Are they an organization with genuine integrity? Do they conduct their business ethically and treat their employees well? Are their compliance programmes and values just window dressing, or do they do everything they can to live by them?

In the era of fake news and false stories, can we believe in them? *Can we trust them?*

This scrutiny is setting a radical and challenging agenda that is shaping the future of business in the field, in the high street, online, on the floors of the world's stock markets and in the hearts and minds of consumers increasingly in touch with and united by shared information and insight on the internet.

It's an agenda about 'authenticity' – and it's only recently that business has begun to wake up to just how real and urgent it is. If you want your business to thrive, your actions and your behaviour must comply with your values, and the terms – both ethical and regulatory – that you set out in your compliance programme must be demonstrably true and alive in your culture, and clearly lived and supported by all who work for and with you.

And yet... we continue to see the destruction and harm caused by systemic non-compliance or the misdeeds of a few, and newspapers abound with examples of corporate and NGO scandals and crimes.

In many of these cases organizations have implemented credible, determined compliance programmes that have simply not been up to the task and have failed to achieve their goal.

But research also tells us that much of this aberrant behaviour is the direct result of organizations ignoring their duty to stakeholders and society, forgetting their mission and failing to make sure those working for them are both mindful of, and motivated by, it.

Indeed, some corporate compliance breaches have been cynical – and inevitable.

Time again we are led to conclude that the organization did not really aim to prevent illegal or unethical conduct; it just wanted to hide behind the defensive curtain of its policies and procedures so it could turn a blind eye.

At other times, the conduct in question was not downright unlawful (even though prosecutors may have subsequently held them to account for it), so the organization did not have policies and training to prevent it. Quite the opposite – they put their pursuit of profit before their mission and their duty to clients, stakeholders and society, and their incentives encouraged their employees to do the same.

So what's going on here? How do you make compliance effective?

Part One of this book sets out to redress the long-held perception of compliance as a dour and tedious restraint holding back innovative ideas and commercial performance – a defence bulwark via which the lawyers can isolate an organization from excessive damage when the inevitable scandal happens.

Our purpose here is to change minds. To establish the critical and central importance of what we and many others call 'compliance and ethics' in helping to deliver, grow and maintain the reputational and commercial success of an organization in this challenging environment. And above all, to show how those organizations that go in authentic pursuit of effective compliance and ethics will gain real advantages in the marketplace over those competitors who continue to see compliance as a tick-box, lip-service, merely defensible exercise.

We look at why compliance is failing. How it has evolved from its first faltering steps. What it actually means, and what it can potentially deliver. What the obstacles and barriers are – including prevailing attitudes – that prevent it from fulfilling that potential. And how organizations – and all those involved in leadership positions – can start to build and harness the benefits of an effective compliance and ethics programme and a culture that supports and lives it.

Whoever you are – whether you are a compliance champion, a compliance sceptic, or simply indifferent and largely bored by the whole subject – we hope to change your mind, and open your eyes to a whole new world of expectations and possibilities.

01

Why compliance isn't working

In this chapter we discuss the underlying causes that make compliance fail, and what organizations can do about it.

Fatal flaws and collateral damage

Horatio: To what issue will this come?
Marcellus: Something is rotten in the state of Denmark.

HAMLET

History is littered with companies that have collapsed or been significantly damaged, not because their commercial strategy has failed, but because they have failed to comply with the law and the ethical values and expectations of their stakeholders and broader society.

When an organization fails like this, it will be punished with the imposition of fines and penalties and receive negative coverage from the media and angry consumers. That will often have catastrophic consequences for all those who work within it and rely on it. Real people are affected. Employees lose their jobs. Investors take a hit. Pensions suffer. So do partners and suppliers and consumers.

But it's not just commercial enterprises that we're talking about...

For decades the aid sector was one of the most highly regarded areas of all human endeavour. Within it were some of the most trusted names and brands in the world. Professionals and volunteers proudly belonged to cultures whose purpose and vision was unquestionably 'good'.

Then, quite suddenly, stories began to leak into the media. Stories about individuals and groups who were able to hide behind the perceived goodness of the organization they worked for to do bad things to the very people they were supposed to be protecting.

That's not all these stories revealed. Even more worryingly, they exposed structural flaws at the very heart of these non-governmental organizations' (NGOs') cultures. It became clear that people did not feel safe or empowered to report the misdeeds of the few – despite knowing about them – and if they did, management and leaders did not act on what they were being told, and tried to keep it quiet.

Why would people fail to stand up and speak out when they saw the values and mission of the organization they so proudly worked for being betrayed? When they did speak out, why didn't those in power act immediately to stop what was happening?

We see this knock-on devastation happening again and again. So what keeps going wrong? Why do organizations keep getting it wrong?

The human factor

Try this...

THE £10 MILLION QUESTION

You're a manager. You've just discovered a way to make £10,000,000. It's illegal. But it's foolproof. Really. No one will ever know.

A couple of people working under you may suspect, but they'll never be able to prove it. Besides, their jobs depend on you, and their families depend on them keeping their jobs.

This is £10,000,000. Guaranteed. You absolutely know you'll get away with it. You absolutely know you can keep people silent. So come on, what would you do? Honestly!

Can you really legislate against human nature? Absolutely. You can, and you must. But that's not enough – you also need to work with it.

Consider any of the corporate scandals in the news today. When the dust has settled, what do you see?

Alone, or collectively, employees have been able to act, or to fail to act, in unlawful or unethical ways – and spread chaos, incur enormous cost and cause so much despair as a result.

Are they incentivized? Authorized? Self-motivated? Or is it the surrounding facts and circumstances – what we will call 'culture' – that influence their behaviour, and make them believe they can, and will, get away with it?

Culture

Culture isn't just a given set of circumstances over which we have no control. It is we – our colleagues and our leaders – who define, shape and 'own' the culture in which we live and work.

This is what we will be exploring through the pages of this book: how to implement a compliance and ethics programme that isn't just a stand-alone within an organization. Instead, it is part of building a culture whose values leaders and employees are invested in, and which is genuinely responsive to the requirement that people behave according to those values and principles. A culture that defends them robustly and lives them fully.

As a result, the organization as a whole becomes trusted and recognized for its integrity and performance. And that gives it a commercial advantage in the marketplace.

In short, this is the practical business guide to implementing an effective compliance and ethics programme that doesn't just protect reputation, but enhances it, and delivers commercial success.

So why isn't compliance doing that? Why isn't it working?

How to be ineffective

Almost invariably, compliance is based on the premise that if you can get people to be compliant at all, it is out of obedience to a policy.

No matter if it's mind-numbingly dull – just lay down the law and show them the sharp end of the stick.

As a result, much of compliance doctrine – and much that is written about it, and much that is done – ends up being routine, tick-box, rules-based stuff. An unengaging necessity.

Fear and boredom.

Our policies, your obedience.

The problem with this approach is that it just doesn't work – because people don't work like that. Yet the idea of creating something that is genuinely effective – because it is genuinely engaging and relevant – doesn't make it onto the agenda.

THE POLITICIAN AND HIS WIFE

In 2003 an elected member of the European Parliament received a speeding penalty that would have resulted in him losing his driver's licence. Although he was the one driving, he asked his wife to say she was at the wheel. She had fewer points and wouldn't lose her licence. She agreed and assumed the penalty.

Some seven years later, and with the MEP now an elected member of the United Kingdom Parliament, the arrangement came to light during the couple's divorce proceedings.

Both received an eight-month prison sentence for perverting the course of justice.

This story illustrates how people will attempt to justify their behaviour even if it is dishonest or illegal. Both parties were presumably well aware that it was dishonest or unethical, and almost certainly illegal, for one party to suggest and the other to agree to this pretence.

The fact they would be committing a criminal offence was not sufficient disincentive, even where one of them was an elected member of the European Parliament, a position of responsibility, and answerable to the public. Instead their only concern was to shift liability for the speeding offence and then avoid being found out. Clearly, and fundamentally, they believed they would get away with it.

And that's the point, that's what experience – and the scandalous history of non-compliance – confirms again and again.

But as we show in this book, it is hard to communicate copious rules and make sure they are understood. People don't have the bandwidth anyway. And people won't follow mere policies and rules if they have enough incentive not to, don't feel the rules apply to them, think they might be able to avoid being found out – or if they just think it isn't 'cool' to be the one who stands up for rules.

Typically, two views prevail about what compliance is there to do, and they're usually found working together.

'Defensible compliance'

The first view sees compliance as fundamentally about creating a defensible set of rules that will protect the organization when – not if – the rules get broken.

When there is a breach of compliance, a defensible programme will either try to insist the organization is not at fault, and instead the authorities should only pursue the individuals concerned; or will accept the organization is at fault, but argue for all it is worth that any consequences are too minor to be considered punishable at law.

All that really matters is that the organization has the best chance of defending the adequacy or reasonableness of its compliance procedures. Defensibility always wins the argument.

In effect this is a counsel of despair. It doesn't really believe that you can or must stop compliance breaches from occurring, only that you can limit the damage to you and your organization when, inevitably, they do. You spend money on compliance to avoid or minimize any fines and penalties.

So defensible compliance usually ends up being all about quantity, not quality. And the larger the organization, the greater the quantity: numbers of compliance officers employed, pages of forms staff are required to complete, how many third parties are put through a systematized process of due diligence screening... and so on.

Clearly, measures like these have a role to play – you cannot simply do without them and expect to create a compliant organization. However, as the history of corporate scandals has shown us, while this approach may protect the organization or limit the damage when it gets investigated or prosecuted, it won't stop there.

Because defensible compliance is about 'protection' rather than 'prevention', sooner or later there will be another non-compliance event, and with it the costs and disruption of the ensuing investigation and defence against prosecution.

This is not a sustainable, or commercially efficient, path to follow. On each occasion the organization's reputation is being trashed all over the internet and the front pages of the newspapers. Stakeholders will increasingly lose their trust, and at some point the courts will find for the prosecution.

We'll look in more detail at this approach to compliance and why it has come about in the next chapter.

Compliance as impediment: doing the legal minimum

The second view, complicit with the first, sees compliance as the 'big blocker', stonewalling energy, creativity, ideas – the enemy of all that seek to do things differently and better.

It's a view that can be summarized in what we once heard a lawyer say:

> Under Delaware law, the directors' duty is to maximize returns
> to shareholders while complying with the law. Accordingly, to do
> more than the legal minimum required for compliance is a breach of
> directors' duties.

Even if this were true, it is of course based on the premise that more compliance means lower returns to shareholders. This completely fails to acknowledge two things:

- Companies increasingly have to satisfy a range of shareholder and stakeholder demands – not just in terms of profitability but also in terms of responsible business.
- Effective compliance can actually increase medium- and long-term profitability.

The Age of Damage

We have entered the Age of Damage – a world of radical transparency where people now have the mechanisms in social media to punish those they don't believe are behaving in the right way. You are only trusted for what you do, not for what you say. You can't just invent a good story about your business, because if it isn't true, you will be found out, taken down and left to plead forgiveness from your investors, regulators, customers and the media.

Like it or not, companies are increasingly having to let their story be told by the people who are experiencing it on the ground. Trying to work with this new reality isn't losing control – trying to work against it is.

At the same time, employees, customers, consumers and stakeholders are increasingly beginning to favour those organizations and brands whose values are their values – organizations that stand for something, have an authentic purpose, and act positively for the benefit of society and the wider environment. Younger people, in particular, are increasingly favouring companies with such values. Making money at the expense of all else is no longer a recipe for success.

Increasingly, there is an appreciable dividend to be gained from responsible business in terms of reputational enhancement, trust, the loyalty of customers and employees, and from society, prosecutors and regulators giving the organization the benefit of the doubt.

So your story needs to be both good and true – a story that's underpinned by a lot more than 'the legal minimum requirement'.

For many if not most organizations this represents a radical departure from the way they've thought about and done compliance. How do you do this? Can you really move compliance out of the silo in the back lot where it's usually housed? What are the building blocks? Who do you have to persuade? How do you demonstrate the positive impact of effective compliance on the bottom line? And who are 'you' anyway?

Those are the questions we have set out to answer – so let's dive right in...

Making compliance effective

IT'S YOUR SHIP

As a United States warship, the *USS Benfold* is armed with cutting edge systems. However, once it was the most poorly performing ship in the whole of the US Navy, with huge issues of inefficiency, low morale, insubordination and failure to follow regulations.

Then Captain Michael Abrashoff took over command, charged with improving the situation. He decided that what he needed to do was to focus on getting everyone on board into the mindset of being the responsible captain of the ship.

So he began a campaign with a simple slogan, 'It's your ship'. He invited every single member of the crew, no matter what their rank, to challenge every process, and every procedure, asking them, 'What would you do? It's your ship. You tell me.'

Soon Captain Abrahsoff had transformed his crew into inspired problem-solvers eager to take the initiative and take responsibility for their actions. And the *USS Benfold* became one of the most efficient ships in the Navy.

Just one of the examples Captain Abrashoff gives is of a crew member he found painting the ship. It was the eighth time this man had painted the same thing within the last 12 months. When asked why, the crewman explained that it was because all the nuts and bolts on the ship rusted, so they had to be continuously painted. Captain Abrashoff asked him what he would do if it were his ship. And the crewman replied, 'I'd change all the nuts and bolts to stainless steel.'

In his book *It's Your Ship*, Captain Michael Abrashoff tells us that this single remark has since saved the US Navy millions of dollars![1]

Within the traditional 'defensible compliance' or 'compliance as impediment' environment, Captain Abrashoff's radical proposal could be seen as a lack of compliance – establishing a counter-current to the existing 'my policies, your obedience' status quo that employees have been expected, or harangued, to comply with.

But look further... This story is saying that we will really only willingly comply with rules and regulations that we can all see make sense, all agree with, understand the importance of, and see as beneficial to us. Rules and regulations that become 'our agreed way of doing things, our agreed way of behaving' – because we all own them.

The vital point of departure for the change in performance is 'trust'. Captain Abrashoff told his crew he would trust them to speak out against what they saw as 'wrong', identifying what needed to be improved and suggesting how that improvement could be made. And he supported that trust through actions. Whether and how far the Captain actually trusted his crew when he began his campaign is not the point; it is what he said and did that mattered and brought about the change. This is important because it is a simple principle of human nature that a leader's assumptions about people tend to become self-fulfilling prophesies.

What creates effective compliance?

Effective compliance happens when:

- we are trusted and empowered, so we are part of defining the things we should do and why we should do them;
- we know that the rules are there for good reasons and to protect us and others as people;
- we know that we will be heard if we believe there's a way to improve something, or if we need to report a betrayal of what we have jointly agreed.

In other words, effective compliance happens if we know that compliance is a living part of who we are and what we choose to stand for. If we are treated and trusted like the people we want to be, the organization and its people work as one. Non-compliance is prevented, and the organization and its people are protected.

We want to stress – this is *not* to say that all the answer lies solely in culture or trust. You need to have the compliance programme fundamentals thoroughly thought through and in place. But what matters is how those fundamentals and their complexities are given life and assimilated into the culture of the organization by everyone within it – especially all those with leadership and management responsibility. That is what makes it effective.

Zero harm

Broadly speaking, many organizations have been very successful in embedding a health and safety culture in which everybody, at every level in every function, is responsible for their own health and safety and those around them. All driven by education, training, incentives (such as health, safety and environmental performance linked to everyone's annual performance bonus) and culture. Compliance is inherently no different.

It is no accident that it is those in leadership and management positions who are most influential in shaping how people behave and perform. This includes middle management, who can often be the *most* influential, depending on the size and culture of the organization and how dominant is the personality of the leader at the very top. But just as for health and safety, everyone needs to be involved, everyone needs to have influence. Each of us, by what we do and say, or don't do and don't say, affects how others think, and what they will say and do – particularly when they're in a challenging situation.

Effective compliance is not just the domain of the Compliance function – but of the entire organizational culture.

Compliance, culture and ethics

Let's go back to the rules of the road. Here's a true story...

THE HIRED CAR

Two senior managers from a UK company were visiting a colleague at the US parent company in the Midwest. They collected a rental car at the airport, picked up the colleague, and drove to a meeting.

At one point they began exceeding the speed limit and the American colleague said, very politely, 'Please don't – Mr Brady wouldn't like it.' Mr Brady was the owner of the company.

The driver slowed down.

Breaking the law could have had serious consequences, including prosecution and disciplinary procedures. But it wasn't the speed limit ('compliance rule') that proved effective here. It was the mention of Mr Brady ('culture'). And that's what the passenger turned to straight away, despite being one voice to the visitors' two. The passenger achieved the desired result by communicating the culture rather than communicating the rule.

In this particular case, the company was sufficiently small and the owner's personality and values were sufficiently influential that he did not need policies and procedures and a complex structure delegating authority to ensure that managers and staff acted in accordance with his wishes and the company's values.

But of course, the structure, scope and personality of each organization is different and many quickly reach a size, headcount and spread where the personal values of a Mr or Ms Brady cannot of themselves assert the influence needed. The challenge is how to create a compliance culture that is felt by and belongs to everyone in the organization. It must resonate personally with each employee through time and remain relevant despite the inevitable changes and challenges that every organization faces.

This takes us to the core of what this book is all about...

In a nutshell

A compliance programme is essential...

Just as the integrity of the human body is dependent on its skeleton, organizations require a robust, well-defined, structured compliance programme.

They need top-level commitment. They need to assess the risks in order to understand how to help their staff navigate them. They need to educate and raise awareness about the risks and the principles and policies that subject matter experts have identified to help them navigate those risks and remain compliant.

A well-managed business will also have procedures and controls that can be leveraged to help keep people on the straight and narrow.

And they need continually to monitor, review and improve all of the above.

But on its own this isn't enough...

Trying to implement a compliance programme that is seen by employees as a series of diktats and a 'blocker' to progress, or one that is merely 'defensible' and only focuses on protecting the organization itself is destined to fail.

It also needs to be part of an ethics-based culture...

If compliance is to be effective, it must also become a fundamental part of the organization's culture and values. And those values need to include, and the programme needs to be a compliance and ethics programme that is informed and motivated by, clear principles of ethics and integrity, and concepts such as fairness, honesty, respect – the things people want to live by.

This is what we mean when we refer throughout this book to 'compliance and ethics'.

So it is owned, shaped and lived by everyone...

Shifting the conversation from one of rules and legal minimum to one of culture and values moves compliance from being imposed upon the organization to a place where it emanates from within each employee across the organization.

When that happens, culture can powerfully influence our behaviours to remain within the rules and norms of compliance and acceptable business conduct. It gives shape, feel, voice and purpose to compliance and ethics. The employees trust the organization and the organization trusts them. And in turn investors, regulators and consumers trust the organization.

And the business gains a sustainable competitive advantage...

When compliance and culture are working together, they prevent damage from happening. They develop an organization that will be more resistant to the inevitable headwinds and occasional storms. They build performance, trust, reputation – enhancing the value of that organization compared to its peers. And so they create real, effective and sustainable competitive advantage.

This only happens when compliance and ethics are an indivisible entity

Culture alone will not create compliance. But no compliance programme will truly work unless it is through culture. To come alive and be effective, the two must be inextricably woven together, like the double helix of DNA. That is why throughout this book we refer to 'compliance and ethics' as indivisibly woven threads.

10 reasons why compliance fails

1. When there is lack of leadership

Too often there is no actual or visible leadership and management commitment to the compliance programme and to the organizational culture of compliance and ethics at the top, or at each level of the organization. In such an organization, senior management talk the talk without credibility or authenticity. They will tend to be compliance sceptics, believing there is no value to the bottom line. Often, they will actually believe compliance is just an irritatingly necessary burden, or something that protects them from personal liability.

2. When 'we only need to do the legal minimum'

When an organization commits to doing only the minimum it thinks necessary, the compliance programme will almost inevitably fail. Effective and sustainable prevention is not a budgetable idea. The focus is on protecting the organization when – not if – the rules get broken.

3. When management are not held accountable for compliance – they see it as 'the compliance function's responsibility'

Unless managers themselves live the programme, and are seen to do so, they give implicit permission for others to ignore or undervalue it. This will happen when compliance is not a big enough priority for the top leadership, and managers know it.

4. When the organization's incentives are not aligned with its compliance objectives

Closely linked to management accountability, this is arguably the single most important reason why compliance fails. Some incentives encourage misconduct – usually implicitly and unintentionally, sometimes explicitly or intentionally. On the other hand, incentives based around, or that reinforce, values and ethics help to create the living culture that makes compliance effective. And they are visible evidence of the leadership's commitment.

5. When the programme isn't 'ethics- and values-driven'

Using the organization's values brings the company's culture, spirit and vision to life, including the need for a culture of compliance with its policies and procedures. Compliance can and should play a key and active role in how any organization tells its story, expresses its purpose and reflects its values.

6. When it over-relies on 'obedience' or 'rules for everything'

A rules- and obedience-based programme fails to understand human psychology. It often produces a 'them' and 'us' mentality, because no sense of ownership has been created.

This approach can even prompt some to resent and deliberately circumvent rules they see as unnecessary, or as 'red tape' or 'there to be broken'.

Similarly, when an organization attempts to prescribe a rule or procedure for every situation, rather than a principles- and ethics-based approach, it is in effect failing to engage and seek the complicit assent of its people.

Finally, if the organization takes such an approach, it will inevitably fail to anticipate situations for which it needs a rule. There are far more ways around rules than there are rules, and people simply don't have the bandwidth for so many rules.

7. When compliance is seen as out of touch and uncool, dead hand, sales prevention

When compliance does not emerge from the book and the arcane jargon in which it has been encoded, its relevance to employees' lives and the business mission is invisible. This can produce real and problematic discontent.

8. When the compliance function acts as an auditor or 'the police' rather than as a business partner

In such circumstances, issues can be driven underground, and compliance is not sufficiently trusted to help spot and navigate problems areas.

9. When there is deliberate scepticism

There is almost always a minority that will undervalue or undermine the importance of compliance principles – and the policies that support them – to the business.

When this scepticism is unchecked, or extends up into the senior leadership, this can be one of the biggest challenges for a compliance programme – especially if the compliance officer has been hired to tick the box and given no budget or authority to implement or update the programme.

If minds stay closed, the prognosis in such circumstances is not good.

*10. When there is wilful dishonesty, often for self-enrichment,
    by a small minority*

Dishonesty among a few will always be a threat, but an effective ethics-based programme actively lived, owned and defended by the majority should drive those few away.

And finally...

Let's be honest – compliance leaders and officers can also be part of the problem rather than the solution. Incompetence, lack of experience or seniority, and demotivation play their part. But often the underlying cause here is that compliance is not seen as vital to developing and delivering the business agenda by the rest of management, and is not properly represented in the boardroom.

Note

1 M Abrashoff (2007) *It's Your Ship: Management techniques from the best damn ship in the navy*, Hatchette.

02

The meaning, origins and role of compliance and ethics

In this chapter we get clear about some of the fundamental terms and concepts in compliance. There's a bit of doctrine here, and a little bit of history, but the purpose is to understand the territory.

Why have compliance?

Long before today's intense spotlight on ethical behaviour, compliance was needed because, without it, organizations and the people who worked for them wouldn't comply with the law. Take this 150-year-old prediction:

> I see in the near future a crisis approaching that unnerves me and causes me to tremble for the safety of my country... corporations have been enthroned and an era of corruption in high places will follow, and the money of the country will endeavor to prolong its reign by working upon the prejudices of the people until all wealth is aggregated in a few hands and the Republic is destroyed. I feel at this moment more anxiety for the safety of my country than ever before, even in the midst of war.

Extract from a letter from Abraham Lincoln to Col. William F. Elkins, 21 November 1864[1]

The fear Lincoln is voicing here is very particular – the corrosive power of business when it seeks ways in which to subvert or avoid complying with the law for its own gain.

Now consider some of the themes that are woven like a tapestry of discontent through the narratives that describe our modern business world... abuse of power... corruption... inappropriate business practices... bribery scandals... sexual misconduct... false accounting... financial collapse and economic crisis... mistreatment of employees... cover-ups... money laundering... misreporting... poor governance... One might say not much has changed, even that Lincoln's words have proved prophetic. But in fact, that wouldn't be altogether true – 'The times, they are a-changin'.'

In recent years civil society, prosecutors, governments, social media, whistle-blowing enterprises like WikiLeaks and groundswell movements like Me Too have taken very meaningful steps to confront and tackle these kinds of behaviours. Multi-billion-dollar fines against certain banks for breach of sanctions. Claims against companies and individuals for tax evasion and the backlash against so-called 'tax-havens'. Multi-million-dollar fines and prison terms following anti-corruption and bribery investigations. The updating of laws to continue the squeeze on sophisticated tax structures. The exposure of individuals who have used their positions of power within organizations to abuse and prey on employees.

So, while it may seem like a question with an all-too-obvious answer, it is worth spending just a bit of time looking at why we need compliance, and taking a quick tour through the history of compliance and how it has evolved.

Compliance: a short history

Before we begin this section, it's important to say that this is a deliberately broad-brush summary, and you shouldn't rely on it for legal advice.

Ethical versus non-ethical origins

Many laws and regulations in relation to subjects such as corruption, bribery, data privacy and modern slavery have their origins in ethics.

They have been transcribed into law because the voting public, NGOs, political representatives or other policymakers have demanded it.

This matters, because what tends to be the case is that those areas of compliance with an ethical origin resonate more readily with people. They align with their personal morals and integrity. This may be one of the reasons why compliance and ethics are often used interchangeably, as shorthand for an ethics-based approach to compliance, aimed at motivating compliance by making people think about the ethical reasons for doing so, including the ethical origins of laws.

Others, such as anti-trust, sanctions and export controls have a commercial philosophy, national security or foreign policy origin. These, without the broad ethical origin, often appear more abstract and may actually conflict strongly with a person's own views.

As such, non-ethics-based compliance is likely to be seen as more formalistic, abstract, less relevant and more the remit of the 'regulatory compliance' function or similar.

This is why, on the whole, an *ethics-based* approach to these areas of compliance doesn't work at all, or in the same way. However, you *can* still have a *principles-based* approach that helps people to navigate these difficult areas by applying broad principles. You can also have an *integrity-based* approach through which you can get agreement that we need to be trusted to act with integrity – which includes compliance with the law and with other standards we have committed to meeting.

As we will discuss later, what seems to be a small thing can make a big difference when developing the culture of compliance and ethics within an organization. How a person views a particular compliance or ethical commitment will determine the degree to which they will embrace it.

The social need

We've said that an organization needs compliance to manage compliance risks and avoid the consequences of non-compliance. But why does society need it? What vacuum is compliance filling, and what forces is it protecting society from?

The simple fact is that people within corporations can tend to get a bit 'excited' and go off the rails in rapid pursuit of business glory, replacing their own behavioural norms and the ethical principles and the interests of society with a very different – and sometimes antithetical – set of commercial 'rules of the game'.

Limited liability

Joint stock corporations were created and permitted by society to encourage entrepreneurialism and risk-taking by protecting the owners of the business from the consequences of insolvency, but one could argue that the concept of limited liability and the separate legal personality of the corporation have in fact been abused.

Limited liability corporations were not invented to permit people in business to behave in a way that would be illegal, or unacceptable to employees, stakeholders, society, and even to themselves, if they behaved in that way in their own personal lives, nor to protect them from the consequences of such behaviour.

In the UK, generally speaking a company can *only* be held liable for the acts of its officers, employees, agents etc if 'a directing mind of the company' (effectively a director) connived or colluded in the relevant misconduct. What this means has been particularly illustrated in the area of health and safety.

Before the Corporate Manslaughter and Corporate Homicide Act 2007 (UK 2007, Chapter 19), companies in the UK could not be held criminally liable unless a directing mind of the company connived or colluded in the relevant health and safety wrongdoing. This was changed after several terrible tragedies exposed significant health and safety failings for which no prosecution could be brought.

The failings of the law were further exposed when in 1993 the UK Health and Safety Executive successfully prosecuted a small open water canoeing business after four teenagers tragically died while canoeing in Lyme Bay on the south coast of the United Kingdom. The company was fined and the owner, who was also the managing director, was imprisoned.

> The moral and ethical iniquity of being able to prosecute a small organization because those with real responsibility for controlling the company's affairs were visibly close to the incident, but not being able to prosecute a larger company because of the greater distance between directors and incidents, was seen as fundamentally flawed.
>
> The Bribery Act 2010 (UK 2010, Chapter 23) followed this lead and it too removed the same 'directing mind' requirement.

If such a view might be considered rather apocalyptic, it cannot be denied that, whatever their personal morality, many employees and leaders perceive that, when they come to work, it's okay to leave their values at home, shedding the morals and ethics they hold dear in their private lives, and instead follow what they perceive as being what we've already called the 'rules of the game' in the corporate world.

They take on a new persona when they walk through the door in the morning and leave it behind at the end of the day.

As a result, compliance programmes have evolved that are designed to exercise control over the conduct of people who work in and for an organization, because society and law enforcers realized the irresponsible behaviour of organizations had got to the point where something had to be done, and that something would not come from within.

The modern compliance programme

The modern compliance programme has its origins in the United States, in particular, the enforcement of laws such as the US Foreign Corrupt Practices Act,[2] and has been further developed in regulated sectors in the United States, Europe and elsewhere.

US companies are vicariously liable for the acts of their employees and others acting on their behalf. US Department of Justice Federal Sentencing Guidelines (see page 89) state, broadly, that in order for a court to determine the appropriate sentence for a company, it is up to the company to show that it had in place a best practice compliance and ethics programme, designed and implemented in accordance with the Guidelines. The programme must be designed and implemented to ensure compliance with the relevant law and prevent the act in question, so that if the act did occur it can be said to have happened despite the company's best efforts to prevent it, and the company should be treated more or less leniently, depending how credible and well implemented its compliance and ethics programme is assessed as being. The Guidelines are supplemented from time to time with additional guidance, sometimes in the form of 'memos', issued by the US Department of Justice or the Securities and Exchange Commission.

What's very clear is that this is not just about defensible compliance; it's about whether the company was really doing all that it reasonably could to prevent – and genuinely did not want – the non-compliance.

Prior to the UK Bribery Act 2010, and the concept of corporate criminal liability under statute, there was less need or incentive in the United Kingdom for the type of compliance and ethics programmes seen in the United States. The same could be said in other European jurisdictions. Early programmes developed in regulated sectors, especially financial services, where the regulator could hold a company liable and impose significant fines and other penalties, if a regulated company could not show that it was doing all that it reasonably could to prevent the relevant wrongdoing.

Then the UK Bribery Act 2010 came along and changed everything, at least in relation to bribery: companies could be held strictly, criminally liable for bribery by officers, employees, agents and other persons performing services for them, and the only defence would be the so-called 'adequate procedures' defence – a compliance programme defence.

The development of best practice

When we follow the story of compliance on from this, and look at how best practice has developed internationally in different areas of compliance, what we see is continuing evolution of this principle in many jurisdictions. In most cases the only defence companies have against allegations that they or their representatives have behaved illegally or improperly is to demonstrate that they had put in place 'adequate procedures' to prevent such behaviour – in other words, a compliance programme defence.

Of course there are inherent dangers in this:

- Those seeking to act illegally or improperly may try to hide behind the cover of a compliance programme.

- Equally, in trying to ensure that companies are protected on this 'adequate procedures' basis, the evolution of compliance programmes, and the core of compliance doctrine, may adopt a defensible rather than preventative approach.

- And lastly, there is little or no discourse about what will actually and effectively get people to comply. Too often this results in a false premise – namely that people will behave properly out of obedience to a policy, or out of fear of the consequences of breaching a policy.

Parallels with health and safety here are very instructive and worth looking at. This is a well-established, mature regime with consequences of failure that are potentially far more tragic and long lasting than in most compliance areas. Organizations have learned that you have to have policies and procedures to establish a good solid foundation – you cannot and must not do without this. But with that foundation in place, it will ultimately be culture, values and incentives that are what will really make the difference between an okay safety record and a truly strong safety record and culture.

In just the same way, an effective compliance and ethics programme may be initiated and developed by the organization's leaders and by subject-matter specialists, but it is put into operational effect by all those performing on the front line, it is experienced by those with whom they interact, and should be recognized by those to whom they report.

The climate today

There is now a real and growing understanding of the damage caused by 'non-compliant' business practices and the importance of stamping them out. But it relates not just to behaviours that are specifically unlawful. Organizations and individuals are increasingly being held to account – and even brought down – for 'unethical' behaviour.

All this could be viewed as good news for compliance practitioners, who now appear to work in a growth area and no longer need to apologise at parties for what they do! But perhaps more to the point, the urgent relevance of compliance *and* ethics is now widely and increasingly accepted – and advocated – as a central part of the corporate culture, not just by those bodies that enforce the law, but by the public, the media and employees themselves.

Indeed, organizations that stay within the letter of the law, but are found out to be acting unethically, are no longer safe from public opprobrium. And the 'grey area' between the two that has been exploited for so long is now being exposed not just in business, but also in areas like sport.

What we are seeing here is the emergence in the public mind itself of an increasingly clear sense that 'compliance' is ultimately not just law-based, but must also be grounded in ethical principles. The two are inextricably entwined, and attempts to separate them no longer wash. It comes down to simple, universal things: 'Don't lie, cheat or steal, behave with honesty and integrity, and treat people with respect at all times.'

So before we go any further, let's try to get clear about what compliance is. Then we'll do the same with ethics, and look where and how it fits into the picture. Without an understanding of these things, it is difficult to appreciate how a programme can be formulated, and why it increasingly matters to an organization, its regulators and investors, and all its other stakeholders.

What is 'compliance'?

Compliance means different things to different people... which means different people can – and do – seek to define it in different ways to suit their purposes... which is a huge part of the reason why it fails to achieve its intended purpose.

So let's begin by assembling a 'typical' definition and try to understand how this variance results.

> **Compliance:** Typically understood to mean complying with laws or regulations, with an organization's rules, policies or procedures, or with a person's instructions or command. If an organization or its employees or other representatives commit a compliance breach, the organization may be liable to fines, penalties or damages, or suffer reputational harm.

Already we've got problems. As most practitioners know, in law 'There's many a slip 'twixt cup and lip'. Bending, or interpreting, or manoeuvring your way around the law can provide you with a great deal of wriggle room. Indeed, room enough to hide objects as big as yachts and Learjets.

In a business, compliance is, in effect, the way in which organizations seek to ensure that they and their employees do what they 'must do', and don't do what they 'must not do'. It is about obedience or conformity with rules or requirements. Most of these are defined or underpinned by law, but they can arise as a result of commitments entered into by the organization or its employees.

Compliance is a form of risk management, and many of the very same best practice principles that apply to professional risk management generally apply to compliance. It involves trying to manage the risk that people who work in or for an organization will get themselves and/or the organization into trouble or cause harm to others if, or when, they do not comply with the laws and other standards that the organization is required to adhere to.

As we shall see, the difference between a compliance approach that is all about preventing the 'if' and one that is really all about mitigating the 'when' can make all the difference to how effectively risk will be managed.

And while it is essential that the compliance rules and requirements are defined with precision, and in some sectors it is imperative that businesses comply with precise minutiae, nevertheless rules and regulations, like the law, are liable to end up with as many holes as a Swiss cheese. That is, unless they are also invested with ethical principles.

So, do you just add ethics and abracadabra – and you've got the magic formula? Unfortunately, it's a great deal more complicated...

What are 'ethics'?

Of course, ethics have been an abiding preoccupation of philosophers and thinkers going as far back as Confucius, Socrates and Aristotle. There are countless definitions, but let's take one that is clear, concise and practical from the contemporary Oxford Online Dictionary (2019):[3]

> **Ethics:** Moral principles that govern a person's behaviour or the conducting of an activity.

Ethics deal with concepts of right and wrong conduct, and often look at this from the point of view of what is deemed to be *morally* good or bad in a society. You can't go very far wrong if you think of ethics in terms of morals – especially in a compliance context.

Morals are of course familiar to us all. Irrespective of where we have grown up, stories, particularly children's stories, abound with a moral at their core. What to do, or what not to do. What to say, what to think, how to act. 'Doing the right thing' or 'Do unto others as you would have done unto you'. These teachings aim to embed the basic principles of behaviour, so we carry them with us as we make the transition from child to independent adult – and from the home to business.

Where this is important in a compliance context, and where ethics are distinguished from compliance, is that ethics turn out to be rather more intangible than might first appear, and are rooted in the social norms, perspectives, principles and values of the community in which you live at any one time, as the word's root in the Greek word $\tilde{\eta}\theta o\varsigma$ (ethos), meaning 'custom' or 'habit', suggests.

Although many laws have their origins in ethics and morals, the reverse is not the case, ie ethics and morals are not generally enforceable in the way that laws are. Laws tend to need to be clearly and objectively defined. Ethics and morals, on the other hand, tend to represent the principles and values that people have come to agree among themselves, often with a high degree of universality and consensus within, and sometimes across, cultures and communities.

But within that consensus, there is room for different personal interpretations.

THE MAN WHO WAS LEFT LYING IN A GUTTER

A man was beaten, his valuables taken, and he was left lying in the gutter. A small group gathered.

One in the group said, 'This man needs help.' A second said, 'The person who did this needs help.'

Neither response is wrong, but they are, very definitely, different. So, is one 'more right' than the other? And what if you had to choose between them?

The fact is, different people see things differently, and when it comes to 'doing what's right' that difference can be deep as a puddle or wide as an ocean.

Where a particular view may be the status quo and the norm locally, it may be seen as ethically wrong in another location. While the views of each are equally valid, different values may be involved and the potential for conflict arises, especially when individuals from each location come together in a common environment – for our purposes the business environment. See also what we say about national, local and organizational culture in Chapter 3.

What about 'business ethics'?

The Institute of Business Ethics offers the following definition:

> **Business ethics:** The application of ethical values to business behaviour.

There is a crucial point being made in this. For while a commercial organization could have values such as performance, innovation and excellence, if it wishes to have an effective compliance programme those business values need to be motivated by explicit or implicit *ethical values* like integrity, sustainability, honesty, respect – values that are about shaping and governing behaviour and – we're back to that word again – providing a *moral* compass.

It's important to note that we're not examining the ethical business strategy of an organization here, but how an ethics- and values-based approach helps an organization manage the risk of its employees and others doing bad things.

These ethical values must resonate with the employees, as it is their behaviours that will to a large extent support or potentially damage the reputation of the organization. They act as leading lights for all the organization's employees to follow, and set out the expectations in which all its stakeholders can invest and trust.

However, once again we bump into differences of perspective and norms among diverse communities and geographies that do not conduce to 'moral clarity' – and indeed can create real moral and ethical dilemmas.

The Human Rights and Business Dilemmas Forum articulates the problem well:

> How does a company address the presence of child labour in its
> supply chain, particularly in locations where child labour is relatively
> common and where there is evidence that removing income-generating
> opportunities will push children into deeper poverty or other forms of
> exploitation?[4]

This difficult terrain can be hugely problematic for businesses, and we return to it briefly in Chapter 8. As we've seen, ethics may be intangible in nature, and views about what is ethically right or wrong can vary at a personal level. But the consequences for an organization that is perceived to have behaved in an unethical manner, even where such behaviour is not illegal, can be enormous: negative media headlines, political shaming, consumer boycotts, collapse of market share.

How then can we arrive at a way of thinking about 'business ethics' that is tangible, useful, applicable – and helps businesses to develop effective ways of avoiding this kind of risk? Well, a nice way of explaining ethics within a business context is 'compliance with the unenforceable'. That doesn't mean 'entirely indefinable'.

Ethics can certainly have porous and contested borders, but for the purposes of this book, when we think of *business ethics*, we are really referring to the legitimate expectations of stakeholders that the business they are invested in, and its employees and representatives, should behave like responsible members of their society, and in accordance with its accepted ethical or moral norms. This is strongly linked to the role a business has, and is expected to have, within society and the community it operates in, as reflected in an article published in the *Daily Telegraph* in 2018: following the collapse of UK construction and services company Carillion, Lawrence Fink, the boss of the world's largest investment firm, reminded companies that, 'as well as making a return for their shareholders, they have social responsibilities too' and that 'society demands that companies should serve a social purpose'.[5]

We return repeatedly to corporate social responsibility (CSR) and its connection to compliance throughout this book.

All this doesn't give us a 'get-out-of-jail-free card': difficult ethical dilemmas, questions and contrary interpretations will always crop up from time to time. But when all is said and done, at the core of business ethics lies a lot of basic common sense.

What is 'integrity'?

Just the smallest amount of research will tell you that many organizations include integrity as one of their core values. Yet few define it. Where so much else is defined and described, why not 'integrity'? Is it even more nebulous than ethics? Just one of those qualities that you know when you see it?

Here's how the Cambridge Dictionary of English (2019) defines it:[6]

> **Integrity:** The quality of being honest and having strong moral principles that you refuse to change.

Other definitions include 'Acting honestly and ethically'... 'Acting in a way that you would be happy to read about in the newspapers'... 'Acting unimpeachably'... Still others span the spectrum from fairness to courage and honesty, but our own preferred definition is simply this: *Doing the right thing even when no one is looking.*

Here's an old anonymous Chinese parable that does a pretty good job of framing all that:

> ### THE PARABLE OF THE EMPEROR AND THE SEED
>
> The Emperor was growing old and felt it was time to choose his successor. Rather than appoint a family member or one of his courtiers, he summoned the young children of his kingdom. He gave each a seed and asked them to return one year later on this day. From what they have grown, he will choose his successor.
>
> One of the children was young boy called Ling. He duly planted, watered and tended the seed. But it didn't grow. Meanwhile the other children in the village boasted of the fine plants their seed were producing. Three months, six months, nine months went by. Ling's seed did not grow. Finally, the day came for the children to gather at the Emperor's palace.
>
> The other children laughed at Ling's pot. Each of them proudly clutched beautiful plants as the Emperor began his inspection. On reaching Ling, he asked about his empty pot. Ling was terrified, but explained quietly that no matter what he did, his seed would not grow.

The Emperor continued his inspection and then addressed the children: 'Little did you all know that a year ago I gave each of you a boiled seed, which would never grow. Each of you substituted the seed I gave you with another. All except Ling. Despite knowing what was at stake and seeing how you all had beautiful plants, Ling had the honesty, courage and above all the integrity to withstand temptation and remain true to his values.

'Therefore, it is Ling who will become our next Emperor.'

There are many variants of this ancient anonymous tale.[7]

However it might be defined, it seems to us that integrity is a fundamental component of ethical organizational behaviour. It is a personal characteristic that points us in the right direction. We will show how it feeds into what it is to be ethical and what it is to be compliant.

Compliance and ethics in practice

Perhaps it is useful to think of each of compliance and ethics in this way: an organization faces a whole range of issues and challenges and varying stakeholder expectations. Some are 'must dos', some are 'ought to dos', and some are 'nice to haves'.

- The 'must dos' are compliance.
- The 'ought to dos' concern business ethics and corporate responsibility.
- The 'nice to haves' are probably just that.

The flow can be illustrated as shown in Figure 2.1.

But this is *not* about separating 'need to dos' from 'don't need to dos'. Effective compliance is about thinking of these as all of a piece, and in terms of what society, the media, consumers and stakeholders expect, we are seeing a movement from left to right, with the nice to haves ending up as ought to dos, and many of the ought to dos ending up as must dos.

Moreover, five years from now the organization's behaviour today will be judged by the standards five years hence. So an ought to do today may well, in five years' time, have become a must do, and other

FIGURE 2.1 The continuous evolution of compliance and ethics: the journey from voluntary to mandatory

Commercial strategy (tied directly to ethical / responsible ideals)	Influential stakeholders (consumers / partners / media / public expectations)	Voluntary initiatives (local / regional / world organization)	Official guidance (government / regulatory)	Compulsory (through application and enforcement of law)
The Body Shop Tom's Shoes The Co-operative Bank	Recycling versus dumping Animal testing for cosmetics Use of corporate tax havens Investor lendingcriteria	UN Global Compact World Fair Trade Organization Voluntary Principles on Security and Human Rights	UK Modern Slavery Act Chapter 8 US Sentencing Guidelines	Anti-bribery laws Anti-trust laws Economic sanctions

must dos or stakeholder expectations will have emerged that may not appear anywhere on the spectrum today.

The process of what is ethical and what should be enshrined in law is constantly evolving, as new issues emerge that are external to the organization, including politics and the changing expectations of consumers, media, employees, partners and customers. The organization has to adjust and evolve with what is 'law', and what is considered to be 'right'.

This also helps to explain why a strong, ethics-based approach sets a high bar that will lead to a strong culture of compliance and a more future-proofed programme. If the organization already has a programme in place to respond to an ethical expectation, it will be ready to assume the same responsibilities, should that expectation become enshrined in law.

So, what is a 'compliance and ethics programme'?

Here is our definition, and throughout this book this is what we mean by the term:

> **A compliance and ethics programme:** An approach to compliance that goes beyond doing the minimum to comply with the law, and goes beyond having a set of rules and procedures to follow. It invites, requires or expects people to apply a broader set of principles, values and personal ethics to what we do at work and how we do it.

Whether 'ethics' precede 'compliance' is a matter of semantics and cultural emphasis within the organization.

A compliance programme without the ethics is designed to achieve strict legal compliance but no more than that. What's more, the absence of 'ethics' is, to our minds, a sign of a lack of understanding that an effective compliance programme also requires a commitment to ethical values.

FIGURE 2.2 A compliance and ethics programme

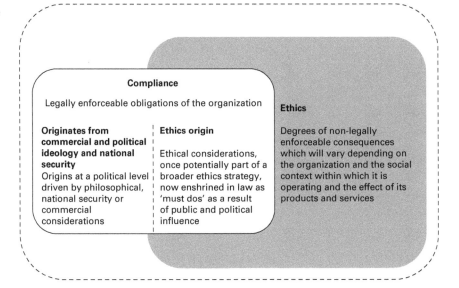

It's not just us. It is pretty clear to practitioners that a compliance programme that is not based on values and ethics is unlikely to convince the US Department of Justice about its authenticity and effectiveness, or the commitment of its senior management.

To be fair, many enlightened organizations do want to do the right thing and certainly want their compliance programme to be effective, but they have not really thought through properly how to do it, and what compliance and ethics really means in this context.

But, unfortunately, there are also those that simply pay lip-service to the term. They make bold commitments to act ethically and with integrity at all times, but when push comes to shove, they will only do so if it is convenient – especially when times are tough.

The consequences of failure

Not having an effective compliance programme carries grave risks. Depending on whose perspective you look at it from, they include:

- individual and corporate criminal convictions;
- imprisonment;
- fines and penalties;
- investigation and remediation costs and disruption;
- debarment or disqualification from tendering;
- damage and harm done to others;
- redundancies;
- termination of employment;
- reputational damage and loss of shareholder value;
- failure and closure of the business;
- ruined lives.

The rewards of success

On one level, the upside to having an effective compliance and ethics programme is the opposite of the downside: you avoid the sanctions and the consequences that result from non-compliance. However, the rewards for an organization are far greater than simply avoiding negative consequences.

If you have an effective compliance and ethics programme, and integrate compliance and ethics effectively into your strategy and your culture, you will enhance your organization's performance, reputation, value – and commercial success. Being seen and known to be an ethically compliant organization – one that champions and effectively maintains ethical behaviours – wins trust, wins admiration, wins positive stories, wins friends, wins custom... wins a real competitive advantage in the marketplace.

We have written this book to help everyone in business – not just compliance officers – harvest those rewards for their organization. So, in the next chapter we get straight down to looking at the barriers to success.

Notes

1 E Hertz (1931) *Abraham Lincoln: A new portrait*, Horace Liveright, Inc.
2 Foreign Corrupt Practices Act of 1977, as amended, 15 USC §§ 78dd-1, et seq.
3 https://en.oxforddictionaries.com/definition/ethics [accessed 24.02.19].
4 HRBDF (no date) Case studies: Child labour, Human Rights and Business Dilemmas Forum. [Online] https://hrbdf.org/case_studies/child-labour/child_labour/combating_child_labour_in_football_production.html#.XJySCKbgrWd [accessed 23.02.19].
5 J Fairley (2018) Caring capitalism, *Daily Telegraph*, 16 January. [Online] www.telegraph.co.uk/news/2018/01/16/caring-capitalism [accessed 24.02.19].
6 https://dictionary.cambridge.org/dictionary/english [accessed 24.02.19].
7 See for example: https://betterlifecoachingblog.com/2010/05/04/the-emperors-seed-a-story-about-integrity/ [accessed 24.02.19].

03

Barriers to success

In this chapter we look at the big – and all too common – reasons why compliance so often never gets to the place where it becomes effective.

'Here be dragons'

There's a quotation that has often been misattributed to the Nazi leader, Hermann Göring: 'Whenever I hear the word culture, I reach for my pistol.'[1] In this chapter we'll meet a number of situations in which we'll find revolvers being pointed at both culture and compliance.

As we've made clear, a living culture that people actively want to support is one of the keys to enhancing the performance potential of a business. But to take root and flourish it needs ethics-based compliance to underwrite and articulate its values. And all the while there are those who regard both culture (unless it's a win-at-all-costs culture) and compliance not as valuable contributors to business success, but as burdensome obstructions to the fundamental purpose of any business – the pursuit of profit.

So be warned: this chapter is all about the obstacles that can and do get in the way of effective compliance.

However, as the saying has it, half the battle lies in being prepared. That's why over the next few pages we're going to take a walk across the minefield and try to map where the dangers lie – the places where traps await, the barriers we are likely to encounter, and perhaps above all what may be on the minds of those who point their pistols!

The dragon of doubt

It's 12 September 1962. John F Kennedy, President of the United States for less than two years, is about to address an audience at Rice University in Houston, Texas. He stands up, and he says something extraordinary... 'We choose to go to the moon in this decade and do the other things, not because they are easy, but because they are hard'.[2]

What makes those words so remarkable is that when they were spoken no one actually knew how to get to the moon – or even that it was possible. But an urgent agenda had been set. 400,000 people from a multitude of different disciplines joined the task. Knowledge was shared. Silos came down. Until the way was found – and seven years later, on 16 July 1969, mankind took a giant leap.

But perhaps the most important thing in this story isn't how the undoable was done. Instead, it's that the voices of scepticism and doubt – and there were many – were unable to halt the progress of such a collective, and united, enterprise.

Of course, there is such a thing as 'healthy scepticism', and doubt, per se, is no bad thing. However, when it has the upper hand, either because it is not directly opposed by the leadership, or is not overwhelmingly opposed by the majority, the dragon of doubt can rapidly incinerate the efforts of any project and make the possible seem impossible.

It may appear that the business case for effective compliance has by now been overwhelmingly made by the plethora of recent organizational scandals, and the fallout of reputational and commercial harm that has resulted. But unfortunately, that's not yet the case. For the foreseeable future, at least, there will always be those who doubt the do-ability – or the point – of creating effective compliance, and remain implacably opposed to what they see as a wasteful investment.

The dragon of doubt remains perhaps the biggest barrier of all to getting effective compliance in place.

However, doubt is not the only obstructive or problematic attitude to be found in most organizations. So, while the exercise is perhaps a little crude, we think it's useful at this point to look at three common attitudes or 'types' that are present in pretty much every organization.

Three attitudes: the sceptic, the champion and the in-betweener

The sceptic

It would be a huge mistake to think that compliance sceptics are 'blind' or 'bigoted'. Often, they are highly intelligent, skilled and educated business people who see their fundamental role as having to choose what will bring the greatest value to the organization they serve. And in the end, 'value' here means commercial value. Their task – and it is a highly challenging one – is to weigh up where and how investment should be made to bring the most benefit to the department or business area for which they are responsible.

So it is not surprising that you may hear them saying these sorts of things about compliance:

'Not on my budget.'

'We do only what we need to do.'

'Unless it delivers value to the bottom line, it is a candidate for cost-cutting.'

The problem here is that they have not yet been persuaded by the mounting weight of evidence that points to the commercial pay-off that effective compliance brings – or even the costs of failure.

In essence this means that while sceptics may be well informed politically, they are often poorly informed about compliance and ethics. And the more senior the sceptic, the bigger the 'blocker' they can become, as others assume they speak with authority and wisdom.

The ethics champion

No doubt we would like to think of these as the heroes and heroines of our story – Promethean figures who bring enlightenment to the modern business world. They are the ones who stand up and say, 'We do this not because it's easy but because it's the right thing to do.'

But without due regard to the commercial labyrinth that colleagues face on a day-to-day basis, championing ethics can backfire – spectacularly. Indeed, even when they are subject-matter experts, politically inexperienced champions can become a real barrier to success – as much of a 'blocker' as the ill-informed sceptic.

The fact is, when the ethics champion asks for more budget or resources, he or she is competing with others who will feel their own cause has at least as much, if not the greater, claim. This is the realpolitik of compliance within a commercial environment, and leaves the ethics champion facing the same fundamental questions and dilemmas as their colleagues:

> 'I know what I need to do, but my organization hasn't the resources to implement all this.'

> 'How can I justify the budget to do what I want to do and do it in the way that will make it most effective?'

Like it or not, in a commercial environment the ethical rightness of something is not necessarily in itself an overwhelming argument. The job is to make the case powerfully and persuasively.

The in-betweener

While most organizations have a cross-section of natural compliance and ethics champions, and equally natural – and often determinedly – cynical sceptics or blockers, there is almost always a large majority in between who don't have a strong tendency either way. More often than not they will go with the flow of the prevailing culture, or follow the direction laid out by strong leaders or personalities, taking the line of least resistance, like a river through a landscape.

These are the in-betweeners. They are not unprincipled. Indeed, they represent an opportunity, because they naturally want to do the right thing – and with a little nudge or affirmation they will do so (we'll talk more about 'nudging' in a moment). But they also represent a significant barrier to success unless or until you have won them over directly, or indirectly – by defeating the leaders, personalities and cultures that will otherwise take them in the wrong direction.

If this sounds like effective compliance is a battle for hearts and minds, that is because it is exactly what it is!

So... who is responsible for compliance?

Some people have more visible and specific compliance and ethics responsibilities than others, including those who have the necessary subject matter expertise. But the reality is we are all ethics experts. It's just that we don't necessarily think that ethics, less still compliance, is what we do. We need to be nudged in the right direction, reassured that this is what we are all expected, and empowered, and indeed informed to do. If we bring our personal ethics, integrity, decency, honesty and sense of fairness to work and don't leave them at home, we will be championing the ethics and values that the organization wants, and making them the basis on which we conduct our business.

And that brings up the thorny problem of human nature...

Psychology and human nature

A compliance programme involves structures, polices and processes. But that's all dust unless the programme is respected, owned and lived by the community of people it is there to represent and protect.

Moreover, people are forever curious about the world around them: when confronted by physical or intangible limitations, they test them. This tension between the desire to explore and the need to conform is characteristically human, and it's something anyone developing, implementing and maintaining a compliance programme must recognize and accommodate.

Rather like Judo, which harnesses, rather than opposes, the movement of the opponent, the aim is to 'pull' people along willingly, rather than push them and so meet with resistance. There's a whole theory around this, which is vital to look at and goes by the rather friendly title of 'nudge theory', so let's take a quick tour right now.

Nudge theory

In recent times, governments around the world have begun to introduce schemes designed to radically reduce single-use plastic, and hugely increase recycling. Taxes, penalties and deposit schemes are all part of the mix. But it was the BBC's *Blue Planet* series that created the real shift in momentum around plastic and raised global awareness of the damage caused by waste plastic.

Incentives and penalties are important, but so too is common assent: a view that becomes the prevailing view of all, and defines 'the way we do things'. But how do you get to that – what can 'nudge' people into a positive pattern of behaviour, and what gets in the way?

During the 1980s, and drawing on the earlier work of the behavioural economist Herbert A. Simon, Richard Thaler and his collaborator, Cass Sunstein, proposed a theory that is now receiving a lot of attention.[3] They were specifically interested in how and why consumers make choices that are often bad for them, and how they might be influenced instead to make decisions that are in their own interests. They came to call this 'libertarian paternalism' – a way of looking at how specifically designed policies can achieve changes in behaviour that 'nudge' people to make the right decisions for themselves.

Why is this relevant to an organizational compliance and ethics programme? Because it offers credible insight into the simple fact that no matter how hard you try:

- people don't instinctively act consistently with what they ought to do;
- and while some 'get' the long-term goal, others just don't – or won't.

In part this tells us that translating the complexity and consequences of compliance and ethics into something so simple that everyone gets it is a big part of the job. But it also tells us that even if we do that, it's not enough!

However, the 'libertarian paternalism' theory offers hope. With the right strategic thinking and by working with, rather than against, the grain of human psychology, people can be 'nudged' into making the right decisions and doing the right thing, whether long term or short term, even when they don't instinctively want to, or don't fully understand why they should. A great example of this is a YouTube video called 'The impossible texting & driving test', which shows a very effective way to persuade young people not to text while driving – by forcing them to text while driving![4]

Nudge theory is not a panacea but, as we'll see in the next chapter, used intelligently it is one part of the wider answer to the whole problem that human beings are... well, human beings!

Once again, we are back to the core message of this book – that compliance and ethics needs to be part of the culture of an organization for it to be successful. And that there are a range of strategic and tactical approaches to achieve this end, rather than blithely expecting people to obey policies.

Danger? What danger? Burning platforms

BOILED FROG

There's a legendary experiment that goes like this:

Place a frog in a pan of water...

Watch it swim...

Now light the gas ring under the pan... Low setting.

Very slowly increase the heat...

What happens?

Unaware of the rising danger, the frog continues complacently to swim...

Until it is Boiled Frog.

(The fact that this is just a legend does not make it any less true!)

It is often said, especially in business circles, that nothing concentrates the mind more, and helps people to focus, than the urgent call to action of a 'burning platform'. There is much truth in this. An organization that has not experienced the cataclysmic effects of a major or scandalous breach of compliance may well under-play, and so under-invest in, a compliance programme. Complacent in their success, or consumed by commercial imperatives and challenges, its leaders and its culture can sleepwalk towards disaster.

When there is no burning platform or recent, scary near-miss experience, this can so often be a barrier to persuading an organization about the downsides of failure to comply. And when the voices of scepticism are also in the ascendancy, it can be difficult in the extreme to get people to believe that the cost of implementing an effective programme and actually behaving in a compliant way, even taking into account the perceived possible reduction in work won and potential profitability, is easily dwarfed by the costs of non-compliance – huge fines and penalties... even bigger investigation and remediation costs... reputational damage... and the painful experience of going to jail or seeing long-standing colleagues going to jail.

The swimming frog fails to see its destiny as boiled frog.

But this is only half the truth. The consequences of actually experiencing such an event can lead to a grossly over-engineered programme on the one hand, and a poorly built programme constructed in haste and panic on the other. In either case, the danger is that an ineffective programme is brought into being built not on shared values or ownership, but on hostile and merely 'defensible' auditability: a programme designed by specialists – and lived by no one.

No frogs swim here.

Unfortunately both these 'before and after' states are all too common. Lethargy followed by knee-jerk reaction. Bolting the stable door after the horse has bolted, or building an airless fortress with policies, processes and controls for the sole purpose of preventing anyone from doing anything again that could be determined by a regulator or court as non-compliant.

Either way, they represent serious barriers to any kind of effective compliance, because they fail to understand the importance of creating a living – and ethically founded – culture that has the positive backing of a community willing and prepared to defend it and give it time to grow.

Silence

The British philosopher John Stuart Mill once wrote that 'Bad men need nothing more to compass their ends, than that good men should look on and do nothing.'[5] We might add, 'and say nothing'.

Silence in the face of unethical conduct, whether it is contractually achieved through gagging orders and inappropriate non-disclosure agreements, or is the result of a culture of indifference or fear, is the great enemy of effective compliance and ethics. And it is the almost inevitable destination for an organization that fails to create a culture that is actively endorsed, valued and protected by its people, or that fails to respond visibly and appropriately when allegations are made.

If your destination is 'silence', then history shows that you can indeed hide, deflect or obscure misconduct, grossly abusive and unethical behaviour or corruption.

But only for a while.

Think of the ancient Greek myth of King Midas who was cursed by the Gods with ass's ears and tried to hide them... In the end he could not bear to keep his secret to himself – so he whispered it to the evening air. But the wind was listening, took up his secret, and blew the truth across town until soon everyone knew Midas had ass's ears.

For Midas, read Harvey Weinstein, and the collapse of Miramax. Or pretty much any corporate misconduct... In the end the listening wind will hear above the silence. The truth will out – and the damage caused by the failure to address an issue early, before it has taken root and spread its destruction far and wide, can, does and will bring an organization that has tried to hide terrible secrets behind silence crashing down.

Of course, silence also raises the issue of whistle-blowing, which we deal with later in this book. While every organization needs to think about how it can provide people with the means to report a breach, and protect them when they do, whistle-blowing is in itself problematic. For example, what should you do in the case of what could be a malicious or 'fake' report?

But there is a vital idea that offers a counter-current to these dangers. It is simple, and at the same it is the hugely challenging goal at the centre of this book...

The most effective way of ensuring your organization is compliant is to create a values-based culture that gives your people the desire to protect, and the role of protecting, the citadel each and every day – before such destructive silence and such caustic secrets can ever take root.

It is the same principle adopted today in the realm of health and safety – that you speak out when you see something unsafe – something that can cause hurt or harm.

The fallacious distinction so many organizations continue to make is between protecting their culture and protecting their reputation. This is both a semantic and logical fallacy. By failing to protect the ethical values that underpin your culture, you are failing to protect your reputation. And in our new world of radical transparency, sooner or later you *will* be found out and brought down.

But for the moment let's leave the last word with the Jewish writer, Nadezhda Mandelstam, 'Silence is the real crime against humanity'.[6]

Incentives

If you don't have the right understanding of the incentives in your organization, how they are structured, what dynamic and culture they create, this will be an impermeable barrier to the success of your programme. And by that we mean hard or explicit performance incentives such as bonuses, stock options and pay rises, softer or less obvious incentives such as doing what it takes to hang onto your job or to keep an office from being closed, and the ones in between, in annual objectives agreed between employees and their managers.

Those agreed performance objectives also perform an important role. So you need to find a way to have ethics and integrity objectives in performance target setting and reviews. However, compliance doctrine places too much emphasis on those types of objectives and insufficient emphasis on the bonus, the pay rise, etc and the softer or less obvious incentives such as those mentioned above. Culture and incentives combine when it comes to promotion and what is the secret to getting on in your organization, and if compliance is not also part of that equation, it will never catch up and become effective.

It is axiomatic that organizations need to strike the right balance between incentivizing high-performance and not creating unintentional non-compliance incentives. When they do not, and merely pay lip-service to values while encouraging ambitious and potentially unscrupulous employees to go hell-for-leather to achieve results at all costs, this can act more in the manner of a 'nudge, nudge, wink, wink theory' (just don't get caught, nudge, nudge, wink, wink, know what I mean, mate...). It's like employing heavyweight boxers and telling them and everyone else their job is really to rock babies to sleep.

Well-managed, enlightened organizations often have a 'balanced scorecard' approach to bonuses, whereby people are rewarded for the overall performance of the company, rather than by achieving targets focused on performance of an individual or team or business unit. This can create dissatisfaction, as high achievers might receive less then they deserve, or perceive that they deserve, and low achievers may receive more. On the other hand, it does encourage teamwork and collaboration, which may be explicit values of the organization and are generally valued. And if you don't have this enlightened approach, you will have significant barriers to compliance and ethics.

Later in this book we will discuss how to overcome this barrier and make sure your organization's incentives are aligned with, and supportive of, what you need to achieve in terms of effective compliance and ethics.

Culture

There's a famous statement often attributed to the late management guru, Peter Drucker: 'Culture eats strategy for breakfast.'[7] It also eats compliance for breakfast.

We come back to the word we began this chapter with: 'culture' – and why people go on pointing their pistols at it. We keep suggesting that it is both the key, and the barrier, to successful implementation of an effective compliance and ethics programme.

But why? What actually is it?

Well, of course it's complicated, and also very simple. So let's start with the complications... Here's a composite of so many typical definitions:

> **Corporate culture:** A culture that aligns to company values and goals.

Hmm... This kind of 'smart' looking definition just hasn't got the point – a point that the majority of businesses still don't get!

Values and ambitions can be very different things indeed. And if you don't align your commercial ambitions with your ethical values – if there is ambiguity, or contradiction, or room for interpretation between them – those with the ambitious energy and talent to drive your business are possibly, probably and hey – inevitably! – going to see your values as... well, in the end, luxuries, irrelevances, constrictions and limitations... after all, not meant to be taken seriously... but rather, a soft 'cosmetic' border you really mean them to find ways to cross, and indeed are 'silently' encouraging them to cross. (Just make sure you aren't seen doing it, and cover your tracks.)

Many corporate cultures continue, usually without intention, but occasionally with deliberation, to be honeycombed with these kinds of imprecisions and equivocations.

So let's be clear about 'culture'. When an organization is vague or ambivalent about the way it expects its values and behaviours to be present when it pursues its business goals, it provides loopholes through which naked, unethical, abusive and illegal behaviour can wriggle its way through. And as it does so, it can also numb, threaten, frighten, intimidate or silence those who try to cry out, 'This is wrong and not what we stand for!'

Our definition of corporate culture that is conducive to effective compliance goes more like this:

> **Corporate culture – our definition:** The positive, unambiguous, visible and accountable alignment, by the leadership and employees, of the (ethical) values and behaviours their organization supports with the commercial ambitions it has, and the roles of power it appoints.

Of course, this means that the building blocks of effective compliance are many, complex and interconnected. We'll talk about them later, but some of the basic barriers you need to consider are these:

- What needs to change in the existing organizational culture?
- What are the variations in culture across different parts of the organization?

- And in a multinational and multicultural organization, what are the variations in which people see, experience, respond to and understand the values and behaviours you are trying to get universal agreement and support for?

To take just three examples...

- Some cultures are much less likely to produce whistle-blowers than others.
- And some cultures see no conflict of interest in appointing their brother's company as a supplier. Quite the reverse – they consider it to be the safe and trusted choice.
- Some cultures have no word for 'integrity'.

This has implications for the tools and tactics used to train, communicate with and motivate people, and for the strategy – how a compliance and ethics programme is designed as an integral part of the larger cultural programme – but also works effectively with *local* culture.

Local culture: Differences on the ground

Local cultural 'variation' can derail compliance, especially in a multinational organization. It's one of the great challenges and barriers to success.

You *have* to ask, what is the local culture within the office, the local area and the country? That can often mean understanding, and finding a way around, 'custom' – *the way we do it here* – especially when, for example, customary culture accepts low-level bribery and corruption as norms of behaviour.

Structuring your programme around the particular culture will help it be understood, valued and retained. But it is also vital to be clarion clear about what your company will and will not do in order to win business – or, to put it more simply, the absolute red line that defines the values and codes of behaviour your business will under no circumstances cross over to win commercial advantage.

The fact is that, in some situations, businesses will face a choice between maintaining their ethical values and standards, and losing a lucrative contract 'simply' because they will not accept local custom.

Ethics and commercialism are apparently in direct and naked opposition, and very often the big money is on the fighter in the commercial corner.

However, of course the actual choice is between immediate – and possibly huge – commercial gain, and potentially catastrophic reputational harm that can cost you billions or bring your business down. Think of Barings Bank... or Enron... or Lehman Brothers... or Freddie Mac... or FIFA... or Goldman Sachs... or Exxon... or Volkswagen... or Cambridge Analytica...

Nevertheless, an absolutely central – and often overlooked – element of business is the willingness to gamble for reward. *We'll take this risk...*

Research has correlated certain cultural traits with the way people see, or resist, corruption. Two common data sets used because of their longevity and broad scrutiny are those of Hofstede's Cultural Dimensions[8] and the Transparency International Corruption Perceptions Index (CPI).[9]

The Hofstede cultural dimensions can be found online, along with some useful tools to understand different cultures as well as improving your own abilities to adapt and work within different cultures. Originally presented in the 1970s, the four cultural dimensions: 'Power Distance Index', 'Individualism versus Collectivism', 'Masculinity versus Femininity' and 'Uncertainty Avoidance Index' have seen much commentary and some expansion since then, in particular to include a fifth dimension 'Long-term versus Short-term'.

While all play a role in a particular culture's willingness to engage in and tolerate corruption, non-compliance or other unethical conduct, the cultural dimension that has repeatedly illustrated a robust correlation is 'power distance'. This expresses the degree to which the less powerful members of a society accept and expect that power is distributed unequally. The fundamental issue here is how a society handles inequalities among people. People in societies exhibiting a large degree of power distance accept a hierarchical order in which everybody has a place, and which needs no further justification. In societies with low power distance, people strive to equalize the distribution of power and demand justification for inequalities of power.

Researchers over the years have generally noted that those coun-tries exhibiting a high power distance culture have a poor CPI rating. For example, Denmark has a power distance of 18 and a year-on-year CPI within the top 5. Vietnam has a power distance of 70 and a CPI typically in the 110–120 range. Venezuela has a power distance of 81 and a CPI ranking in the 160s.[10]

Undoubtedly the Cultural Dimensions and the CPI have their flaws; however, each is nonetheless a well-respected reference from which more refined and localized investigation and analysis can be made. But why is this important? Because if the underlying dynamics of a culture can be understood, then the most efficient and effective means by which compliance requirements can be embedded can also be understood.

Take a high power distance country. The underlying cultural analysis suggests that people are accepting of the hierarchical order, which in turn means that they are likely to accept the inherent inequalities of corruption. So telling an audience not to tolerate corruption – to call the hotline and to speak up – may receive polite nods and warm smiles... But in reality, your words are falling on deaf ears. At the same time, it may also mean the same audience is more likely to obey a policy or instruction not to engage in unethical, or at least carefully defined, non-compliant conduct.

Local 'personal leadership' culture – the dangers, and benefits, of charismatic leadership

Another seminal piece of research by Stanley Milgram published in 1965 demonstrated the ease with which people will obey authority and inflict upon another person what they believed to be potentially life-threatening electric shocks.[11]

Many of us will have worked in, or heard stories about, office conditions or cultures in which, for whatever reason, there is abso-lute and unquestioning loyalty to a particular manager or person in authority. What he or she says goes, even if the subordinate knows it is wrong. To an outsider, and even to the individual when questioned, it may seem irrational, illogical and fundamentally wrong. But this can be an extremely impenetrable barrier to overcome.

Personal loyalty to a leader is a hugely powerful force and can be a fundamental asset in developing effective compliance. But only if the leader in question is fiercely advocating the right behaviours that are shaped by the ethical values of the company. The danger is that 'cultism', not culture, prevails.

Of course, these cultural perspectives on 'leadership' and 'obedience' cut both ways. Just as it can undermine and prevent implementation of the organizational culture and programme of compliance and ethics, getting the 'authority' on board can be leveraged to galvanize unwavering support for the programme and culture. While they may 'agree' with you, they will 'follow' the immediate authority.

Resources: 'The cuckoo in the nest'

There is no doubt: social scrutiny of business is only going to increase. But if you think that is in itself necessarily a reason for organizations to provide budget and properly resource an effective compliance and ethics programme, think again.

However serious your organization is about compliance and ethics, there is now a regulatory culture of compliance that is in danger of imposing an intolerable burden on even the largest organizations. New laws, new standards and changing public opinion bring with them additional compliance burdens, and to manage them effectively implies increasing costs. There is an expectation that, even if you try to use existing tools, procedures and strategies you will nonetheless have to conduct a risk assessment and include appropriate provisions in your policies, procedures and controls, training, contract terms, internal audit protocols and assurance reporting. Managing this additional burden, none of which is your making, receives few words of thanks, however efficiently it is undertaken.

This produces a very common perception that the Compliance and Ethics function is about managing the 'downside', whereas other functions are about creating the 'upside'. And, of course, such a perception is inimical to generous budgets!

Let's also be absolutely clear: having inadequate resources is one of the big reasons compliance fails. We are not talking about resources to make 'more compliance'. We are talking about the proper allocation and efficient use of resources to deliver 'effective compliance and ethics'. This includes budget, people, technology, training, advisors and consultants and a proper learning network.

The dynamic is fundamentally different where the organization itself, or a senior decision-maker, has experienced the consequences of a non-compliance event. With or without an independent monitor, the case for change is demonstrably made to management at every level, and the consequences for a few individuals will have become part of the legend of the organization. The compliance officer does not have to spend a disproportionate amount of time persuading the business to accept a new policy or procedure – the prosecutor/monitor/external lawyers are going to insist on it.

INDEPENDENT COMPLIANCE MONITOR

It is quite common for companies that have been investigated by prosecutors and regulators, and which often enter into some form of settlement agreement, to agree to the appointment of a compliance monitor. This can come in different forms, but essentially the organization agrees to the appointment of an independent or semi-independent consultant, whose role is to monitor the design and implementation of compliance and ethics programme enhancements and provide periodic reports to the prosecutor or regulator. It is a form of more or less independent assurance that the organization really has implemented the new or revised programme necessary to prevent the non-compliance reoccurring. We refer to this type of monitor occasionally throughout the text and explore this subject in a little more depth in Chapter 13.

However, while prior experience of such an event can be a great catalyst for change, we have also seen how overreaction can create a straight-jacketed organization hell-bent on imposing defensible compliance at all costs. This is the opposite of an environment in which truly effective compliance can thrive.

The Compliance and Ethics function must argue its case just as robustly as any other function. It must do so clearly, providing justification and, where possible, measurable targets. It must use what resources it can scrounge, and what resources it is given, wisely and efficiently, failing which the broader business will be justified in challenging and clawing back allocated resources.

Management time and attention

Even with everything else in place, if there is lack of commitment from the management, whether at the top, or at country, region or business unit level, a compliance and ethics programme will fail. Classically, this is often referred to as 'ensuring compliance is a regular agenda item', but it also means that the compliance officer should have direct access to a senior management that understands the positive role of compliance and ethics within the value chain, to discuss concerns, obtain support for initiatives and keep senior management abreast of implementation progress and problems.

This is often where the dragon of doubt begins to breathe its fire!

An effective compliance and ethics programme only works if it is resourced as an essential element of a successful and sustainable business and is embedded within the business as a whole. It is not a peripheral activity. It is not a 'nice to have', and nor is it a one-off project, no matter how high profile and expensively resourced.

If we want to turn it into 'business speak', a compliance and ethics programme is a marketing, design, development, implementation and feedback exercise. No different to any service or product the broader business is offering its customers. It's just that the customers are primarily internal to the organization, rather than external.

With any product or service it takes time, effort and support to secure a contract or sale, customer satisfaction and repeat business. It is no different for in-house customers. However, experts must give the users something that works for the organization and for them. If they cannot, it will be 'ineffective'.

In addition, the expert needs feedback. For now, take it as read that, just as the organization must resource implementation of the programme, it must resource the means by which customer feedback is generated and conveyed. Without resources to monitor the programme, and to engage with relevant people and groups inside and outside the organization, there will be no feedback. And without feedback, there is limited opportunity to genuinely improve the compliance and ethics programme.

In short, inadequate resources are a significant barrier to developing, implementing, monitoring and enforcing an effective compliance and ethics programme.

Poor skills, bad approaches

A FTSE 250 General Counsel once compared their organization's view of the Compliance and Legal groups: 'Legal help me. Compliance tells me what I can't do.' It is a negative perception, and not seen as a contributor or partner to developing the business.

The fact is, a rubbish compliance officer is a major barrier to effective compliance and ethics. The reasons can be many. Lack of technical competence, lack of experience, absence of inter-personal skills, failure to understand how vital marketing and communication are. The ability to package the technical, business and personal skills and approach is the 'key' to unlocking the acceptance by the broader business of the need and purpose of compliance and ethics, as well as the opportunities that it can create. More on this in Chapter 14.

Short-termism

We're leaving this to last, because it's a message – and an issue – that we can all too easily forget about. The business environment is necessarily impatient. It may talk about sustainable long-term goals, but in any given moment it wants to see rapid results and visible returns on investment.

Compliance and ethics are a daily, monthly and yearly focus. It requires time, effort and resources to be proactive and strategic, on top of the resource-consuming reactive/tactical stuff. What's more, the environment, and national and international legislation, are moving all the time. What is effective today is ineffective tomorrow. The programme must keep moving to accommodate today's regulatory and social environment and anticipate what it will be tomorrow.

Notes

1 'The comment is often attributed to the Nazi leader Hermann Göring, but the origin of the line is found in the 1933 play Schlageter by the German dramatist Hanns Johst. In the play, a character says, "Wenn ich Kultur höre... entsichere ich meinen Browning! [Whenever I hear the word culture... I release the safety-catch of my Browning!]" Schlageter was a nationalist play based on the life of Albert Leo Schlageter, who was court-martialled by the French and shot in 1923 for taking part in active resistance to French occupation of the Ruhr. It was popular with the National Socialist regime, which may help explain the attribution to Göring' (http://oupacademic.tumblr.com/post/75094913460/misquotation-hanns-johst).

2 JF Kennedy (1962) Moon speech: Rice Stadium. [Online] https://er.jsc.nasa.gov/seh/ricetalk.htm [accessed 28.03.19].

3 RH Thaler and CR Sunstein (2008) *Nudge: Improving decisions about health, wealth, and happiness*, Penguin Books.

4 RydBelgium (2012) 'The impossible texting & driving test'. [Online] https://www.youtube.com/watch?v=HbjSWDwJILs [accessed 23.02.19].

5 JS Mill (1867) Inaugural address delivered to the University of St Andrews, 2 January.

6 N Mandelstam (1970) *Hope Against Hope*, Harvill Press.

7 First attributed in 2004 by Mark Fields, later CEO of Ford.

8 https://geert-hofstede.com [accessed 24.02.19].

9 https://www.transparency.org/research/cpi/overview [accessed 24.02.19].

10 https://hofstede-insisghts.com [accessed 24.02.19].

11 S Milgram (1965) *Some Conditions of Obedience and Disobedience to Authority*, Sage.

04

Looking for answers

In this chapter we try to gather the scattered flock of answers together, and assemble them into what collectively will deliver effective compliance and ethics – and make commercial organizations succeed in our highly exposed and highly competitive environment.

Mission impossible?

In this chapter we'll be talking a lot about blood, sweat and tears. And if you happen to be a compliance officer, they're mostly yours.

To put this bluntly, we believe that if business leaders are to succeed in the highly competitive landscape of our world today, the 'ethical compass' that guides their enterprise must be deeply integrated into the 'commercial purpose' of their enterprise. This is no longer a 'nice to have' but a '*must* have'. Without it, businesses will not succeed.

The effort of achieving effective compliance and ethics will add hugely to the value of any organization that makes it. But it isn't an easy thing to do. The road is long, the spectrum of requirements is wide – and when you begin, the task can seem overwhelming and discouraging: one mission you might choose not to accept.

So let's start by looking at a famous story, 'The man who planted trees', by the French writer Jean Giono, that is all about a long and apparently impossible task.

THE MAN WHO PLANTED TREES

Travelling through Provence just before the First World War, Giono writes that he found himself in a desolate region of barren hills and empty valleys. 'There must once have been a spring or well here... but it was dry... The five or six houses, roofless, gnawed by wind and rain, the tiny chapel with its crumbling steeple, stood about like the houses and chapels in living villages, but all life had vanished.'

As dusk fell he met a shepherd returning from the hills who took him back to his house. After supper, the shepherd fetched a small sack and poured out a heap of acorns onto the table. 'He began to separate the good from the bad. I smoked my pipe... When he had set aside a large enough pile of good acorns he counted them out by tens, eliminating the small ones or those which were slightly cracked... As soon as he had one hundred perfect acorns he stopped and he went to bed.' The next day the shepherd began to plant his acorns carefully and methodically on the hillside. 'For three years he had been planting trees in this wilderness. He had planted 100,000. Of these, 20,000 had sprouted. Of the 20,000 he still expected to lose about half to rodents or to the unpredictable designs of Providence. There remained 10,000 oak trees to grow where nothing had grown before.'

Giono writes that he left the shepherd then, and shortly afterwards, the war broke out. It was more than a decade before he returned to that region.

When he did, he found that all through the intervening years the shepherd had continued planting trees, and the landscape was now astonishingly transformed. 'The hills were covered in oak and beech, and Creation seemed to have come about in a sort of chain reaction. The brooks, dry since the memory of man, ran again with water. The wind, too, scattered seeds. As the water reappeared, so there reappeared willows, rushes, meadows, gardens, flowers.' Farms now prospered in the valleys, and the ruined village rang to the sounds of children and the school bell calling them to study.

Giono closes the story with these words: 'When I reflect that one man, armed only with his own physical and moral resources, was able to cause this land of Canaan to spring from the wasteland, I am convinced that, in spite of everything, humanity is admirable.'

Here is a carefully constructed story about what delivers real transformation. Right at the centre of the lexicon are words like persistence, patience, focus, precision. There are clear messages about being methodical; of doing each small thing in a way that gives it the very best chance of succeeding; of expecting that only a percentage of your efforts will bear harvest; of never losing sight of the greater vision – that from small acorns mighty oaks will grow.

Of course, this is also a fable written to give hope to those who seek to bring about change – a story that tells us one individual really can make a difference. Which, for our purposes at least, is what is fundamentally wrong with this story. Because if you try to walk the arid hills and unresponsive valleys of your organization with the aim of achieving fecund change *all on your own*, you are going to fail. You need everyone else. Why? Because compliance is fundamentally a consequence of the community and culture it helps to frame and which frames it.

So is it all about culture?

Developing a thorough, detailed and extensive compliance and ethics programme along the lines described in the following chapters of this book is essential. But if that programme merely exists within the lofty boundaries of its own well-defended hill, and does not work its way actively into marketing, communications, the boardroom, the shop floor, the field staff, the commercial agenda, day-to-day operations – and the very DNA that defines what and who a business is – it will remain, at best, a defensible programme only.

As a result, your business itself will remain at risk, and there is no way you will benefit from the huge commercial advantages of having employees, stakeholders and consumers believing in the integrity of your brand.

But does this mean the answer is all about culture?

No.

Culture is the main blocker and the main solution – but that is also an entirely inadequate thing to say. You need to put in place the right tactical details, practical steps and building blocks – an effective compliance and ethics programme helping to shape and underwrite the culture that delivers effective compliance and ethics. The two require each other.

They also require everybody's assent.

The art of persuasion

It takes time to persuade men to do even what is for their own good.

THOMAS JEFFERSON[1]

The need for effective compliance may seem clear – open any national newspaper on any day and you'll almost certainly find at least one article describing the compliance or ethical failings of an organization or public figure. And yet day after day such articles continue to appear. People still require persuasion.

The good news is that we are at a moment when the many things that contribute to effective compliance and ethics, and how they must converge and work together, are quite well understood. Things like psychology – what motivates compliance... the role of culture... the role of leaders... the importance of policies and incentives... the alignment of the commercial agenda with ethical values... the role of communication, training and storytelling... and, not least, the expectations of increasingly mature and knowledgeable stakeholders.

Effective compliance and ethics is all about bringing people and agendas together to achieve not just common agreement about, but common ownership of, and responsibility for, the values and behaviours that underpin the whole organization. Agree what is right, do what is right, defend what is right – together.

But, of course, getting that level of agreement is the whole of the challenge.

Since we are still among the shepherds, it is worth citing the old adage, 'The shepherd always tries to persuade the sheep that their interests and his own are the same'. In the world of business these interests may never entirely converge, but the closer they are aligned the more compliant and ethical the organization is likely to be – and the greater that organization's potential for competitive advantage.

How? Well, we are back to where we began this book – with Aesop's questioning tale about what most effectively persuades people to do what you want them to do. We are under no illusion: it cannot be all carrot and no stick; and it cannot be all vision and inspirational leadership with no palpable programme or confirming detail.

Re-thinking the integration of compliance and ethics subject-matter expertise within the organization's strategy and the planning and execution of its work helps get you ahead. Re-thinking the long-term organizational culture of compliance and ethics and implementing an effective compliance and ethics programme will keep you ahead. This is also about how you actually persuade people at a tactical, training or policy level, not just how you persuade the organization that it needs effective compliance and ethics.

One size doesn't fit all

An effective compliance and ethics programme is holistic and multi-dimensional. It cannot just be top down. It also has to be bottom

FIGURE 4.1 An effective compliance and ethics programme is holistic and multi-dimensional

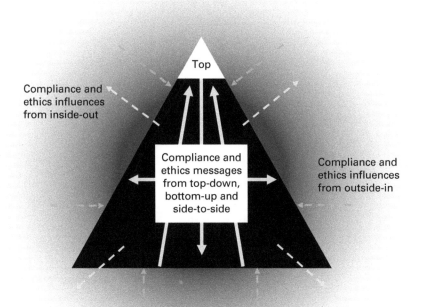

up. From one side to the other side. From inside to out. And from outside to in.

It cannot simply be ideological or theoretical. It must be inspirational, but also practical and relevant. It must be looked at from all angles and from the perspectives of everyone within the organization – from the boardroom to the back room to the front line.

Every programme is different – no one size fits all. While the components may be well defined at a conceptual level, how each is implemented is unique to the organization. Its size, its operations, its geographic spread, and its sector and risk profile.

In Chapter 5 we look closely at the question: what size fits a small or medium-sized enterprise (SME)?

Personal versus business values

We've already talked about this issue as a barrier, but it is worth expanding on it here. Many, it may even be a majority, seem to think that different morals apply when you come to work, and that acting honestly and fairly is incompatible with good commercial business practices. It's as if business says, 'Leave your personal values at the door when you arrive at work.' We are confronted with what seem to be competing and mutually incompatible ideals: do the right thing *or* do whatever it takes to be successful in business.

It is true that there is a real and growing understanding that success is correlated with doing the right thing. To take just one example, David Jones, the CEO of Havas and founder of One Young World, has actually written a book entitled *Who Cares Wins* in which he puts forward the idea that if you are a business in today's world, 'If you do not do good, you will no longer do well'.[2]

But this is not yet a ball that you are likely to find on most of the putting greens where 'hard-nosed businessmen' play.

The highly respected Professor Roger Steare goes further by exploring how love is the strongest motivating factor for most people.[3] Yet so many people, not least leaders in business, leave love at home and allow other factors to dominate at work.

We know many readers will blanche at the idea of trying to implement a culture that encourages more love at work – and yet the principle of 'caring for each other' is one of the primary drivers of effective approaches to zero harm in health and safety, and is now recognized as a core characteristic of high-performance teams. To discount this kind of thinking is the route to failure precisely because it dismisses the way in which the vast majority of people are most effectively touched and engaged. As the old proverb has it, 'Connect with the heart, capture the mind.'

There is also the question here of what we might call the 'home self' and the 'work self'. When a business really does ask people to leave their personal morality and perspectives at the door (or allows them to think that they should), there's a very real problem of exactly how that business is then going to connect in any meaningful way with its employees. Take this all too common account from a newly arrived Human Resources (HR) employee:

> Every day I showed up at work, met with many managers and many teams. I watched and listened. I asked questions such as 'Why are you doing this?' The most common answer was, 'Well, it's required.'

The problem isn't just about how you connect, but whom you are connecting with, as this wonderful Japanese tale makes clear:

THE CALLING CARD

Keichu, the great Zen teacher of the Meiji era, was the head of Tofuku, a temple in Kyoto. One day the governor of Kyoto called upon him for the first time. His attendant presented the card of the governor, which read: 'Kitagaki, Governor of Kyoto'.

'I have no business with such a fellow,' said Keichu to his attendant. 'Tell him to get out of here.'

The attendant carried the card back with apologies.

'That was my error,' said the Governor, and with a pencil he scratched out the words Governor of Kyoto. 'Ask your teacher again.'

'Oh, is that Kitagaki?' exclaimed the teacher when he saw the card. 'I want to see that fellow.'[4]

The challenge for the corporate environment is to connect with the person and pick up where home and education have left off. But until the corporate mission is truly aligned to explicit ethical values of the company, the suspicion will remain that if you behave ethically and put personal moral values before commercial imperatives, you are likely to come up against a glass ceiling.

Simplicity

When something works, is helpful and is simple, people want to use it, and you can pretty much leave it to them. Think your tablet, your smartphone, your car. However, behind the simplicity there is often incredible complexity, understood by only a few with the relevant expertise.

Compliance and ethics is no different. Behind every effective compliance and ethics programme are layers of complexity that only those with subject-matter expertise will truly understand. It's their job to keep that complexity under the bonnet. The 'user interface' of compliance and ethics has to be accessible, intuitive, simple – clear. And that goes for the clarity with which an organization lays out and unfailingly supports its values.

The aim isn't to constantly police for non-compliant behaviour, but to create a culture in which employees are able to agree, support and defend values, behaviours and processes that conduce to their own personal morality, or that they can clearly see support them and the (ethically aligned commercial) goals of the organization they are a part of.

This is about getting the crew to take responsibility for their own ship!

Simplifying complexity to enable others to easily use and benefit from what you understand, but they don't, is one of the hardest things to do. It takes an open mind and clearness of mind. Usually it cannot be done alone.

Think back to how often you have been burdened with a problem. You explain what it is to someone – a friend or colleague. They listen and they offer a word or two of guidance and, eureka, you find you are on the path to finding a solution. Is that person cleverer than you? Maybe. Maybe not. Simply what they have is a clarity of mind and therefore the ability to see what you cannot see. You are in the fog. They are not. You see the trees, they the wood.

Simplifying this complexity down to a few words, a story, an example, a picture that connects with the heart and captures the mind of each person will help to bridge the transition between home and office. It will bring them with you on your journey.

Storytelling

The night is black, the forest blacker.

So we gather round the fire.

The wood sap sizzles.

The Storyteller begins.

We see his words catch alight in the flames –

and his story becomes ours...

Compliance experts are not hired as great storytellers – at least not yet. And yet stories light fires that warm hearts and connect minds. They are fundamental to how we communicate and understand each other – and to how a community connects to its members. To get where they want to go, most businesses will need to ask a lot of their people. Great storytelling can make people want to give a whole lot more.

There's just one golden rule: they have to be genuine – stories that people can believe in, stories about 'me' and 'us'.

Instead, so many businesses try to exert editorial control on the stories that are told about them within – and beyond – the premises. A single voice, a single 'approved' point-of-view. Other voices are filtered, awkwardnesses or bits that don't quite fit the mould are bowdlerized, inconvenient truths are avoided.

There always appear to be good reasons for this level of control, at least to those who are trying to exercise it. But it has an almost inevitable consequence: things that should get discussed don't, and people end up not believing, or not caring about, what you are trying to tell them.

During the final decades of the Soviet Union, the official state-controlled newspaper of the Communist Party was *Pravda*. It had the reputation of being the least believed newspaper in the world – and the irony that *Pravda* means 'truth' was not lost on the Russian people. This is monocular storytelling – the world seen through a single Cyclops eye. If you are not of the Cyclops race, it's just not the way your world looks. And if you are of the Cyclops race, your stories are likely to be regarded by everyone else with disinterest, scepticism or even derision – as a vehicle to propagandise your own self-interests.

The day-to-day moral and human dilemmas thrown up by compliance and ethics provide precisely this kind of authentic story-telling – a balance of stories that can engage people in real and honest ways in the problems and challenges that can arise in their business. They offer the crew ways of exploring how they would fix the problems so their ship runs better.

Let them come to you. Catch them when they do. But don't rush it. Collecting good stories takes time and it takes time to tell a good story.

As we said at the start of this section, compliance experts are not – yet – hired as great storytellers. However, they do know people who are: people who live in Marketing and Internal Communications who are trying to create a community that can believe in itself and its mission. Compliance needs Marketing; and though it may not know it yet, Marketing needs compliance!

Once again, our message is clear: no one can achieve effective compliance and ethics on their own. You have to join forces, share skills, persuade and convince – until everyone is on your side.

Whatever your own skills as a storyteller, the most important thing is to reveal your own heart. People's perception of you will be shaped by what others hear you say and see you do. Word of mouth is the most influential marketing tool. If your heart is connected and your mind is captured, more likely than not the excitement and enthusiasm for what you are talking about will be apparent and infectious.

Hire the right people

People are the fundamental starting point of any organization. They must work together. They must complement each other. They must rely on each other.

Everyone, of course, is different. Additionally, we are differentiated and categorized by grade, compensation, benefits, office size and location, job title and responsibilities. However, if we focus on what is truly important for an organization to succeed, we will find that by connecting everyone by their common values and commitment to honesty, integrity and ethical behaviour we have located the heartbeat of the organization and from there we can capture the mind.

It all starts with whom we choose to employ. It is axiomatic that an organization's employment procedures should include vetting and screening of candidates, ethics- and values-based competencies and interview questions. But getting the right people and building the right culture that they want to belong to is more than just a matter of process.

In the same way that due diligence is not the be-all and end-all of third-party risk management but just one information gathering part of assessing the character and trustworthiness of the third party, hiring procedures should be getting at a more basic point:

> Hire the sort of people you want to work with – people who are likely
> to embrace, uphold and indeed be attracted by the organization's values
> and its commitment to acting ethically and in accordance with the
> values that we as individuals would generally consider non-negotiable.

It is true that broadly speaking every organization employs a cross-section of society, including a few bad apples (or 'bad actors'); and the regulators and prosecutors recognize that even the best compliance and ethics programme will not necessarily prevent a determined bad apple from committing a non-compliant act, often motivated by self-enrichment. But organizations can also develop a distinctive ethical culture and perpetuate it by hiring people 'in the same ethical mould' – even if they may be diverse in many other ways. It is possible to attract, recruit and retain 'ethical people' who will actively help to keep your organization compliant.

Compliance: with us, not against us

Compliance is often seen as the 'party pooper', the spanner in the wheels of business. The politer version of the frequent comments about compliance (less so about ethics) is that it is like jamming a stick in the wheel. Slamming on the brakes. Adding costs. Making the organization uncompetitive. A deal-killer. Sales prevention.

Business exists to do business. To move forwards, create deals, sell goods and services and generate a return. It employs large numbers of people to create and execute that business. When they feel they are unable to do what they have been recruited and employed to do, the natural reaction is frustration.

But if the culture of that business is based on ethical values, and if management and those on the deal-making team see compliance and ethics as their responsibility just as much as it is the responsibility of the Compliance and Ethics function, this sense of compliance as a 'pedantic policeman' is minimized, and choices that may place the reputation of the business in danger down the line are far less likely to be made. Compliance becomes a lighted path, and the conversation moves from 'Thou shalt not...' to 'Is this who we are?'

In this kind of organization the Compliance and Ethics function is much more like a business partner. However, it is also critically important that the function retains its independence or autonomy professionally and, in our view, personally. It must be able to stand up for those things it is there to safeguard and ensure – and that can sometimes mean sailing against the prevailing winds. This is something that many regulators and prosecutors attach a lot of importance to.

It is very hard to foster a culture of management accountability and responsibility for compliance and ethics if the compliance officer or function acts, or is seen to act, as a policeman rather than as a business partner. If a compliance officer is a member of the relevant management team, and shares the management team's aims and, crucially, incentives, he or she is much more likely to have the trust and confidence of that management team, to be told things in good time, to understand the business and to have access to the planning and other information necessary to perform the best possible role. Equally, advice given by the compliance officer is much more likely to be listened to and accepted, and the management team is less likely to view compliance and ethics as the compliance officer's responsibility rather than their own, shared responsibility.

Bureaucracy can be good!

Bureaucracy is part of the problem with compliance, but it is also part of the answer. You need to be smart about it. Only use it for good reason, and make sure people can see and believe that you do not implement policies, procedures and controls for the sake of it. Challenge the need for every policy and procedure – and that includes those recommended by your external adviser, auditor or compliance monitor.

The right bureaucracy is not only useful but essential. Not only can policies, processes and procedures help with corporate governance and custodianship of the organization's assets, they can also provide clear pathways and actually speed up and simplify actions and decision-making.

Also, many people like processes and are happy and comfortable operating within them – engineers, for example. So although it may sound like a statement of the obvious, you can improve compliance by reducing bureaucracy and making sure people can see that you have done so on the one hand, and using it smartly where it is useful on the other.

While many people may not conform, be compliant or act in an ethical manner simply out of obedience to a policy, a well-written policy can provide a reference point against which certain principles can be determined.

Clearly you need a programmatic approach, including adequate risk assessment, policies, procedures and training: we know this from safety and indeed other management systems. But they will only take you so far, so rather than saturating people with policies and procedures and then topping off with some culture and values, try to have only the *necessary* bureaucracy (some of which can actually help shape and support the organization's culture) and then dedicate more of your and your staff's precious time and energy to culture and values.

Ensure the structure is visible to those within the organization and that its relevance can be understood and articulated by them. Ensure also that it can be presented in a clear, structured and comprehensible manner to external stakeholders, whether investors, regulators, partners or clients.

Show that it is not bureaucracy for its own sake, but complementary to, and in harmony with, the organizational culture of compliance and ethics that the programme is there to support and nurture. You need to leverage and integrate the existing bureaucracy.

Look carefully, critically and boldly at what is needed and whether what is in place, or being considered, is actually necessary. Reduce where possible and amend and alter when appropriate. It is too easy to continue adding to and tightening the bureaucracy until it strangles the organization and its freedom to be what it is – an environment of innovation and commercial opportunity.

Readers concerned about SMEs will be pleased and relieved to read the above, but it applies equally even to the largest organizations.

Ultimately, improving compliance culture and taking an ethics- and values-based approach is fundamentally the opposite of the 'more bureaucracy' approach.

Integrated compliance and ethics

This follows on quite logically from the point about bureaucracy. How an organization manages different compliance risks, and some legal and other types of risk, can and should be integrated. In this way, bureaucracy and duplication can be reduced or eliminated and the same policies and procedures can, to a greater or lesser extent, be leveraged to manage the different risks.

Although we often use anti-bribery/anti-corruption to look at the broad issues of risk management throughout this book, the same general, programmatic approach works for any form of compliance or conduct risk and for other risks such as fraud, money-laundering, export controls, sanctions, other forms of economic crime, competition law/anti-trust, data protection, information security, etc.

Different types of compliance risk would use essentially the same principles and many of the same policies, procedures and controls, and would only differ in certain respects. For some risks, such as data protection and information security, the compliance programme may be less informed, underpinned and motivated by ethics, honesty or integrity but, primarily, by a culture of complying with the organization's policies.

A further benefit of this approach is that some risks, and some risk managers, can benefit from taking a compliance and ethics programme approach. For example, when an organization says that it does not really know how to manage information security risks, this is because it does not take a compliance and ethics programme approach. It has information security policies and e-learning, but nobody knows where those policies are, they are not drafted in a way that makes them easy to understand or engaging, and people are not motivated to comply with them (either through being punished for non-compliance or through any attempt being made to sell them to employees).

For each type of risk there will be a different risk assessment and quite possibly a different risk owner or risk expert, but as far as possible the same programme should be used to manage the risk.

A culture of responsible accountability

Let's start with an interesting story...

A CURIOUS CASE OF UN-ACCOUNTABILITY

A company had a fleet of vessels. Given the nature of the company's work, safety was a significant risk and a big deal for everyone at every level.

A triumvirate comprising the captain, the chief engineer and the operations manager had joint accountability for leadership, performance, quality and safety. Some of the vessels had more complex operations and therefore more significant safety risks than others.

At one point, in an attempt to improve the safety record, a safety manager was appointed to some of these vessels. Although the safety manager was a specialist whose time and attention were totally dedicated to safety, the company found that the safety record on board those vessels actually deteriorated. It was recognized that this was because the leadership triumvirate consciously or unconsciously took the view that safety was now someone else's responsibility.

The same is true of compliance and ethics. For compliance and ethics to be effective, they must be everyone's responsibility. *But* – it must also certainly be the responsibility of accountable management.

Management at every level, but especially at the country or business unit management team level, have to understand and accept accountability for the compliance and ethics programme at a reasonable level of detail in order to help its effective implementation; they also have to walk and talk the same commitment. If the management team gets this, then the information that top-level management and the board ask them for by way of assurance about the effective implementation of the programme is the same information they want their own staff to provide to them.

Incentivizing accountability

In addition to making sure that short-term incentives achieve the right balance of business performance and respect for the organization's culture and values, an organization needs to look at how to incentivize ethical behaviour, just as it may be familiar with incentivizing safe behaviour.

Many organizations include overall safety performance as part of the formula for assessing whether the organization has achieved its business performance targets. It may say that no bonus is payable, regardless of financial performance, if the safety performance is below a certain threshold; or that the bonus payable cannot 'max out' unless the safety performance is exemplary. And if it really cares about safety, it almost certainly should say it.

Such approaches are familiar and relatively well embedded, although there is always a risk that they create a culture of suppression of safety incidents and manipulation of safety data, whereas the organization above all wants to be confident that all safety incidents and potential incidents are reported and addressed.

For an organization's compliance and ethics programme to be assessed as 'best practice' or 'world class', it will be expected to have found a way of including ethical targets and measures in employee performance management. This makes perfect sense in theory but is difficult to achieve in practice. To take one example from our own experience, a company rolling out a group-wide code of conduct e-learning programme might also set a group-wide performance target whereby 100 per cent of employees have to complete the e-learning in order for the short-term bonus to be payable, or to be payable at the top level. This would give a lot of profile to the e-learning and encourage senior management, indeed managers at every level, to accept accountability for employees within their business unit doing the e-learning on time, otherwise everybody's bonus would suffer.

So far so good – a very good example of an organization-wide ethical performance target, which of course could and would be included in each individual's performance objectives of the year. However, most organizations will require that all eligible employees complete any mandatory code of conduct e-learning that is rolled out, so this particular performance objective ceases to have the same value.

Organizations will continue to need to work out how to include ethics or integrity or compliance in their corporate performance objectives, in the same way as they may already do for safety and may well be attempting to do for other values, such as teamwork, innovation... and so on. In Chapter 13 we explore how this concept is fine in theory but difficult in practice.

The key test should be: if an employee is going through their performance appraisal at the end of the year and has failed to deliver the targeted results, but the reason for this is that they have stood up for what is right, will the organization's culture and systems ensure that they are rewarded and not penalized for that action? When and if an organization does reward such a situation, and makes it clear to others why it is doing so, that is the moment when its commitment to thriving commercially within a framework of compliance and ethics will be believed. Now that *is* a story!

What's in it for me?

Focus really hard on what motivates compliance.

Nothing – no effort, no policy, no training, no communication, no great idea – will work unless doing the right thing, acting with integrity, being honest and treating people fairly, is rewarded and recognized every bit as much as making money – *but not to the exclusion of making money*.

A little nudge can deliver big change...

Incentives and motivations to behave ethically come in many different, often more subtle, forms, not just in the form of bonuses, performance objectives and performance reviews.

In Chapter 3 we talked about nudge theory – the idea that with the right strategic thinking and by working with, rather than against, human psychology, people can be 'nudged' into making the right decisions and doing the right thing, even when they don't instinctively want to, or don't fully understand why they should. Used thoughtfully, and with the right expertise and advice, this is a highly valuable addition to the suite of tools that together add up to effective compliance and ethics, defining 'the way we do things here'.

Technology: friend or foe?

In many respects you can say the same of technology as you can say of bureaucracy: technology can be a master rather than a servant, and many of its obvious applications to compliance involve processes.

Technology is a two-edged sword. It will certainly change approaches to compliance – something we take a parting look at right at the end of this book. On the positive side it can make compliance and ethics more efficient and accessible; it can be used to increase bureaucracy but also to make procedures less intrusive and, overall, faster and thus less bureaucratic. (Imagine, for example, being able to use technology to link your calendar and your expenses claims and automatically create a record of what hospitality was provided to whom, when, where and at what cost.)

Technology can also be used to get the message out there in a faster, more consistent and more engaging way; it is a tool to overcome budget and resource limitations; it can find, identify, extract and process information that can be useful as reference points, data points indicating trends, and for developing strategy.

But as the debate about artificial intelligence (AI), Big Data and privacy gets ever more intense, it is really important to recognize that people are now highly sensitized to 'technology intrusion'. Misuse this tool, and it – and the company as a whole – will be seen as 'Big Brother' – an organization bent on control that all those not trying to do the controlling don't want to work for.

What if doing the 'right thing' *ethically* looks like the 'wrong thing' *commercially*?

The fact of the matter is, there *will* be times when an immediate commercial benefit is in apparent conflict – or even direct collision – with an ethical position.

So let's briefly anatomize this with an example:

THE BIDDER WHO WITHDREW

Nathalie is a regional Head of Contracts. She received a phone call from a bidder in a multi-party tender process. The bidder told her that they would be withdrawing from the tender process because they had serious concerns that the bid process was being rigged by at least two of the other bidders, and based on that belief the bidder did not wish to be associated with the process.

Nathalie duly accepted the withdrawal. But, of course, this now left her with all sorts of dilemmas: Were the allegations correct? Should the tender be put on hold? But if so, what about the delays and all the knock-on effects? And what if the contract were awarded to a bidder who was subsequently found to have been rigging the market? Would the organization then be exposed to possible accusations of endorsing, or failing to properly check on, corrupt practices that it had been alerted to?

But hang on – let's look at this from the point of view of the bidder for a moment and how difficult it must have been for them to make the call. Instead of creating this terrible stink, involving a client in all sorts of difficulties, and thereby possibly wrecking a lucrative commercial relationship, they could have just kept quiet and proceeded anyway. However, they concluded that their values (ethics and integrity) and protecting against a potentially serious risk to their reputation were worth more to them than remaining in the bid process.

We do not doubt that they had had serious discussions about what to do. We do not doubt that there was a robustly made argument to let things lie and not withdraw. We do not doubt that those involved were placed in a hugely problematic position: Do the (ethically) right thing; or do the (commercially) right thing.

The choice seems very stark here:

> Take the immediate pay-off of this single opportunity, and convince yourself that the risk of possibly catastrophic reputational and legal consequences is remote...

or...

> Insist on the value of integrity, and hope that by not winning this contract you can survive long enough to enjoy the commercial benefits of the loyalty and trust you thereby build in your employees and stakeholders.

However, given that we live in an online world where companies and individuals who go against the fundamental values society regards as precious will be found out, and brought down, there is perhaps less choice than would first appear. Would such a business be successful in the long term if it was willing to work for customers who could not be trusted to operate cleanly and honestly...?

A lot has been written about the importance of an organization's decision-making process and the culture that emerges when it chooses integrity and doing the right thing, or otherwise. Make no mistake – embedding a culture of ethics and integrity requires process, repetition, visibility and consistent courage. As the old adage goes, you have to do something 13 times before it becomes habit. If an organization truly wants to uphold its commitment to acting with ethics and integrity, it needs to encourage and have a process for these factors to be taken consistently and visibly into account in all its decision-making.

In it for the long term

A good compliance and ethics programme is like good wine. It takes time to mature.

In case anything we have said thus far suggests otherwise, it is worth being clear that an effective compliance and ethics programme is a long-term game. It is an effort that must continue through every day, every week, every month and every year. A moment's hesitation or an 'Okay, just this once' under pressure can undo years of hard work to develop the organizational culture of compliance and ethics.

Stop saying 'compliance'!

Compliance is so necessary in business. But wow – it's also such a turn-off word! So maybe it's time we used a different vocabulary...

'*Trust.*'

Now there's an important word! We don't use it as often as we should, but this is largely because it's the actual and desired outcome of our compliance and behaviours. It is what we want employees, clients and other stakeholders to do: to have belief in who we are, what we do, and how we do it – commercially focused and competent, ethically aligned.

Or how about '*integrity*'?

Our 'integrity programme'... our 'commercial integrity'... our 'employee integrity'... our 'social integrity'... our 'environmental integrity'... our 'reputational integrity'... our 'market integrity'...

The bigger point is that actually we should be talking not about compliance or ethics... but about the behaviours, values and culture that everybody cherishes, everybody wants to talk about, wants to own – wants to uphold.

Keep it alive

Finally, this isn't a 'do it and it's done' exercise. The abiding challenge is how to keep the hearts and minds of many different people alert and engaged. That requires the efforts, expertise and talents of many different people… staying creative, innovative, dynamic, listening, staying honest… finding ways to keep it interesting, relevant, useful – and alive… month in and month out… year after year.

As Nelson Mandela writes in his autobiography, *Long Walk to Freedom*, 'I have discovered the secret that after climbing a great hill, one only finds that there are many more hills to climb. I have taken a moment here to rest… But I can only rest for a moment… for my long walk is not ended'.[5]

Notes

1 T Jefferson (1790) Letter to the Reverend Charles Clay, 27 January.
2 D Jones (2012) *Who Care Wins: Why good business is better business*, FT Publishing.
3 R Steare (2014) *The Power of Love in Business*, Roger Steare Consulting Limited.
4 V Karve (2019) Academic and creative writing journal, 13 January. [Online] http://karvediat.blogspot.com/2019/01/humor-in-uniform-rankophilia-fake-olq.html [accessed 16.02.19].
5 N Mandela (1995) *Long Walk to Freedom*, Abacus.

PART TWO

After broadly surveying the landscape, we will be looking in some detail at the specific elements and components that, when properly combined, will deliver a best practice programme to manage and bring to life effective compliance.

However, there's no magic or infallible recipe that will work in every case, precisely because each organization is a special case. And of course, as we discuss in Chapter 5, organizations vary in size – what may work for a large multi-national organization won't work for an SME, while most SMEs can use personal culture in a way that a multi-national cannot.

What is certain is that achieving effective compliance and ethics is a long-term undertaking, and there are likely to be moments when everyone involved will come up against the equivalent of what marathon runners call 'the wall'. This is especially so in larger organizations.

Momentum slows. Progress appears to grind to a halt. Obstacles and attitudes just won't seem to shift. Purse-strings are drawn tighter and resources diminish. Disinterest, boredom or hostility seem to prevail. Disagreements emerge. The value and purpose of what you are trying to do come under attack, and the mission begins to seem impossible.

These are an inevitable part of the journey, and you will encounter most if not all of them. But no matter how intransigent or entrenched the difficulties may be or appear to be, they are not insuperable, and the value that accrues to your organization in terms of creating a powerful sense of purpose, real employee engagement, and authentic belief and trust in your brand, is immense.

We know that existing employees and new talent are increasingly looking to work for 'authentic' companies that provide them with purpose and meaning, who care about things they care about, whose values are their values, who they can trust and respect. And that this 'sea-change' in what people expect from business is happening among stakeholders, customers and consumers too.

Effective ethics-based compliance lies right at the heart of those organizations that will succeed and thrive in this new environment of expectations.

To remind us all that compliance and ethics doesn't just exist within a programme or a theoretical discussion, but is engaged day to day in the life and problems and challenges and decisions people encounter, each chapter in Part Two ends with a short section we have called 'Across the minefield: Compliance and ethics meets real life'.

05

The anatomy of a compliance and ethics programme

In this chapter we take a quick tour of the basics of a best practice programme along with an overview of the key points we'll be developing through Part 2.

The road to compliance

Before we begin, a word of warning...

It is an easy short cut to descend directly into detail, and is the failing of many texts on this subject: 'Build the bits and the whole will take care of itself.' That doesn't work, in the same way that building an engine transmission, body and dashboard doesn't result in a Rolls-Royce. As the opera singer Beverly Sills once said: 'There are no short cuts to any place worth going'.[1]

We've also made it very clear in Part One of this book that simply implementing a rules-based management system without developing an ethics-based culture will not achieve effective compliance, or give organizations, investors, partners, customers or regulators the confidence they are looking for.

There is no short cut to effective compliance and ethics. It takes time – structure and culture have to align!

Starting points

The old spiritual song 'Dem bones', written in the 1920s by the great African-American author and songwriter, James Weldon Johnson, provides many school children with their first anatomy lesson in how the parts of the body are all interconnected to work as one.

To work, effective compliance and ethics must be holistic, integrated and interrelated. And while each part may be separately described – just as we do in the following chapters – each must exist and work in harmony with the others. It is a living thing. And like anything that lives, the whole needs to be greater than the sum of its parts.

So, as we'll repeat more than once, having a view of what the 'whole' should, or must, look like for your particular organization is the critical starting point. It will be different in every case. It needs to be scalable, risk-based and proportionate, depending on whether the organization is an SME, a large, listed company, or some other form of organization.

However, in every case it is also vital that you take a methodical, coherent approach and cover all the fundamentals described by national and other applicable laws and guidance issue by lawmakers, ministries, regulators, NGOs, international standards organizations and other key global organizations.

For reference, we provide a select few at the end of this chapter.

What about small and medium-sized enterprises?

SME-focused readers be reassured: compliance and ethics programme expectations and requirements for SMEs are different, in that account should and would be taken of each organization's size and resources, as well as the risks it faces. Pretty much all the guidance referred to at the end of this chapter makes it clear that a compliance and ethics programme should be (i) risk-based and (ii) reasonable and proportionate, having regard to the organization's size.

In fact, US Compliance Programme Guidance (see Chapter 8 of the US Department of Justice Federal Sentencing Guidelines, referred to at the end of this chapter) even includes some very useful statements on this very subject, which we reproduce in the next box and would find it hard to improve upon.

Similar reassurance for SMEs will be found in the UK Ministry of Justice guidance, ISO37001, the Transparency International Business Principles for Countering Bribery SME version (2008) and in most if not all respected guidance (see 'Useful sources of guidance', page 102).

There are two key points to note:

- an SME is expected to demonstrate the same degree of commitment to ethical conduct and compliance as a large organization; but

- it may meet the requirements with less formality and fewer resources.

OFFICIAL COMPLIANCE PROGRAMME GUIDANCE RELEVANT TO SMEs

Excerpts from Compliance Programme Guidance, Chapter 8 of the US Department of Justice Federal Sentencing Guidelines:[2]

A) In general. Each of the requirements set forth in this guideline shall be met by an organization; however, in determining what specific actions are necessary to meet those requirements, factors that shall be considered include: (i) applicable industry practice or the standards called for by any applicable governmental regulation; [and] (ii) the size of the organization [...].

(B) [...]

(C) The size of the organization.

(i) In general. The formality and scope of actions that an organization shall take to meet the requirements of this guideline, including the necessary features of the organization's standards and procedures, depend on the size of the organization.

(ii) Large organizations. A large organization generally shall devote more formal operations and greater resources in meeting the requirements of this guideline than shall a small organization. As appropriate, a large organization should encourage small organizations (especially those that have, or seek to have, a business relationship with the large organization) to implement effective compliance and ethics programs.

(iii) Small organizations. In meeting the requirements of this guideline, small organizations shall demonstrate the same degree of commitment to ethical conduct and compliance with the law as large organizations. However, a small organization may meet the requirements of this guideline with less formality and fewer resources than would be expected of large organizations. In appropriate circumstances, reliance on existing resources and simple systems can demonstrate a degree of commitment that, for a large organization, would only be demonstrated through more formally planned and implemented systems.

Examples of the informality and use of fewer resources with which a small organization may meet the requirements of this guideline include the following: (I) the governing authority's discharge of its responsibility for oversight of the compliance and ethics program by directly managing the organization's compliance and ethics efforts; (II) training employees through informal staff meetings, and monitoring through regular 'walk-arounds' or continuous observation while managing the organization; (III) using available personnel, rather than employing separate staff, to carry out the compliance and ethics program; and (IV) modelling its own compliance and ethics program on existing, well-regarded compliance and ethics programs and best practices of other similar organizations.

Key programme components

A compliance and ethics programme may be designed to address many kinds of ethics and compliance risks – some will be universal, others specific to the given organization or sector. For example, pharmaceuticals, banking and insurance are subject to rigorously enforced regulatory requirements without which they are not permitted to conduct business. It is the same for some other sectors, such as aviation, shipping, road haulage and utilities. But any programme is typically broken down into several essential components that apply both at the 'macro' (organizational) level and at the 'micro' (risk specific) level.

The number and terminology may vary, but fundamentally the principles and substance are the same, reflecting an international and cross-sector consensus derived from management systems generally, and lessons learned from specific programmes such as health and safety. Indeed, the main components of a credible and effective compliance and ethics programme are the same as they are for a safety or quality management system, or indeed for a management system approach to managing any risk – especially conduct risks. The difference between this book and almost all other authoritative sources and guides is the emphasis we are placing on the vital importance of an ethics-based culture in achieving effective compliance.

The nine components used in this book

For the sake of clarity, we will refer to nine programme components. We describe them in brief below, and then explore each one in more detail through. They are illustrated in Figure 5.1.

1. Top-level commitment

This is typically the first in every list – and for good reason. Without clear leadership and support it is practically impossible to implement and maintain an effective compliance and ethics programme. In effect it is the keystone – the foundation – and it may be all a small organization has.

Also known as 'tone at the top', it refers to the determination and commitment of the highest level of the organization's management to defining, developing and fostering the organization's compliance and ethics programme and its enforcement and ensuring that the organization and all who work in and for it will behave ethically and in accordance with its values, applicable laws and that programme.

Such commitment is clearly and regularly communicated and demonstrated by the words and, critically, the deeds of senior management. This normally includes such things as a 'zero tolerance of bribery' – but this simply isn't enough.

The commitment that matters most is visible support for and belief in the importance of developing an authentic culture of trust that, at its heart, values and respects people. It means a personal and active

FIGURE 5.1 The nine components of a compliance and ethics programme

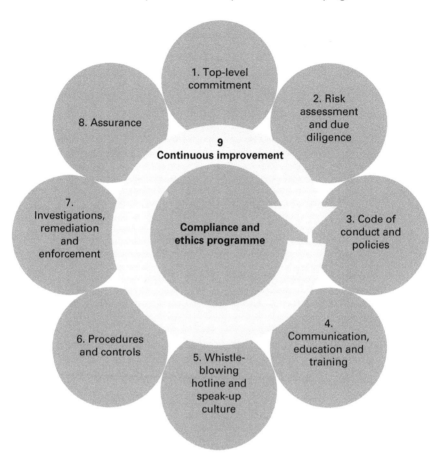

engagement, voiced authentically and consistently, in a culture whose perspectives and values go beyond, and challenge, the pursuit of profit and gain at any cost, placing 'who we want to be' right at the centre of company targets, and backing that up conspicuously (for example through the incentives and bonus criteria).

This requirement for a more personally exposed leadership approach – in effect for *emotional competence* – is now increasingly understood as a business imperative.

On an everyday level, it also means dedicating sufficient resources and management time to the compliance and ethics programme, including finding time for it on the agenda for meetings.

And on a final note here, this isn't just about engagement from the senior leadership, but from every level of management.

2. Risk assessment and due diligence

A compliance and ethics programme cannot be effective or efficient if it is not based on a well-informed understanding of the risks.

This requires some person or people to examine and understand the sector, the business generally, and its operations more specifically, within the context of all applicable compliance and ethics risks and responsibilities and to develop a rigorous assessment of the compliance and ethics risks. These risks are likely to include such areas as bribery and corruption, competition/anti-trust, sanctions and export controls, money laundering, environmental regulation, human rights, modern slavery and data privacy.

Together with relevant background and any risk management and/or risk mitigation actions, these must be explained to and signed up to by management.

There are some key points to pull out here, which we will develop later in this book:

- The design of every compliance and ethics programme starts with an understanding of the risks.
- A programme will not be effective unless risk assessment is done at the right times and in the right ways.
- This is a sword and a shield – stakeholders expect compliance and ethics programmes to be risk-based and proportionate, but they must be based on a good understanding of the risks.
- Due diligence plays a key role – but is not the be-all and end-all. It is an information-gathering tool to enable risk assessment to be effective.

In order to design the programme, in practice this means conducting:

- an enterprise-wide compliance risk assessment to assess the relevant compliance risks in the sector(s) and geographies in which the organization operates, with the types of client, partner, supplier and other third parties the organization works with, and given its business model(s);

- third-party compliance risk assessments before the organization engages with specific third parties;
- country compliance risk assessments before entering new countries;
- project- or transaction-specific risk assessments to understand how the relevant compliance risks may materialize and are managed in a specific project or transaction.

Only then can the remaining components be developed and implemented so they are effective and fit for purpose.

3. Code of conduct and policies

Once you have assessed the risks, you are then in a position to draft appropriate policies to educate people in them. This starts with the code of conduct and, for many small organizations, it may end there.

If you are taking a values-based approach, this is the document or website or app in which you can communicate and help embed the key principles and values and what they mean when applied in a compliance and ethics context.

A code of conduct defines the risks to the organization, and each policy needs to capture the latest subject matter expertise, and be written in a way that ensures all people who work for or with the organization understand how to adhere to them and recognize the value generated by adhering to them. You cannot expect somebody to comply with a policy if they are unaware of it, cannot find it, do not understand it, or do not believe it is important or will be enforced.

But... is that really the best a 'code of conduct' can be – the most it can achieve?

It is startling to see how so many codes still exist only within their own terms of reference – as if they do not belong to the larger story the enterprise is trying to tell, or the wider mission it is trying to accomplish. And while many companies do now offer a website on which their code sits, it is remarkable to us how few organizations are taking their code into the social media spaces and places where most people live and discuss things and share stories.

While codes do at times have to deal in arcane points of law or regulation, in the main they engage with almost all the big issues that people care about. They offer dramatic scenarios. They ask everyone, 'How do we work?' and 'What do you think is the right thing to do?'

Fundamentally, they ask and describe who we are. They deal in authenticity.

A code of conduct is potentially so much more than a single document, website or app. It can and should spill out into the daily life of the community of employees, promoting and provoking dialogue and discussion – a rich source of stories, challenges, honest recognitions and reflections that become part of the life-blood of the organization and how it is trying to become something everyone believes in, and everyone wishes to protect.

We still use the term 'code of conduct' and talk about 'policies'. But maybe we should start to say, 'This is who we are' and talk about 'our stories' and 'what we all stand for'...

Depending on an organization's size, sector and risks, it is likely to need further policies, sitting beneath and expanding upon the code, to provide more guidance in complex or risky areas.

4. Communication, education and training

The next step is to make sure that all relevant people are aware of and understand the organization's code of conduct and other policies – what the expected standards of conduct are and what you should do if faced with a particular risk or situation.

Of course, the immediate, and critical, purpose here is to create understanding, so you can clearly warn people against certain courses of action and make them aware of the consequences if they take them, just as a No entry street sign clearly says, 'Do not drive down here!'

Communication is a two-way process and includes channels for obtaining feedback on the policies, so that:

- they can be adjusted to improve their application and relevance to the business and understanding by those who must adhere to them;

and

- people can report conduct that is inconsistent with those policies. (This is where a whistle-blowing policy and helpline come in – see the next component.)

This component also includes communication of the organization's compliance and ethics commitments to external stakeholders and other third parties, and collective action.

But why stop there?

Once again conventional thinking can and does mean that so many compliance programmes remain cut-off from the broader life of the organization – an island unto itself.

'Communication, education and training' can and should also be about involving others, such as marketing and internal communications, and other arenas, such as the company newsletter, town halls, social media, story vehicles, vision and values statements, awards and incentives schemes, even the annual report, to begin linking and embedding the programme into the culture and storytelling of the organization.

5. Whistle-blowing hotline and speak-up culture

A key part of embedding a compliance programme and an ethical culture is the establishing of trustworthy whistle-blowing procedures to create a speak-up culture in which people can see that the organization is serious about upholding the programme and defending the values that underpin it, and will always support those who speak up.

The ability for people inside and outside the organization to confidently raise a concern or make a complaint is, rightly, regarded as absolutely fundamental to an effective compliance and ethics programme by legislation and regulatory guidance. It is also a critical means by which the organization can gather feedback on how it is perceived, and what is happening on the ground.

However, while the 'whistle-blowing hotline' is referenced continually by compliance and ethics programmes, it is only one of many potential communication lines. Indeed, most organizations have several communication lines – both internal and external. For example, a customer feedback or customer complaint line. These are usually run by Marketing or the Sales department, so the information and insights they provide do not necessarily get back to the compliance and ethics programme.

There are also often local call-in lines when there is a specific project or a CSR or human rights feedback line that is set up for local communities to use in connection with a CSR project. This is a prerequisite if you are adhering to the Protect, Respect and Remedy Framework described within the Guiding Principles on Business and Human Rights.[3]

Internally, employee surveys potentially provide a rich source of feedback and a reality check on how successfully a company's ethical culture is being lived, valued and supported. However, the learning opportunity, and an authentic, visible and coordinated response from right across the leadership is all too often missed.

This in itself creates a lack of trust and belief, and when this is also accompanied by failure to act, or inconsistent action in response to whistle-blowing (see item 7 below), cynicism and scepticism rapidly undermine the effectiveness of any programme. 'Why should I bother?'... 'No one is listening'... 'If I do speak up, will I actually be branded a troublemaker, or lose my job?'

We strongly believe that all these communication tools should be integrated strategically. Each one is a source of useful information and will give a view on how people are behaving and how the organization is perceived. Such an approach offers a valuable means of developing competitive advantage.

More specifically, the various data points will give feedback on how the compliance and ethics programme – and each of the risk areas it covers – are being complied with, and how the organizational values are being lived.

Finally, in our view there is a problem with the word, 'Whistle-blowing'. It carries a cargo of danger and risk to the whistle-blower and a pejorative load as well. We would rather use the more general, and less charged, words 'Speak up'.

6. Procedures and controls

Once the organization has the appropriate policies and has communicated and educated appropriately, it can then assess whether the relevant risks are adequately managed, or whether additional procedures and controls may be necessary in order to manage the risks down to an acceptable level.

Examples include financial controls for controlling expenditure, and procurement procedures for controlling the way in which suppliers, subcontractors and consultants are selected, engaged, monitored and paid.

For many well-managed organizations, this will be a matter of leveraging, or integrating, existing procedures and controls and adding in any compliance and ethics specifics, such as contractual clauses or due diligence questionnaires and screening.

7. Investigations, remediation and enforcement

This goes hand-in-hand with the whistle-blowing hotline and speak-up culture.

If you really wish to make sure your compliance and ethics programme is as effective as possible, you need to seek out, obtain and utilize any and all feedback that you reasonably can.

This may include:

- comments about what works or what does not work;
- what's confusing or poorly understood;
- what is too bureaucratic or clunky and so will probably be circumvented because it is too difficult or time-consuming and makes the business inefficient and insufficiently agile;
- allegations, suspicions or reports of breaches or failures of, or weaknesses in, the programme.

This last category involves what are commonly known as 'whistle-blowing cases'. It includes not just information brought to the organization's attention by an internal or external whistle-blower, or via an internal or external whistle-blowing channel, but also breaches, or control failures or weaknesses, that are detected by internal audit or by compliance monitoring, or that a manager observes or suspects.

It is an unfortunate fact that, from time to time, a situation comes to light that requires investigation. If such investigation reveals that the organization or certain people who work in or for it cannot or will not comply with your programme, then you need to get to the bottom of it.

You may have discovered an individual who needs to be removed from the company, or you may have discovered a broader problem with the culture. Or it may simply be that the relevant policy or procedure is poorly understood, too complicated and time-consuming, or simply does not work. Whatever it is, you need to understand the facts and decide what changes are necessary.

The nature of the investigation may be quick and light and result in no finding of any wrongdoing. However, it may also require instruction of specialist advisers – and even a decision to self-report to the authorities.

The ability to undertake these investigations at short notice, at the required level of detail and with the required level of technical expertise is important. With technology, speed is of the essence to avoid deletion or amendment of vital data.

Remediation – and transparent reporting of it – sets the tone for others, as they see how the organization responds. It is a story opportunity, and stories of action get passed down the grapevine. So do stories of inaction.

It also makes a vital contribution to continuous improvement.

8. Assurance

Once the programme has been designed in accordance with the above principles and rolled out, the next step involves monitoring and auditing, as well as establishing appropriate metrics and reports. Any lessons learned should be used to address control weaknesses or failures and continually improve the design and implementation of the programme. In this book we discuss this component and the final component (continuous improvement – see below) together in Chapter 13 under the heading 'Assurance and continuous improvement'.

9. Continuous improvement

A compliance and ethics programme is not static. It must continuously adapt as the organization and its internal and external environments evolve.

Continuous improvement is a process and a culture, and it fundamentally depends on the quality of feedback – and the quality of response to it. Feedback is part structural and process, part cultural and psychological. People find it hard to give feedback. People find it hard to receive feedback. However, without both we either remain static or head off randomly in a direction.

Sources of feedback are many and various – though still too few of them are actually harnessed by organizations and their Compliance and Ethics functions to learn about the effectiveness of the design and implementation of their programme. Such sources and tools include whistle-blowing allegations and other internal investigations, audit findings, the results of or impressions formed during monitoring visits, the results of external certification or benchmarking assessments, customer and employee feedback – and so on.

The key is that the organization recognizes that a compliance and ethics programme is not a one-off project but is something that requires continuous improvement. It is vital to find out about the control weaknesses or control failures and use that knowledge to improve the programme.

Here, as with communication, training and education, each person with responsibility for compliance and ethics must have the skills to combine intellectual and scientific concepts of capturing information, identifying data points and giving them meaning, with the art of integrating the data points into the organizational culture of compliance and ethics and thereby generating life, value, opportunity and improvement from the raw hard data of feedback.

It is a positive cycle. Gather feedback. Generate and implement improvement. Gather feedback... And so on and on.

The role of Compliance and Ethics Committees

Compliance and/or Ethics Committees can play an important role, depending on the size and structure of the organization and the type and number of risks that it faces.

In our experience, such committees fall broadly into three categories and have different purposes:

1 A Compliance and Ethics Committee as a Board Committee, performing the governance, scrutiny and assurance role traditionally associated with Audit Committees or other Board Committees with names such as Business Practices Committee or Corporate Governance Committee.

2 A Compliance and Ethics Committee as an Executive Management Committee, comprising some or all members of the organization's most senior executive management, whose role is to agree and support the compliance and ethics programme strategy, objectives and initiatives, and to receive periodic reports that may go into more detail than those provide to a Board Committee.

3 A Compliance and Ethics Committee as a cross-functional Compliance Committee, attended by the head of each 'compliance' function (eg Compliance and Ethics, Data Privacy, Sanctions and Export Controls, Anti-Money-Laundering, HR, Health, Safety, Environment and Quality (HSEQ), Finance, Quality, etc.) at which best practice can be shared, policies and procedures and initiatives can be combined or leveraged, and duplication and gaps can be identified and avoided or addressed.

The reader will doubtless appreciate that each type of committee may have a role to play relative to one or more different parts of the programme's anatomy.

'Hanging in the balance'

How a compliance and ethics programme and its components fit into the structure of an organization, and work through its key relationships, will of course be different in every case – from the complex interrelationships of a large company to the simpler proximities of an SME.

But in every case the effectiveness of the programme depends in large measure on the personal, visible, consistent commitment given by its leadership, and the level of planning and best practice that has gone into shaping the it. When any of these things fails, or is not working properly, the programme will fail.

As we have tried to stress, no one organization is the same as another. The profile of its risks, where it currently is on the path to effective compliance, what has happened in the past, what is happening now, its size, structure, geographic spread and commercial focus, the make-up of its leaders and people, its future ambitions and sense of purpose, perhaps above all the character of its culture, will all add up to what makes your organization distinctive and unique.

Reflect, plan and execute accordingly for where you are going, where you plan to be and what might come up in the meantime. Be pragmatic but allow some margin. It is a balancing act. Travelling light, or doing 'less', presents obvious risks of failure, although prosecutors and regulators will have some sympathy for SMEs trying to strike a sustainable balance (see the discussion earlier in this chapter). But overloading the wagon, going overboard to do 'more', also has the potential for failure.

It is how you and all those involved understand and respond to these things, creating the combination that works for your special case, that will make all the difference, and ensure that the whole is ultimately greater than the sum of its parts.

Useful sources of guidance

NATIONAL AND GOVERNMENTAL ORGANIZATIONS

- Chapter 8 of the United States Department of Justice Federal Sentencing Guidelines[4] describes seven elements, as listed on page 104. The legislation and guidance are supported by other memoranda and guidance notes issued from time to time by the US Department of Justice and the US Securities and Exchange Commission. Note also the specific guidance for small organizations, discussed earlier in this chapter.

- The UK government Ministry of Justice guidance notes to the UK Bribery Act 2010[5] lists six elements shown in the box below.

- The Brazilian government Comptroller General (CGU) issued guidance entitled Compliance Programs – Guidelines for Private Companies[6] (Programa de Integridade: Diretrizes para Empresas Privadas) (CGU Guidance) clarifying the elements of compliance programmes set forth in the Clean Companies Act[7] and further regulated by Decree 8.420/2015.[8]

- Article 17 Loi n° 2016-1691 du 9 décembre 2016 relative à la transparence, à la lutte contre la corruption et à la modernisation de la vie économique, otherwise commonly known as Sapin II, offers eight procedures by way of guidance. Furthermore, the French Agence Française Anti-corruption guidance in support of Sapin II 2016 to prevent and detect corruption.[9]

- Italian legislative decree nr. 231/2001 and the compliance programme guidance contained or referred to therein.

- The Australian government Attorney General's Department Crime and Corruption website.[10]

World and non-governmental organizations have also contributed enormously to the discussion and are source of valuable guidance. Here are a few of them:

- The United Nations Office on Drugs and Crime which provides a range of useful links to compliance related source material.[11]

- The Organization for Economic Co-Operation and Development[12] and in particular the 1997 OECD Convention on Combating Bribery of Foreign Public Officials in International Business Transactions and its Associated Good Practice Guidance.

- Transparency International Business Principles for Countering Bribery 2013 and SME version 2008.[13]

- The Global Infrastructure Anti-Corruption Centre (GIACC), unlike many other bodies, does not attempt to organize the elements of a compliance programme into six or seven buckets. Instead, it lists 22 measures for an organization's compliance programme (see page 107), as well as slightly different programmes for governments, funders, project owners, and institutions/associations.[14]

- The *International Chamber of Commerce (ICC) Ethics and Compliance Training Handbook*.[15]

INTERNATIONAL STANDARDS

- Additionally, emerging international consensus has matured into various international standards (ISOs). Some, such as 19600, are perhaps too generic to be of great use, in our view, while others, like 31000 are, in our view, unhelpful. ISOs do have their critics and their limitations.

- However, 37001 has significant value and could play a really important role in anti-bribery compliance. It reflects a clear, broad-based international consensus regarding best practice anti-bribery compliance programme content; and the credibility of, and organizations' familiarity with international standards and the process and benefits of being audited and potentially certified against them could mean that this standard will gain significant traction.

US DEPARTMENT OF JUSTICE FEDERAL SENTENCING GUIDELINES
Seven compliance program elements

1 The organization shall establish standards and procedures to prevent and detect criminal conduct.

2 (A) The organization's governing authority shall be knowledgeable about the content and operation of the compliance and ethics program and shall exercise reasonable oversight with respect to the implementation and effectiveness of the compliance and ethics program.
(B) High-level personnel of the organization shall ensure that the organization has an effective compliance and ethics program, as described in this guideline. Specific individual(s) within high-level personnel shall be assigned overall responsibility for the compliance and ethics program.
(C) Specific individual(s) within the organization shall be delegated day-to-day operational responsibility for the compliance and ethics program. Individual(s) with operational responsibility shall report periodically to high-level personnel and, as appropriate, to the governing authority, or an appropriate subgroup of the governing authority, on the effectiveness of the compliance and ethics program. To carry out such operational responsibility, such individual(s) shall be given adequate

resources, appropriate authority, and direct access to the governing authority or an appropriate subgroup of the governing authority.

3 The organization shall use reasonable efforts not to include within the substantial authority personnel of the organization any individual whom the organization knew, or should have known through the exercise of due diligence, has engaged in illegal activities or other conduct inconsistent with an effective compliance and ethics program.

4 (A) The organization shall take reasonable steps to communicate periodically and in a practical manner its standards and procedures, and other aspects of the compliance and ethics program, to the individuals referred to in subparagraph (B) by conducting effective training programs and otherwise disseminating information appropriate to such individuals' respective roles and responsibilities.
(B) The individuals referred to in subparagraph (A) are the members of the governing authority, high-level personnel, substantial authority personnel, the organization's employees, and, as appropriate, the organization's agents.

5 The organization shall take reasonable steps—
(A) to ensure that the organization's compliance and ethics program is followed, including monitoring and auditing to detect criminal conduct;
(B) to evaluate periodically the effectiveness of the organization's compliance and ethics program; and
(C) to have and publicize a system, which may include mechanisms that allow for anonymity or confidentiality, whereby the organization's employees and agents may report or seek guidance regarding potential or actual criminal conduct without fear of retaliation.

6 The organization's compliance and ethics program shall be promoted and enforced consistently throughout the organization through (A) appropriate incentives to perform in accordance with the compliance and ethics program; and (B) appropriate disciplinary measures for engaging in criminal conduct and for failing to take reasonable steps to prevent or detect criminal conduct.

7 After criminal conduct has been detected, the organization shall take reasonable steps to respond appropriately to the criminal conduct and to prevent further similar criminal conduct, including making any necessary modifications to the organization's compliance and ethics program.

UK MINISTRY OF JUSTICE GUIDANCE ABOUT PROCEDURES THAT RELEVANT COMMERCIAL ORGANIZATIONS CAN PUT INTO PLACE TO PREVENT PERSONS ASSOCIATED WITH THEM FROM BRIBING (SECTION 9 OF THE BRIBERY ACT 2010)

1 Proportionate procedures

A commercial organization's procedures to prevent bribery by persons associated with it are proportionate to the bribery risks it faces and to the nature, scale and complexity of the commercial organization's activities. They are also clear, practical, accessible, effectively implemented and enforced.

2 Top-level commitment

The top-level management of a commercial organization (be it a board of directors, the owners or any other equivalent body or person) are committed to preventing bribery by persons associated with it. They foster a culture within the organization in which bribery is never acceptable.

3 Risk assessment

The commercial organization assesses the nature and extent of its exposure to potential external and internal risks of bribery on its behalf by persons associated with it. The assessment is periodic, informed and documented.

4 Due diligence

The commercial organization applies due diligence procedures, taking a proportionate and risk-based approach, in respect of persons who perform or will perform services for or on behalf of the organization, in order to mitigate identified bribery risks.

5 Communication (including training)

The commercial organization seeks to ensure that its bribery prevention policies and procedures are embedded and understood throughout the organization through internal and external communication, including training, that is proportionate to the risks it faces.

6 Monitoring and review

The commercial organization monitors and reviews procedures designed to prevent bribery by persons associated with it and makes improvements where necessary.

GIACC ANTI-CORRUPTION COMPLIANCE PROGRAMME

The Global Infrastructure Anti-Corruption Centre lists 22 measures that together constitute of an anti-corruption compliance programme for small, medium and large organizations in the public, private and voluntary sectors:[16]

1 Anti-corruption policy.

2 Anti-corruption programme.

3 Board and management responsibility for the policy and programme.

4 Communicating the policy and programme.

5 Compliance manager.

6 Resources.

7 Employment procedures.

8 Training.

9 Gifts, hospitality, entertainment, donations and other benefits.

10 Facilitation payments.

11 Risk assessment and due diligence.

12 Implementation of anti-corruption measures by controlled organizations and by business associates.

13 Decision-making process.

14 Contract terms.

15 Financial controls.

16 Commercial controls.

17 Reviewing and improving the programme.

18 Reporting.

19 Investigating and dealing with corruption.

20 Records.

21 Independent assessment and certification.

22 Working with other stakeholders.

Across the minefield: compliance and ethics meets real life

A kick-back to an estate agent

I was on the train one morning on the way to London and I was sitting next to a man whose friend was standing in the aisle on the other side of me, without a seat. The two had not seen each other for a while and were exchanging news.

It turned out that one of them was a property developer in London. He told his friend with some pride and no embarrassment that he bought a property in London for about £100,000 below its market value and only needs to spend about £25,000 to renovate it. His friend assumed he will then sell the house as soon as possible and make a quick profit.

The man replied: 'No, I need to hang onto it for a year, as I did a deal with the estate agent.'

Double standards

Reports were coming in of terrible weather likely to lead to flooding of the city. A meeting of regional management was called to discuss implementation of information bulletins and emergency lines of communication.

Company policy and values expressed the importance of all staff receiving equal treatment; however, it was clear that all discussion of emergency support and evacuation plans from the areas of potential flooding was limited to the expatriates.

'It's up to you'

You get a text. It's about a supplier we're using. There are all sorts of allegations: abuse of human rights, illegal immigrants, appalling working conditions. The text comes from one of the suppliers we didn't choose.

What's the right thing to do?

A shipment you urgently need has been held up in customs. If you don't get it, work will come to a stop. A local official says it's no problem – if you just pay a small, unofficial fee they'll let the shipment through.
Would you pay? Should you pay?

After work you all go to a bar. One of the team says they've got some really cool drugs – going cheap if anyone's interested. There are quite a few takers, and everyone has a great time.
No harm done?

You receive a case of wine from a supplier as a thank you. You get the team together to share the wine. Then someone says that it's really expensive.
Just drink up?

Notes

1 JL Mason (1996) *Conquering an Enemy Called Average*, Insight Publishing Group.

2 2005 US Federal Sentencing Guidelines, Chapter 8, Part B, §8B2.1. Effective Compliance and Ethics Program, Commentary Application Note 2 (c) (iii).

3 https://business-humanrights.org/en/un-guiding-principles [accessed 17.02.19].

4 https://www.ussc.gov/guidelines/2015-guidelines-manual/2015-Chapter-8 [accessed 17.02.19].

5 https://www.justice.gov.uk/downloads/legislation/bribery-act-2010-guidance.pdf [accessed 17.02.19].

6 http://www.cgu.gov.br/Publicacoes/etica-e-integridade/arquivos/programa-de-integridade-diretrizes-para-empresas-privadas.pdf [accessed 17.02.19].

7 http://www.planalto.gov.br/ccivil_03/_Ato2011-2014/2013/Lei/L12846.htm [accessed 17.02.19].

8 http://www.planalto.gov.br/ccivil_03/_Ato2015-2018/2015/Decreto/D8420.htm [accessed 17.02.19].

9 https://www.legifrance.gouv.fr/affichTexteArticle.do?cidTexte=JORFTEXT000 033558528&idArticle=JORFARTI000033558666&categorieLien=cid (French original: https://www.economie.gouv.fr/files/files/directions_services/afa/2017_-_Recommandations_AFA.pdf, and English translation: https://www.economie.gouv.fr/files/files/directions_services/afa/French_Anti-corruption_Agency_Guidelines.pdf).

10 https://www.ag.gov.au/CrimeAndCorruption/Pages/default.aspx [accessed 17.02.19].

11 http://www.unodc.org/unodc/en/index.html [accessed 17.02.19].

12 http://www.oecd.org/about/ [accessed 17.02.19].

13 https://www.transparency.org [accessed 17.02.19].

14 http://www.giaccentre.org/ [accessed 17.02.19].

15 F Vincke and J Kassum (2013) *ICC Ethics and Compliance Training Handbook: Anti-corruption guidance by practitioners for practitioners*, International Chamber of Commerce.

16 http://www.giaccentre.org/ [accessed 17.02.19].

06

Top-level commitment

In this chapter we discuss who and what makes up top-level commitment (sometimes simply referred to as 'tone at the top'), why it is so crucial, and what will make it fail or succeed. We examine how this tone and commitment must be communicated at every level of management – not least because, for many who work for an organization, the key role model is the local manager.

Introduction

The first principle articulated by the UK Ministry of Justice 'adequate procedures' compliance programme guidance is 'reasonable and proportionate procedures'. As discussed elsewhere in this book, you need reasonable and proportionate policies and procedures, based on a well-informed, rigorous and methodical risk assessment. But before all those things, the sine qua non has surely to be top-level commitment.

A compliance and ethics programme does not get off the ground unless the most senior leaders of an organization have decided to put one in place. And it will not become effective unless that leadership actively supports it and the values, behaviours and policies it frames.

A good example of it in action would be a compliance officer giving a training presentation and then the chief executive officer (CEO) getting on stage (as has happened to one of us) and saying, 'I would just like to reinforce what has just been said by explaining to you why compliance is so important to me personally'; or the CEO accompanying the chief ethics and compliance officer (CECO) to present jointly on compliance and ethics to clients, partners or major suppliers.

This illustrates an important point: even if an organization has none of the other elements of a compliance and ethics programme – even if arguably, in the case of a small or medium-sized enterprise, it has less or no need for them – the first and indispensable element of ensuring that its people work in compliance with the desired behaviours is top-level commitment.

Tone at the top...

Top-level commitment includes, and is often referred to as, 'tone at the top'. In other words, how senior management demonstrates and communicates top-level commitment to the organization's values by setting an example, talking the talk and walking the talk.

... and everywhere else

But while 'tone at the top' is fundamental to an effective compliance programme, the effectiveness of the compliance and ethics programme is reliant on the management commitment and tone of every person at every level, irrespective of title or tenure. By this we mean that every person gives expression to their core values of honesty, integrity and ethical behaviour with confidence and, when necessary, courage.

Everyone has a sphere of influence. If everyone gives expression to their values, they push these vital principles up, across and down. Gradually as everyone's sphere of influence overlaps with everyone else's, the common commitments to honesty, integrity and ethical behaviour become an unbreakable bond between everyone – from CEO to the most junior intern.

It becomes culture.

What senior leadership commitment looks like

Good, effective top-level commitment requires that the most senior managers:

- set the tone and lead by example;
- visibly support and incentivize the ethical values of the company;
- establish zero tolerance of misconduct (eg bribery, fraud or bullying);
- commit to implementing an appropriate compliance and ethics programme;
- provide adequate resources to give effect to the above, including making someone of sufficient credibility, gravity, authority and expertise accountable for designing, implementing and overseeing the programme;
- are demonstrably committed to upholding and enforcing the programme in a consistent way across the whole of the organization;
- ensure that compliance and ethics is a regular agenda item at management and other meetings, in the same way as safety should be for an organization where safety is a significant risk.

It is interesting to note that the US Federal Sentencing Guidelines state quite specifically that:

> The organization's governing authority shall be knowledgeable about the content and operation of the compliance and ethics program and shall exercise reasonable oversight with respect to the implementation and effectiveness of the compliance and ethics program.[1]

It is not the role or intention of this book to examine or compare such guidelines. However, properly overseeing the implementation and effectiveness of the programme is clearly a reasonable and sensible element of top-level commitment, even if it is not always spelt out so explicitly. We examine this more in Chapter 13 under 'Assurance and continuous improvement'.

THE AIRCRAFT CARRIER COMMANDER

There was once an aircraft carrier commander who knew every nook, cranny and rivet of his ship. He would carry out a detailed tour of inspection of all corners and decks of the whole ship every day, so he could have, or appear to have, the same detailed knowledge and level of care as the person responsible for each section or part thereof.

This encouraged all crew members to operate to the highest standards and take pride in the details, knowing that they were important and would be noticed.

A key element of an effective compliance and ethics programme is for management to be responsible for compliance. That means not just saying all the right things but understanding and taking ownership of the details and requirements of the programme – and leading by example.

Who is the 'top'?

The simple answer is the organization executive leadership: typically referred to as the chief executive officer, the chief operating officer, chief financial officer, general counsel and other executive positions that the company may appoint depending on the nature of the organization. SMEs and NGOs/public sector organizations will be different.

The more accurate answer is: 'It depends'.

Why? Because the people who make up the 'top' are not necessarily the people at the 'top'. This is likely to be most true of a family-owned organization, where one or two members of the family may not be involved in day-to-day management but are nonetheless highly influential. Or an executive chairman of a private company. But the same situation can exist in other kinds of organizations. For our purposes, 'top' means the people with most influence.

Once the organizational top has been identified, we can then reflect on who occupies that position.

Where is the 'top'?

So let's look at where the organizational 'top' might be – ie the top top.

The common assumption is that the organization is an autonomous independent organization. The reality is typically quite different and could be:

1 A standalone organization listed on a public exchange.

   a. Traditionally the visible 'top' will be the executive management team. However this will receive guidance and will be influenced by the board of directors.

   b. Depending on the nature of the organization, the board may be more or less 'hands-on' in its guidance to the executive management. The board should be expressly bound by the organization's values, code of conduct and corporate policies, but how much the board will drive the discussion and influence the tone will be determined by the make-up of its members and the culture of the board as a group and of their meetings. Much of this is, in turn, driven by the chair.

   c. Indeed, a valid question worth asking is: 'Should a board have on it at least one person who has expertise in compliance and ethics and/or who is willing to take a lead and be vocal on the subject?' Arguably yes, if the organization is within a high-risk sector or region and almost certainly 'yes' if in a regulated sector. But one could justifiably argue 'yes' in all cases where an organization is above a certain size, given the consequences of a non-compliance or unethical event.

   d. The board may be as far as the 'top' goes. However, where the organization has one or two major shareholders who either individually or together can assert control, then arguably they become a de facto 'top' given the influence they are capable of asserting upon the direction of the organization. On the face of it, this may seem inappropriate, and over the years assertive or 'activist' investors have received mixed media coverage.

   e. However, that is not to say all assertive or activist investors are narcissists! Many genuinely want to protect and grow the value of their investment and see the organization contribute positively to the economy and society – which should in turn help protect and grow their investment.

2 So, is the actual 'top' the executive management team, the board, or the assertive or environmental, social and corporate governance (ESG) investor(s)?

   a. Wholly owned or controlled by one or several private individuals who may or may not be on the management team (including many SMEs).

   b. This could include a young SME with a headcount of around 50 employees and a very simple board structure, or a family-owned business.

   c. Family businesses can be complicated affairs. There may be one, some or no members on the Management Committees. They could simply be shareholders. And there could be family within the business units working through their 'apprenticeship' as they develop the skills and mature before taking the reins.

   d. Typically, wherever they sit, family members will be highly influential in setting the tone of the organization. Interestingly, this can be the case where a family business has been listed but the family still own a large shareholding and/or remain in management positions within the organization.

   e. Therefore, while the 'top' may be the Management Committee, the actual 'top' may be a dominant family member.

3 A partnership, with or without a management board, or an association of members with an employed management and a members' Management Committee.

   a. Both reflect an interesting dynamic. The partners or members wear three hats: They work in the business; they run the business; and they are responsible (liable) for the business. Collectively they are the 'top'.

b. In any partnership or membership of any size, there will a management structure whereby partners or members are elected to represent the broader partnership or membership. Are these now the 'top'?

c. In partnerships or memberships beyond a certain size (numbers or financially), specialist management is typically installed. This management is employed by the partnership or association. The employed management team will manage the organization and will typically then report into an Executive Committee comprised of elected partners or members. Where is the 'top'?

4 A separately branded division of a larger organization or a wholly owned or a 'controlled' subsidiary of a holding company.

a. In these cases, the actual top goes beyond the divisional or subsidiary executive management. They will be receiving direction from the parent organization that in turn will have its own 'top'.

b. In other words, the division or subsidiary is an investment of the parent. In turn the parent is an investment of its owners.

c. How engaged, assertive and active each level of investor is will determine where the 'top' actually is and therefore the 'trickle-down effect'.

We are not directing you to any default, standard or typical arrangement. All the above scenarios are intended to demonstrate is that it is important to step back and think about where the 'top' actually is.

Why is this important? Because the top-level commitment and tone are of critical importance in the development of culture, or in identifying how an existing culture might be undermined.

But remember – it's not *just* about culture but also resourcing, empowering and enforcing a compliance and ethics programme.

The reality here is that whatever the executive management say, the influence (whether actual or perceived) of the activist investor will dominate. Where the organization may have had a culture of ethics – integrity, sustainability, and community engagement – this will gradually be eroded and overridden by the certainty of dramatic change.

The executive management, as they have for years, may well continue to communicate regularly on ethics, integrity and the organizational values. In the meantime, the activist investor is radically changing the board and making statements about radical divestments for short-term gain. Anyone within the organization will be looking up confused: 'Which way are we going?' 'If I'm not going to be part of this organization going forward, why should I care?'

Everyone within the organization will focus on their future.

But conversely, where the investor has a reputation for taking very long-term positions, this is likely to have a positive influence on the culture.

The point is this: the 'tone' and the 'top' must be aligned. So, given that alignment of the top and the tone is critical, what can you do about it?

- Analyse where the misalignment is occurring, why it is occurring and what the gap(s) actually look like.
- Reflect on where the organization is and where it wants to go in terms of a culture of organizational compliance and ethics.
- Reflect on where the actual 'top' is headed.
- Ask if the two can be reconciled and if so, by what means.
- Ask who (and it may be more than one person) will be important in (i) creating the tone and (ii) effecting alignment in tone. In other words:
  - Who are the champions?
  - Who are the sceptics? (We discuss this in Chapter 3)

The 'top' is relative

While identifying the top is an important step, in reality the 'top' is the local management. This is because of proximity and immediate ability to influence at a personal level, set compensation and benefits, and determine things like who is employed, who is promoted and who is made redundant – as well as profit and loss accountability and thus control and disposition of resources.

However the very top is structured, what is important is that it sets the overall 'tone' and demonstrates and demands the necessary commitment, and that it is amplified and made applicable and relevant at each management level. Management at each level must take responsibility for setting the 'tone' at the 'local top'. For local management and the corporate executive alike to rely on announcements from the latter getting through and being followed on the basis they are the 'top' is sidestepping a vital responsibility. It also misunderstands how they are seen by all those for whom they are responsible.

Yes, corporate management in Sydney might set the overall organizational tone, but the country management in South Africa, Brazil and the United States need to grasp the tone and messages and translate them into actions and words that the local business will understand and heed while at the same time reflecting the broad organizational culture.

This is often called 'the tone in the middle', but that term can apply equally, if not more so, to the unseen influencers – the experienced middle managers, project and plant managers who know the ropes, have 'been there and have the T-shirt'. Often it is these people whose example and leadership are followed, for better or worse, just as with safety. They are a powerful support if they are 'onside' or can be won round, but they can be powerful blockers otherwise.

Quite simply, people more readily and consistently pass on messages from those they like and/or respect.

We cannot just stop at regional, country, project or divisional management. We need also to take the 'top' to a functional level. Just as workforce look to the local management team, so employees within a function look to functional leadership. So the 'tone' must cascade down from the 'very top' through layers of operational management (eg Sales and Marketing, Tendering, Operations) *and* through the layers of functional management (Finance, Procurement, etc). It is a matrix.

Ideally each person will adopt a tone and convey a message that is aligned and consistent with everyone else, albeit with the nuances necessary for the people they are responsible for. Inevitably that is not always the case. Everyone, at any particular time, will have their own personal perspectives and challenges. Given the importance of 'tone' in the creation and integration of an organizational culture of compliance and ethics, it is vital those with compliance responsibilities recognize the matrix, that it is imperfect – and that it needs their support.

The point is that at each level, there is a 'top' to which all those below will look. This 'top' is in reality often much more influential than the very top (the board and executive management'). The 'very top' can be distant, remote and dislocated from the day-to-day operational business reality. The 'local top' is typically from the same country and is likely to also be from or at least in the same region or town. It is this 'local top' that makes the day-to-day decisions concerning things like working conditions, salary, job prospects. So the 'voice' or 'tone' of this 'local top' is crucial to the development, effectiveness and authenticity of the local compliance and ethics programme.

Organizations are quite linear in how they operate, with communications travelling more quickly and more effectively up and down, rather from side to side. The fact is, people are more likely to listen to and cooperate with those they see as 'like us round here' rather than 'different from us round here.' In an organizational context, this means people that work in the same business unit or function, rather than those from another function or business unit. Designing and implementing the tone should recognize this tendency.

In other words, while top-down delivery of messages, culture and expectations is absolutely fundamental to any compliance and ethics programme, in practice it is the 'local top' that reinforces and generates the effectiveness of the programme on a day-to-day basis and embeds it into the activities of each person, from the most junior to the most senior.

Looking for champions – and working with them

For the compliance officers, relationships with the 'local top' at each level and in each part of the organization should be developed and nurtured. These will be your champions. Your eyes and your ears. If they are valued and appreciated they will find and take the time to proactively feedback valuable information to you in context.

Some will be more accustomed or inclined to work with you. Others less so – in which case you will need to work more on the nature of the relationship. Key to this is to explain the contribution your compliance and ethics programme can make to the success of their business unit – operationally and financially, and to them personally – success increases the chances of bonus and promotion, etc.

If each 'local' part of the organization is effective, then the whole is likely to be effective. If one 'local' part of the programme is not functioning, it is a hole in the programme and a fundamental weakness that could potentially be large enough for the organization to fall. No one other 'local' part of the programme can directly compensate for that missing part of the programme.

It's about everyone in a management position.

Whether the compliance officer is part of the management team or not, it is those in management positions who are not compliance experts that in fact drive the organizational culture of compliance and ethics. The corporate executive drives the broad organization-wide conversation... all the way to the local management who will amplify the messages while incorporating localized nuances.

It is through everyone working collectively, and together, that effective compliance and ethics becomes embedded within the organization and takes root as part of a living culture. The business leaders lead the charge. This is so important for business leaders, not just compliance officers, to acknowledge:

> Each business leader at each level must be a champion. Each business leader at every level must set the tone and recognize s/he is seen by many as the 'top'.

This is one of the features that distinguish leadership from management.

What makes top-level commitment?

Top-level commitment is comprised of four elements:

1 written words;

2 spoken words;

3 inaction;

4 action.

Let's take them in order.

Written words

Note that out of the four elements, it is only written words that are fixed and can be returned to time and time over for reference and guidance. It also tends only to be the written word that can be audited or demonstrated to a regulator or prosecutor. So just as there can be an overreliance on policies that are too numerous or complex for employees to cope with, so there may be an overreliance on the written word for setting and explaining the tone.

Accordingly, it needs to be approached with care and attention. It will be the reference point for the months and years to come: used as a guide to position and steer the culture of the organization and as a means to screen new hires or discipline those who deviate.

The other three are transient, and to resonate they need to be personal. But they may be more authentic and ultimately more influential.

Written words are what define compliance policies. They can also do a great job of clarifying, positioning and guiding people.

Tone – and some measure of how committed a leadership is to creating and maintaining an ethical organization – will be enshrined in the 'values'. The order they come in... the way they are positioned... any symbols used... how they are defined... and where, when and how often they appear.

These things will also be enshrined in the code of conduct... the way it is written... typeface, graphics, layout... how is it marketed... where it is positioned in the organization... hard copies or exclusively online.

Whether it is just explanatory or capable of being enforced. Who speaks to employees only and with a separate code of conduct for contractors, consultants and suppliers? To what extent it features and is deployed in the organization's storytelling and day-to-day conversations.

All these points sound silly, but they are not. They are crucially important. The code of conduct is a critical document in the arsenal of the compliance and ethics programme and although we will go into the code of conduct in more detail in Chapter 8, for now, our point is simply how a code contributes to the 'tone'.

Most policies, and certainly those concerning compliance and ethics, will be reviewed, approved and signed off by the executive management or the board. Who signs them, how they are drafted, where they are located and how they are referred to (frequency, context and manner) will determine whether they become mainstream within the operational, compliance and ethical culture of the organization.

For example, are the critical policies given acronyms that are remembered and referenced by everyone when required? Even if people don't know precisely what the policy says, do they 'know' what it means in terms of culture and expected behaviour?

It doesn't have to be scientific. At the end of the day one is utilizing marketing skills to influence a natural compliance and ethical response.

Spoken words

So far we've talked about the written word. So, a few lines on the spoken word. The more the values and culture of compliance and ethics are incorporated into introductions, meeting agenda, structure and process, and discussion points and actions, the more they will become an integral part of the way discussions are held and the way decisions are made.

Engaging in external conversations within the frame of your own organizational values and cultural reference points immediately puts the discussion, decisions and actions within your own organization's frame of reference rather than the other party's. It gives you an immediate competitive advantage as you are working within, or can retreat to, your own comfort zone. One notices this when meeting with, or negotiating with, some of the very large multinational organizations with very strong cultural reference points. The meeting and greeting, the introductions, the material on the walls, the meeting structure and layout and distribution of action items.

The point is that the more the conversations become part of the daily conversation at every level within the organization, the more the conversations will become the norm within organizational operations generally, both internally and externally. The more the conversations are had, and the less 'fanfare' there is around each conversation, the more the 'tone' becomes normalized and embedded within the organization from top to bottom and from side to side. When the 'tone from the top' becomes the 'tone from within', whether in written or spoken word, that is a sign things are working!

Inaction

Picture the CEO actively calling up the compliance and ethics experts to the stage and the positive lasting association that is created. Now picture the abject frustration and disillusionment when no action is taken to address a non-compliant or unethical event, and those involved get away with it.

Inaction undermines all the hard work over weeks, months, years to build a compliance and ethics programme. It damages morale. And it has a profoundly negative impact on future efforts to promote a culture of speaking up, giving feedback, or whistle-blowing. It's so important for those at the 'top' to recognize this. People across the organization listen to what is and what is not said and watch what is and is not done.

The 'tone' is fragile. It has blazoned across it 'HANDLE WITH CARE'.

Failure by the people at the 'top' to be consistent, and frequently and visibly consistent, can create fractures within the tone and the culture. If those fractures get big enough, no written words, policies, procedures or system of controls can prevent things from shattering into a thousand pieces. Take the following real-life example:

VISIBLE INACTION

A manager was caught knowingly and wantonly circumventing anti-corruption and travel policies after arranging a business trip to visit some operational facilities.

The planned multi-stop itinerary would have enriched him and a colleague and enabled two government officials accompanying them at the company's cost to engage in tourism and shopping.

The trip was cancelled but, for reasons that remain unexplained, no disciplinary action was taken.

This situation presented the organization with an opportunity to act decisively and visibly. It didn't. While the leadership was 'tone deaf', the organization heard it 'loud and clear'.

Consistent visible action

The simple fact is, if people see that others, particularly others in influential positions, are not living by the 'rules' then why should they? No-one is 'above the law' but sometimes people think they are and this has the potential to create a larger and longer lasting issue to solve.

If a scientific approach is needed, it is a well-researched phenomenon that first impressions set expectations. In the service sector this is a critical response to understand. A good first impression creates space for a person to remain satisfied overall and give a positive review even if there are instances of dissatisfaction. A bad first impression requires a higher and more continuous level of satisfaction before the person will 'forget' the initial dissatisfaction and register an overall sense of satisfaction. Where there is prolonged or regular dissatisfaction, naturally that will be the lasting impression.

The same applies to tone at the top. Starting out with a robust and consistent message, words and actions from the outset, the tone will continue to resonate even where there may be the odd hiccup. However, if the first time the compliance and ethics 'tone' is challenged and the 'top' fails to respond appropriately and robustly either through actions or inaction, or words spoken or unspoken, the effort to create a robust and effective culture of compliance and ethics is immediately undermined. Whatever is next said or done, however passionate, is met only with cynicism and scepticism.

Here is a real-life example of how top-level action can successfully be made visible:

VISIBLE ACTION FROM THE TOP

When I was giving an annual presentation to a gathering of all members of an organization's global Sales and Marketing function, the chief executive (who had been present on the first day and given a presentation alone, but whose presence was not needed on the second day), stayed behind to listen.

At the end of my presentation, he climbed up onto the stage and asked the audience for a couple of minutes of further attention on this topic. 'Let me just underline a couple of key things that our chief ethics and compliance officer has just said. This is why compliance and ethics is important to me, this is why it is important to our organization and to you.'

Why

So we have examined the 'who' and the 'what'. Now we turn to the 'why'.

Top-level commitment is critical in the dissemination and integration of the organization's values, the development of an organizational culture of compliance and ethics, and the implementation of an effective compliance and ethics programme.

This is not argument. It is a statement of fact.

As we stated in Chapter 5, it is the hook from which the organization hangs. Without it, the organization will fall. A body without a head. A car without a steering wheel. A phone without a battery. Picture it as you will.

Let's look at it from two perspectives:

- top-level commitment as an 'enabler';

and

- top-level commitment as an 'enforcer'.

Top-level commitment as an 'enabler'

So how do you give a face to compliance and ethics? By the commitment of resources, authority and money. The commitment, or non-commitment, of resources speaks volumes about a leadership's commitment to compliance and ethics and the presence, credibility and authority it wishes to give them within the organization.

The size and resources of the organization and the risks it faces dictate what resources the organization can and will devote to compliance. At the very least, it must give a senior manager responsibility and authority for assessing and understanding the risks and overseeing the design and implementation of a suitable programme.

Even if the organization can only commit part of one person to this role (in other words, making compliance an additional responsibility of someone who already has responsibility for other, reasonably compatible areas, such as Finance, HR, Risk Management, Audit or Legal) that person is still performing an important office or function, and Compliance must be understood as a function in the same way as those others just mentioned. Moreover, the person chosen must have sufficient seniority, credibility and, above all, authority to perform the role effectively.

The chief ethics and compliance officer has to be able to speak and act with the authority, and as the mouthpiece of the chief executive.

If the CECO belongs to the Legal function in an organization that values it and gives it appropriate authority, then they can draw some authority from that function too, but subject to the same limitations.

Whether adequate resources are available is fundamentally a leadership decision and a decision within the hands of those who hold and manage the budget. A critical skill of leadership is to create time and space to determine whether others have reflected on what resources they need to successfully deliver their responsibilities and create additional value. Whether a leader asks, listens and acts, or does none of these things, speaks volumes. Even if resources are not ultimately secured, just asking, listening and being available to help, offer ideas and contribute can prove highly motivational. However, ultimately 'effectiveness' is a function of adequate resources: people, technical, financial, time and a show of commitment by the 'top'.

Why is the 'show' important? Because very often the CECO has a role without true influence or authority. They have to influence but do not have line management authority to help do so, or to insist on anything. So they have to draw their authority from personal qualities, gravitas and interpersonal skills but also from the chief executive of the organization. When others have 'more important things to do' it helps enormously when the 'top' reinforces the importance of the particular compliance or ethics activity and visibly supports the compliance and ethics expert responsible. This is 'tone at the top', and it makes a huge difference.

But 'tone' isn't just something that is projected or transmitted – it's also something that is received. Compare:

1 A CEO stands up at the annual leadership conference and gives a talk about the importance of the organization's values and its culture of ethics and compliance.

2 A CEO stands up, calls up the CECO to stand with her/him, and gives the same speech.

From the CEO's angle the tone being *projected* is the same. Same speech. From the audience's angle, the tone *received* is completely different. The second gives explicit and unconditional support to those responsible for the creation, implementation, maintenance and enforcement of the organization's culture of compliance and ethics.

This is tone at the top 'enabling'.

Positioning compliance and ethics

The CECO should be a member of the senior management team, or at the very least attend relevant, or relevant parts of senior management team meetings. This is one of the most fundamental and visible manifestations of top-level commitment. The same is true of country, regional and business unit compliance officers, if such a network or function is established. If not, they will not have sufficient authority and credibility, nor will they have sufficient understanding of the business and of management priorities, nor sufficient advance notice of potential issues that they can help prevent.

We examine elsewhere the multifaceted skills, experience and characteristics of the ideal or model CECO, but from the point of view of top-level commitment, the key point is that if someone too junior and ineffectual is appointed they will not be able to do an effective job, and senior management will have failed to fulfil a key part of the commitment expected of them.

(In some cases, one wonders if senior management of an organization have chosen someone quite junior and ineffectual in order to ensure that Compliance does not get too powerful and does not interfere too much with the organization's work and, especially, its profitability.)

Budget and resources

Top-level commitment also means that senior management must devote adequate budget and other resources to compliance and ethics to enable the Compliance and Ethics function to do its job and the programme to be effective. This can include budgets to hire appropriate staff; to purchase external expertise and services for risk assessment, programme design, implementation and testing/auditing/benchmarking; to purchase or enhance existing information technology (IT) systems; to pay for e-learning and a whistle-blowing helpline provider; to provide adequate Communications support; to investigate whistle-blowing allegations and other allegations or suspicions of non-compliant conduct, and so on.

Management time and attention

Even with lots of resources and budget, the compliance and ethics programme can still be ineffective due to lack of top-level commitment if the most senior management, as well as the country, region or business unit management, do not dedicate sufficient time and attention to the topic. Classically, this is often referred to as 'ensuring compliance is a regular agenda item', but it also means that the CECO should have direct, frequent access to senior management to discuss concerns, obtain support for initiatives and keep senior management abreast of implementation progress and problems.

Fostering culture

Ultimately, top-level commitment is fundamentally about fostering the appropriate culture. Throughout this book we have been concerned to stress the critical importance of culture and values in embedding an effective compliance and ethics programme.

Culture comes from the top of an organization (although it may be interesting and instructive to examine how culture may also come from the bottom up). It is certainly true that middle management performs a key role in setting the tone and leading by example: in simple terms, the larger and more geographically and culturally diverse an organization, and the more siloed, the more distant people working in and for the organization are from the most senior leaders who they may not even know and to whose opinions they may be indifferent. So yes, top-level commitment includes middle management commitment, but either way that commitment must include fostering the right culture.

Where an organization has values that include integrity, honesty, ethics or something else compatible with 'doing the right thing' then it is easier and more powerful to build that culture on such value(s). But whatever approach the organization takes and wherever it starts from, the compliance and ethics programme is unlikely to be effective and the top-level commitment is likely to be criticized or critically at fault, if senior leaders fail to foster that culture and to demand that compliance be a matter of culture.

One leader of an organization that we came across repeatedly emphasized the need for a culture of compliance. Sometimes this was shorthand for an ethical culture, but sometimes he really meant it in the sense that 'We have policies and procedures for a good reason, and you must comply with them. It is not just about an ethical culture but about making sure that the system of internal controls works in the way intended, so that we are good custodians of our shareholders' assets.'

Top-level commitment through 'enforcement'

Without the threat of enforcement, without examples of enforcement, without clarity of tone when it is needed, without consistent visible action, there is no stick to complement the carrot. We discuss this topic at the beginning of Chapter 12, in which we examine the importance of robust but fair investigations, remediation and disciplinary procedures as one of our nine components.

In conclusion

Top-level commitment therefore has two sides to it:

- The enabler: *The creator. Inspirational. Motivating. Evocative. Innovative.*
- The enforcer: *Decisive clear demarcation of what is, and what is not, acceptable through action, words and the consistent pursuit of disciplinary due process.*

Across the minefield: compliance and ethics meets real life

The psychology of being challenged

Marie works for a company that designs large, highly specialist equipment that it then operates. A colleague of hers, let's call him Nigel, is responsible for overseeing the design and construction of this equipment. Recently, whenever Marie left work, when most people have already left, she would walk past several large, detailed plans left spread out on various desks in the open plan area outside his office.

One morning Marie sent Nigel a message for him to read when he got to work. 'Are those plans not confidential at all?' Later that day, he replied: 'Not especially. I suppose somewhat, but I figure the office is safe.'

'Look,' said Marie, 'this is not me speaking as the compliance officer. I am not even sure whether we have a clean desk policy, and if we do, it is not my policy or necessarily my responsibility to enforce it. I am thinking more from an industrial espionage perspective. Are these not the sorts of plans that a competitor might be keen to get their hands on – especially if they came from another country? And if you really wanted to get your hands on these plans, it would not be that hard to pay someone to get them for you one evening.'

'True, true. Perhaps I will roll them up a bit.' So he rolls up the plans and leaves them on one of the open plan desks, where they remain to this day.

According to Marie, Nigel is a fairly senior manager, a very sensible, responsible person. He is better placed than most to appreciate the confidentiality and value in these documents, and the possibility of someone being willing to pay or steal to get them. They are his clear and sole responsibility, and they embody some of the design expertise that he has provided or presided over. Yet he cannot see the point of doing what Marie suggested. She thinks he sees it as a tedious, compliance-related procedure, and possibly doesn't like the fact that someone challenged, in the gentlest way, his ability to think it through himself and work out how to operate sensibly and safely.

Stopping the rot?

A member of staff was disciplined and removed from the organization for gross misconduct. Three months later it was announced that he had joined a competitor organization as head of department. His ex-manager from the old organization felt that it would be the doing the right thing to alert the new organization as to why this employee had been released.

What happened next?

'It's up to you'

You're really worried about someone on your team who seems to be in great mental stress. But when you tell them you're concerned, they beg you not to say anything to anyone.
Should you do what they ask?

You've just been promoted and are about to meet an important overseas customer. Someone on the team tells you that the customer always

expects 'a nice gift' whenever he has a meeting with the company, and suggests an idea. It's not excessive.
Carry on regardless?

You're right in the middle of bidding for a valuable new contract. Someone on your team finds out what the two other competitors are offering.
Take advantage?

It's Tuesday and all the talk at work is about an amazing new deal that the company expects to secure and publicly announce on Thursday. Nothing has been confirmed, but on the strength of the rumour, a couple of people say they're going to buy some shares.
That okay?

Note

1   https://www.ussc.gov/guidelines/2015-guidelines-manual/2015-Chapter-8 [accessed 17.02.19].

07

Risk assessment and due diligence

In this chapter we explore how to properly go about compliance risk assessment, show the role that due diligence may play, and provide some guidance on good and bad practices and perspectives.

Before we begin

This book is about compliance and ethics programmes generally, but for the sake of both illustration and precision, we use specific examples, such as anti-bribery/anti-corruption programmes and risks, to explore the issues in appropriate detail. However, the same general, programmatic approach is applicable to any form of compliance or conduct risk.

Conduct risk is a risk, not of something external (such as a hazard or market conditions) impacting the company's performance or sustainability, but of people working in or for the company doing something unlawful or unethical and thereby causing legal and reputational harm to the company, themselves and others.

The type of compliance and ethics programme described in this book would work equally well for other risks such as fraud, money-laundering, export controls, sanctions, other forms of economic crime, competition law/anti-trust, data protection, information security... and so on.

The psychology of risk

We are about to look at the importance of assessing risk, how to be methodical in doing it, and how you go about putting adequate measures into place to manage it. But once you are in the midst of your own methodology and processes, it's easy to lose sight of the fact that so much of the risk an organization faces comes from how human nature can subvert your processes, or justify finding a way around them.

One of the greatest problems in achieving effective compliance has this very issue at its centre, and makes the compass give confused readings or even appear to point in the wrong direction. For example, one of the reasons why bribery risk is so hard to manage is that a business man or woman may view the failure to pay the bribe as a serious risk to the achievement of the business objectives. Where the norm is for bribes to oil the wheels of commerce, risk becomes relative to the norm. And so it becomes all too easy to justify participation in bribery as simple 'needs must' common sense ('If we don't pay this small bribe we won't be able to do our business').

Even where the bribery and corruption are on a much larger scale, people can – and often do – re-characterize what they are doing in terms that could almost appear 'ethical'. For example, 'Our competitors will almost certainly be offering bribes to clients who accept and expect them as a matter of course and custom, so if we do too it's simply a matter of ensuring that business is conducted fairly, on an equal playing field.'

When this is the case, and business objectives are apparently being supported by non-compliant behaviour, it is very possible for people to view compliance as simply a nuisance – words heard but not meant to be listened to. This in itself is a serious risk. Business-focused people forget, put to one side, or simply minimize the risk that even an apparently 'minor' non-compliance event can end up damaging an organization in ways that ambush its objectives, and indeed can bring the whole house down.

The equally often ignored corollary is that authentically upholding its own compliance and ethics gives an organization reputational and other competitive advantages in the market place that actively contribute to the achievement of its objectives.

So let's set out our stall for this chapter:

> Compliance is a form of risk management, and many of the very same best practice principles that apply to professional risk management generally apply to compliance.

But at the same time compliance risk management is also a special case and, as this book consistently argues, cultural dynamics – including the way commercial imperatives and behaviours sit within a clear, and clearly upheld, ethical framework – play a vital part in its success.

The problem with assessing risk

Often, and especially in business, risk is defined or discussed in terms of the uncertainty of an event occurring that could have an impact on the achievement of objectives. However, while a non-compliance event may have very serious consequences for the organization in terms of fines and penalties, as we've just seen, people may not see it as having an impact on the achievement of the organization's objectives – quite the reverse. For example, giving bribes to win a contract may achieve the objective of winning the contract (although of course the payer is never sure if they paid enough to win the contract or paid the right person).

That's why in the case of compliance, when risk is defined around business objectives, the classic risk assessment calculus of 'likelihood x impact' can end up giving you the wrong answers. 'Impact' needs to be understood in a more holistic way.

The immediate output of a risk assessment will be:

- What is the chance of a non-compliance or unethical event?
- The potential causes of such an event arising.
- If such an event occurs, how serious might the consequences be?
- The specific actions that can be taken to prevent, or reduce the chance of, such an event arising.

For certain categories of compliance and ethics risk, the key is to say they could all have significant consequences, in terms of fines and penalties, investigation and remediation costs, and reputational harm – regardless of whether it is a big or small bribe, or whatever.

As we've explained, compliance risks are different from the usual external or market risks that business leaders are more or less experienced at recognizing and assessing. They are most similar to safety risks, but whereas safety risks include the risk of something bad happening to staff, as well as the risk of staff doing something unsafe and causing harm to themselves or others, and getting the organization in trouble; compliance risks (also known as conduct risks) are the risks of people doing something bad and getting the organization (and themselves) into trouble.

And, of course, ethical risks *are* risks of harm to others, whether or not they get the organization into trouble.

One can also talk about the risk of the organization failing to comply with certain laws and regulations (or governance codes and requirements) and suffering damaging consequences, but those are really legal and regulatory risks, not conduct risks. They don't happen because an employee does something bad (either for self-enrichment or because he thinks it is clever or what is expected of him) but because the organization failed to find out about its legal obligations and/or to put in place procedures for remaining in compliance with them.

Why risk assess?

A compliance and ethics programme can and should be risk-based, but it cannot and will not be effective, or efficient or truly credible, if it is not based on a well-informed understanding of the risks. For that to happen, risk assessment must be done at the right times and in the right ways across the whole landscape of risk that a given organization faces.

This means that somebody who understands the relevant compliance risks generally and within the relevant sector, and who has consulted with and understands the relevant business conducts a rigorous, methodical assessment of the risks. This is then explained to management, who sign up to it.

Unless you do this, you cannot know if you have:

- the right policies, procedures and training in the right place, for the right people;
- the right resources;
- the right amount of weight given to those risks when evaluating the potential, sustainable profitability of the organization or a particular strategic move into a new market, or a particular project or piece of work.

Risk assessment really is a critical part of your planning and, as we all know, *to fail to plan is to plan to fail.*

What is 'reasonable risk management'?

It is not realistic or sustainable to expend infinite time, effort and resources in managing a risk down to the point where it has a zero likelihood of occurring, and prosecutors and regulators do not expect an organization to do so. Instead, the compliance and ethics programme will be considered reasonable and defensible, and in our view effective, if reasonable efforts and procedures have been expended and implemented in a genuine effort to understand the given risk and manage it down to a reasonable level.

This is absolutely *not* the same as saying, for example, that a certain amount of bribery is acceptable. A key element of a credible and effective anti-bribery compliance programme is for the organization to have, and clearly state, a zero tolerance of bribery. This is a two-edged sword, and there is no 'get-out clause' here. If bribery occurs and an organization is having to defend the 'adequacy of its procedures' – in other words, the reasonableness and effectiveness of its compliance and ethics programme – the prosecutor or regulator will accept that the programme should be risk-based, but it will also require that the organization can demonstrate that it conducted a rigorous, well-informed, methodical risk assessment.

When to risk assess?

Typically, an organization may need to conduct risk assessments (and, where appropriate, due diligence) at the following times or stages:

1 when it has decided to design and implement a compliance and ethics programme;

2 when assessing a potential move into a new market, sector or country;

3 when considering a change in its business model, such as greater use of agents, distributors, joint venture partners, or outsourcing or sub-contracting;

4 when it contemplates engaging with a particular joint venture partner or other third party;

5 when contemplating a particular project, transaction or piece of work;

6 when it wants to test or validate the implementation of the compliance and ethics programme across the business or in individual countries or business units.

It is in relation to points 4 and 5 that due diligence will primarily be relevant or necessary, especially in relation to specific third parties. When people talk about due diligence, they are primary referring to third-party due diligence. However, due diligence is also necessary in order to gather sufficient information for a move into a new country, and to some extent for other aspects of point 3 above.

A note on 'risk assessment' versus 'due diligence'

Here we expand a bit further on what we have already said about this subject.

Due diligence is a part of risk assessment but, as we shall explain below, it is often only a small part of it. Nevertheless, to our own great frustration, many practitioners use these two terms synonymously, or more often say 'due diligence' when they mean 'risk assessment' – especially in relation to third-party risks. As the former chief compliance officer of a very large UK plc once memorably said to one of us: 'Yes, tell me about it. Due diligence is the side show that has become the main event.'

This may be because of people's obsession with that which is defensible instead of that which is effective. Having loads of due diligence files gives you a warm feeling that the prosecutor is going to be impressed when you have failed to identify or properly manage a third-party risk, and the third party has paid an enormous bribe and got your organization into deep trouble. 'Never mind the quality of our programme, feel the width of our due diligence.'

ANTI-BRIBERY AND ANTI-MONEY-LAUNDERING

The comparison between anti-bribery compliance and anti-money-laundering compliance is interesting in terms of risk assessment and due diligence.

With anti-money-laundering, and for an organization such as a bank for which money-laundering is a core risk, risk assessment is mostly about due diligence. In designing its programme, the bank should have assessed the types of money-laundering risks it faces and the types of customer, geographic location, transaction size or type, or other features that make a client or transaction risky.

After that, it is essentially a matter of running due diligence to try to spot whether the transaction or customer does indeed appear to implicate money-laundering.

The compliance/conduct risk for the bank, not dissimilar to anti-bribery compliance risks, is that employees would rather just have as many customers and transactions as possible, in order to make money for the bank and for themselves (through bonuses).

By contrast, in the case of bribery the risk is that an employee may wish to appoint a third party in order for that third party to pay the bribe. But

> the risk with many third-party types is not that they are potential bribe payers, or at least not that they are engaged for that reason. Rather, the business would simply prefer not to have to deal with bribery risks and due diligence and, instead, just get the cheapest third party or the one most likely to get the work done quickly and effectively.

It can also be important to look at what due diligence is appropriate from a compliance and ethics perspective. Let's take an example:

WHAT'S APPROPRIATE?

One company is considering buying another. The in-house Mergers and Acquisitions team may be inclined to leave the compliance due diligence until the end, and to attach as little weight as possible to the findings of such due diligence.

When asked to summarize what showstoppers or other factors have been uncovered by due diligence that might have a material impact on the value of the business being acquired and the price to be paid, compliance issues might be left off the list.

To be fair, this is partly because, unless the compliance due diligence has uncovered some sort of smoking gun or other evidence of something very suspicious, for the most part the due diligence may simply identify gaps or weaknesses in the target business's compliance programme. However, if the due diligence uncovers some unlawful or otherwise unsustainable business practices that cannot be permitted to continue post acquisition, the purchaser will be forced to revisit the assumptions upon which it has based its valuation.

Risk assessment in compliance and ethics programme planning and design

Each risk area does have its own particular characteristics. However, to help make the discussion clear, we'll focus here primarily on corruption risks as an illustration, although the same fundamental points will be true to a greater or lesser extent for other types of compliance risk, and indeed other types of business risk.

Your anti-corruption compliance risk assessment has to take place at a number of levels and stages. This may sound complicated, but bear with us. It is logical, and it will save a lot of time, money and wheel-spinning in the long run.

Being methodical

We've said an organization needs to conduct a methodical, thoughtful and well-informed enterprise-wide risk assessment when designing its programme, in order to understand the risks it may face in some or all of its parts.

This needs to be conducted either:

- at the outset:
  - to inform the design of the compliance and ethics programme from scratch;

or:

- if working with an existing programme:
  - to enable the business and Compliance to do a gap analysis;
  - to work out which risks do not have appropriate or adequate measures in place to manage them;
  - to identify which procedures are not sufficiently well implemented and embedded;
  - and to understand which risks are not managed enough and, by the way, which are inadequately understood by management (whose responsibility it ultimately is to manage them).

This risk assessment looks at:

- the organization's business model;
- the countries, markets and sectors in which it intends to operate;
- the types of client and other third parties it would expect to work with;
- whether it has much or any choice but to work in certain countries and for or with certain clients and partners, or client types and partner types;

- and, as a result, the different ways in which the relevant compliance risks may manifest themselves.

Such a risk assessment may involve some due diligence at this design stage, eg to understand the compliance risks in a particular country. However, it will not typically involve due diligence into specific third parties or projects.

To give two obvious examples, when it comes to bribery risk assessment:

A pharmaceutical company will engage thousands of sales representatives whose role is to interact with thousands of healthcare professionals and other customers (a significant percentage of which may be public officials, if they work for a state-funded healthcare organization), and to attempt to persuade those customers to prescribe its products.

By contrast, a construction company or oil and gas contractor typically performs large, complex projects for a private or state client, and it wins work through a winner-takes-all, competitive tender process, or sometimes by negotiating a project award and not having to submit a tender as part of a competitive process.

It follows that the bribery risks for those two types of organization, particularly the risk of bribery to win work, are very different and the way to manage those bribery risks may be very different.

Due diligence into a healthcare customer is unlikely to be relevant, whereas it could be very relevant for a construction or oil and gas client.

Getting a clear understanding of the risks

In conducting this enterprise-wide risk assessment, care needs to be taken to ensure the Compliance and Ethics function and the business both understand all the different ways in which the relevant compliance risks might manifest themselves.

The CECO should have a reasonable understanding of the risks faced by an organization of this type, and should certainly have some expertise in the relevant area of compliance in general. He or she should explain any preconceptions to the business leaders and draw out their own views and experience of compliance risks. They know their business best, and good business managers tend to have a good general sense of the risks that they face, although this is much truer of strategic, operational and even hazard risks than it is of conduct or compliance risks. In any event, the CECO and the risk methodology will need to spell out and flush out very clearly the many different and often increasingly subtle ways in which the relevant compliance risks may manifest themselves.

First of all, the organization, with the help of the CECO, needs to identify and agree the scope of the compliance risk being addressed. Is it purely anti-bribery, for example, or is it anti-corruption more broadly? In many cases, for reasons which we will explore elsewhere, it makes sense to have an anti-corruption programme that can manage not only bribery risks but, without a great deal of difference or addition in terms of policies, training, procedures and controls, also manage other forms of risk, most obviously fraud, theft and dishonesty.

The risk assessment methodology should then break the risks down to a reasonably granular level of detail. In the case of a corruption risk assessment, it might or will probably start by showing that corruption risks include bribery, fraud (including false claims), perhaps cartels and other forms of competition/anti-trust law breaches, and the associated/overlapping areas of conflicts of interest, and gifts and hospitality.

It should then break it down further by showing how each risk can take many forms. The following illustrates how this might be done in the case of bribery for a construction or energy company:

TYPES OF BRIBERY RISK

- Bribery by the organization as a corporate decision of its senior management or directing minds.
- Bribery by the organization through its employees.
- Bribery by third parties acting on behalf of the organization, eg agents, consultants and other intermediaries.

- Bribery by any of the above means to win work or to win an advantage in performing work.

- More subtly, bribery by any of the above means to pre-qualify to bid for work, to influence the specification for a tender, or to get work certified or paid.

- Perhaps subtler still, bribery by deliberate or reckless channelling of money or benefits through a supplier or subcontractor that is owned by or pays a kickback to a public official or client representative.

- Bribery of public officials to obtain visas, permits or licences.

- Facilitation payments: providing money or benefits of relatively modest amounts to a public official to expedite or facilitate the performance of a service which the public official is already duty bound to perform – in other words, paying someone to do what they are supposed to do rather than, as is the case with most forms of bribery, paying somebody to breach a duty owed to someone else or to perform that duty improperly.

Once there is a good shared understanding between compliance and the business about these various forms of bribery and corruption, the next step should in the risk assessment should be to gauge how likely any of these risks are to occur in the organization's business; in the countries and sectors in which it operates and with the clients, partners and any kinds of third parties with which it will work.

As part of this process, the risk assessment should take into account whether the organization will have to work with third parties and, if so, to what extent the provision of services or goods by those third parties will involve corruption pinch points, ie situations in which you are likely to face a bribe demand (for example, use of a logistics agent to get people or materials into countries or ports).

General risk assessment tips

This book and this chapter do not attempt to set out a comprehensive risk assessment process in every detail but merely to illustrate the type of process that is appropriate and the reasons for it. The pointers discussed here are relevant to the enterprise-wide risk assessment but also, in whole or in part, to other compliance risk assessments.

Grading the risks

As part of the risk assessment, the organization should grade each risk. Classically, as we've seen, this involves multiplying the likelihood of a risk occurring by the impact of it occurring.

In the case of corruption risks, one can assume that the impact is high, since, as we've also seen, the consequences for an organization of a bribery conviction or settlement can be so damaging. We're not talking about the likelihood of being found out (although a cynical, unenlightened approach might include this factor).

Assessing the likelihood of a risk occurring is more art than science, but a rough scale of 0 to 10 should suffice. The aim is not to get this risk score exactly 'correct' but, broadly, to identify which are the higher risks and to gain a sense of comparative risk when comparing different risks. A scale of nought to five may also suffice: zero, very low, low, medium, high and very high. Or dark green, light green, yellow, orange, red and dark red.

This is an assessment of the likelihood of the particular risk occurring in the absence of any compliance and ethics programme within the organization. In other words, before taking into account the effect of any existing or planned policies procedures and controls. For example, when a large contractor is participating in competitive tenders to win major projects for very large private or public sector clients, it may assess the risk of bribery being used successfully to win the work from the client as being:

- **low,** even before taking into account the organization's planned or existing compliance and ethics programme controls, when the client is a blue-chip multinational private company;
- **medium,** when the client is a national oil company in a high corruption risk country; and
- **high,** when the client is a state municipality in a high-risk country inviting tenders to build infrastructure.

Managing the risks

Once the business has a reasonably complete and well-informed map of the risks, the organization can then assess what policies, procedures and controls will be appropriate to manage those risks. As part of this, it should assess to what extent the existing policies, procedures and controls any well managed business will have can be used, leveraged or adapted to manage the specific risks identified.

For example, if an organization has a large supply chain and spends a large proportion of its revenue on suppliers and subcontractors, it will almost certainly have a sophisticated system of supply chain management or procurement procedures and controls. Even if these were not designed with bribery in mind, they were almost certainly designed to guard against fraud against the company and, more basically, to ensure that the company's money is wisely spent, and that best quality and value are obtained. (We will look at this more closely in Chapter 11.)

Repeating and refreshing the risk assessment (and continually improving the organization's understanding of the risks)

Compliance risk assessment is an ongoing process that needs to be refreshed regularly, as well as revisited when the organization changes its operating model or moves into new sectors or markets. Nonetheless, based on the current risk assessment, the CECO can design and/or enhance and implement the policies, procedures and controls appropriate to manage the risks identified – starting with, or placing particular emphasis on, the highest risks identified.

As mentioned earlier, this form of enterprise-wide risk assessment can be repeated once the programme has been implemented, and periodically thereafter, or at the region, country or business unit level, to assess whether in the opinion of the business and the Compliance and Ethics function, the identified risks have indeed been reduced to the intended level. And bear mind, it is almost never realistic nor expected to reduce the risk to zero.

Country risk assessment

It is important to understand and factor in the level and types of corruption and other associated risks that an organization is likely to encounter in a given country, taking into account the organization's chosen sector and business model. Due diligence is often required to get a really good, practical understanding from companies and risk consultants with actual, first-hand experience, as well as from publicly available information such as the Business Anti-Corruption Portal.[1]

Such due diligence can open one's eyes to:

- whether corruption is very likely or even inevitable in certain circumstances;
- whether the consequences of resistance will be delays and costs or physical threats to managers being summoned to a meeting by someone with a pearl-handled revolver;
- whether the organization can or must enter (or stay in) that country, or whether it is impossible to do business there ethically and sustainably, in compliance with the law and without exposing staff to unreasonable risks;
- what additional or different procedures, controls and resources (including compliance officers and money) will be needed to manage the risks.

If it is sincere in its commitment to do business without corruption, an organization has to be willing to accept that there may be some countries in which it cannot operate. If an expert tells you it is impossible to get the type of visa or permit you will need without suffering unsustainable delays unless you pay bribes, then on what basis can you determine that you know better and can prove them wrong?

As well as at the programme design stage, a country risk assessment needs to be conducted when the organization is contemplating entering a new country, or if there have been significant changes in a country.

Project/transaction risk assessment

Once the organization has assessed the risks and decided in which markets and countries, with which third-party types, and with which business model it can operate, it has the information necessary to design, implement, test and continually improve a fit-for-purpose compliance and ethics programme. That programme needs to include processes for assessing risks and, if appropriate, implementing additional risk mitigation procedures, for certain projects or certain types of work (and, as we discuss in the next section, for dealing with certain third parties or third-party types).

The aim is to assess whether a project, transaction or piece of work has the same features that you recognized or assumed when conducting the enterprise-wide corruption risk assessment and designing your compliance and ethics programme, or whether it represents a type of work that has significant differences in terms of corruption risk type and likelihood and how best to manage them. In other words, are the organization's existing procedures and controls still fit for purpose, do people need training on different risks and stratagems for dealing with them, are more resources needed? Moreover, each project, transaction or piece of work may throw up specific risks and corruption pinch-points that can only be identified or addressed in the context of that project.

(We are talking here generally of construction and oil and gas work, and other sectors that are project-focused, but the same will be true to a greater or lesser extent with other sectors. The pharmaceuticals sector faces very different corruption risks, but the key is to identify when the organization is doing something different from its normal core business operations, and that throws up more or different risks.)

To continue with the project theme, when contemplating bidding for a new project, the organization needs to assess what corruption risks are entailed by that project and, in particular the third parties with whom or which the organization will need to work. For example:

SAMPLE SUMMARY OF A PROJECT CORRUPTION RISK ASSESSMENT

- Who is the client? Do we already know and trust them? Are they blue chip and subject to high regulatory and stakeholder scrutiny and demands? Are they private (which tends to mean a lower risk of corruption) or public?

- What type of tender process are they operating? Is it genuine and robust or is it vulnerable to subversion?

- Are we likely to lose to a corrupt competitor, such that we may as well not waste our time and money bidding, unless we are confident that none of the other bidders is corrupt?

- If we win, is the client likely to preside over a corrupt project?

- Will we be able to get our work certified and paid?

- Are there any local content requirements, such as offsets or other requirements to support the local community or work with particular partners or suppliers that may not meet our usual criteria or be part of our pre-approved supplier base?

- Do we want or need to work with a consortium or joint venture partner, and if so what do we know about them?

- Do we believe we need to work with a commercial agent or consultant? If so, why?

- How have we selected any partner(s), agent or consultant, and how will we ensure visibility and, as far as possible, control over what they may do when they are working with or for us?

- Which suppliers and subcontractors will we need, and have many of them been nominated by the client or by any public official, formally or informally?

- Will all suppliers and subcontractors be pre-approved, preferred providers or new providers qualified through our normal processes?

- Will all suppliers and subcontractors be appointed pursuant to a competitive tender process and otherwise in accordance with our normal supply chain management/procurement procedures?

- Are our normal compliance and ethics programme elements appropriate and adequate to manage the risks identified pursuant to the above project risk assessment, or do we need to put in place additional controls and resources?

Third-party risk assessment

Now we turn to the dreaded subject of third-party risk assessment and due diligence. Third-party risks are some of the highest risks and hardest to manage for many organizations in many sectors. In some cases, historically, this is because organizations have been willing to work with agents and intermediaries in countries and markets that they do not really understand, and to place their trust in someone whom they do not know very well to navigate those risks and help them win work. Many of the biggest bribery cases have resulted from this business model, when misplaced trust has been placed in an agent who will receive a very large success fee if they help their principal (the organization that appoints them) win work. Whenever an organization needs to work with any type of third party, there are increased compliance risks.

When you think about it, so much of this book highlights the nature of compliance risks and why they are hard to manage effectively, even with an enlightened, values-based approach. We identify many of the factors at play, such as motivation and incentives, human nature, business pressures and so on. These risks are magnified when the people whose conduct you are trying to influence and control are not employees of the organization. They are not steeped in the organization's culture and values. They may not have the same incentives and motivation (financial or otherwise). They do not play on the same team. They work for other organizations with different values, and the organization has much reduced visibility and control over what they do. And by 'they', we are referring sometimes to individuals (such as consultants, advisers or intermediaries), but very often to organizations that in turn employ individuals.

As already mentioned, the design and implementation of an organization's compliance and ethics programme needs to take into account the different types of third party that the organization is likely to need to work with, and to include procedures and controls for managing the risks associated with those third-party types. Those procedures and controls should include procedures for assessing the risks associated with specific third parties, as and when they are identified and appointed. This includes due diligence, which we will come to shortly, but it also includes understanding if and why a particular third party or third-party type brings a heightened likelihood of particular corruption risks occurring within a particular transaction or project.

Before evaluating what information your organization already has about the relevant third party and, if necessary, conducting due diligence to ensure that the organization is fully informed and has identified any red flags, the organization should consider, first and foremost, the legitimate business justification for choosing and appointing the third party.

'RED FLAGS'

A red flag is a term commonly used in due diligence and risk assessments to denote a sign of a possible risk or problem. It does not mean that such risk or problem is actually present, or that it is an impediment to proceeding. But it usually means that further work will be necessary to ascertain whether there is really a problem and, if so, whether it can be mitigated adequately before proceeding

---

An organization should have a culture supported by a process, or a process supported by culture, of challenging choices and decisions before they are made by asking questions such as:

- Why do we need a third party of this type?
- What will they do for us and how will we remunerate them?
- Do we understand the risks that that implies?
- How have we chosen the particular third party?
- Are they manifestly qualified to perform the work, and have we chosen them on merit?
- Are we paying more than fair market value for their services?

Only if the organization can answer these questions satisfactorily, might we then turn to due diligence.

Due diligence: The side show that has become the main event

For many practitioners and their 'victims', due diligence has become the be-all and end-all of third-party compliance risk management. This is a dangerous mistake. In its proper sense, 'due diligence' can most usefully be thought of as 'the process of obtaining information necessary to enable a properly informed assessment of the risks presented by the relevant third party, project, country, etc'.

However, it may be that your organization already has enough information to assess the risks, or that obtaining more information, or conducting a screening or other due diligence process won't reveal any further information and/or would not reduce the risk posed by the third party. What is far more important here is the risk assessment and the business justification for the intended engagement or transaction.

Let's take the example of engaging agents and consultants. Suppose your organization wishes to engage a commercial agent to help it win work or to obtain payment for, or some other advantage in relation to, work in a high-risk country. For most types of organization and in most sectors, this may represent the highest type of third-party corruption risk.

An agent is legally or ostensibly authorized to act in the name of its principal, so in that very obvious sense the organization is likely to be held legally and reputationally responsible for what its agent does. More to the point, commercial agents are often compensated by way of a success or contingent fee. The same may be true of a consultant, in which case they represent an equally high risk, regardless of what you call them.

Depending how an agent is incentivized and remunerated, they may stand to gain more than fair market value for their services when they are successful, but to gain nothing if they are unsuccessful in winning work for their customer or principal. This can create a huge incentive and opportunity for the agent to use part of their compensation (especially as it exceeds fair market value for the relevant services) to attempt to bribe others to award work to their principal.

This is why compensation arrangements such as these represent such a corruption risk.

Nonetheless, having assessed the risks on the basis of the information already available and interrogated the reasons why the third party should be used and the terms of its engagement, if the risk assessment deems the third party to represent more than a low risk of corruption the organization will then very likely need to conduct due diligence into the third party.

You will often (at least if you work in compliance!) hear people say, 'I have done my due diligence into this agent and it has revealed nothing untoward. Therefore I am entitled to go ahead with the proposed engagement of the agent.'

When you think about it, the due diligence process, if rigorous and effective, may help you to confirm whether the agent is who they say they are is, whether they have a proper established business, accounts etc. It may also tell you whether the agent has been the subject of any criminal or civil investigation, litigation or convictions, and whether there is any adverse media associated with this person. Or it may simply draw a complete blank and lead you to believe that there are no such red flags. But even if your due diligence is fully effective and reveals the 'whole truth' about the agent, you are then going to trust them more than you would trust your brother, and with the mother of all corruption incentives: a large success fee which they will only receive if your organization wins the work, and nothing if it does not.

Moreover, you have to assume that your third-party due diligence is not effective: the agent may have done or attempted all manner of goblinry and simply not been caught; or a supplier you are looking at may be linked with some hidden public official ownership or financial interest or other relationship.

So our approach to due diligence with any high-risk third party, including agents, consultants and joint venture partners is this:

- Does the information available to you about this third party really give you any reason to believe you can trust them?
- And if you assume your due diligence is ineffective or incomplete, and that your trust proves to be misplaced, what corruption incentives and opportunities have you created, and do you have the ability to manage the resulting risks?

> **TIP**
>
> Corruption risk is all about incentives and opportunities. This is true even at the more basic level, where, for example, a police officer has an opportunity to abuse their power by demanding a facilitation payment, or a pharmaceutical sales rep has the incentive to provide some sort of improper inducement to a doctor to generate prescriptions and thus a good bonus.

Third parties' compliance programmes

When you are conducting due diligence into high-risk third parties, many authorities emphasize the need for you to assess the third party's compliance programme, or at least their system of internal controls. If a high-risk third party has a credible system of internal controls, or indeed a credible compliance programme, it probably tells you something about how well-managed its business is and, if you exercised any audit rights, whether such an audit might provide you some degree of assurance.

However, if we think about it, if the high-risk third party is a small organization (let's say, employing 10 to 30 people), or if it is based in a low compliance maturity country, you would not or should not really expect it to have a compliance programme. The owner/managers of such an organization may not need a compliance programme in order to be reasonably sure that the enterprise and its people will behave in the desired way. Moreover, a compliance programme may not be relevant for mitigating the risks that the third party represents to your organization.

Take a commercial agent, potentially the highest risk type of third party. The biggest risk is that the managing director, or the managing director and the finance director together, will deploy a significant amount of the agent's money in an improper way (and in a way that an audit would not reveal, since they are perfectly at liberty to transfer the agent's money into other bank accounts before utilizing it). This risk is not mitigated by policies and procedures designed to control how others within the agent's organization spend money, manage conflicts of interest, disclose gifts and hospitality, appoint suppliers and subcontractors etc.

Worrying about whether the agent has a credible gifts and hospitality policy is like rearranging the deck chairs on the deck of the *Titanic*: the agent is a high risk, not because their employees may provide inappropriate gifts and hospitality, but because of the opportunity and incentive you have provided for them to engage in 'grand bribery'.

Of course, an audit can tell you a number of useful things about a third party: how well it is managed, whether it uses a credible accounting system, as well as whether there are any specific large or suspicious payments. As with many elements of a compliance and ethics programme, if you have a right of audit and do not exercise it, this may be to your detriment; if you exercise a right of audit and do not look for or notice such payments or other obvious red flags, this could also reflect badly on you. Moreover, negotiating a right of audit and exercising that audit right can help convince the third party about your seriousness. One significant risk with a third party is that they do not believe you are sincere in your commitment to anti-corruption, so anything you can do to convince them of your sincerity helps to reduce the risk.

The same is true when it comes to training of third parties, as discussed in Chapter 9.

Any organization that has a large number of suppliers, subcontractors or other third parties with which it needs to engage will wish to outsource at least part of the due diligence process, or at least use software and other platforms that systematize the process and make it manageable and efficient. But you cannot design a process that enables you to feed in a bunch of names and spew out those names that have 'passed'. At best, you can design a process that gives you a risk weighting of some sort. For example, you could create a workflow that assesses whether there is a low, medium or high risk at each of a number of toll gates, such as:

- In what country is the third party based?
- Did our screening identify the third party reliably?
- Did the screening corroborate any of the information we already have about the third party?
- Did the screening throw up any adverse media or other red flags?

THE PROBLEMS OF THIRD-PARTY DUE DILIGENCE

Third-party due diligence is a real headache for organizations. It can be expensive to do it effectively, and inefficient and ineffective to do it without dedicated specialists who understand what they are doing and why. But it is very difficult if not impossible to outsource the whole third-party risk assessment, due diligence and approval process. There are a number of reasons for this:

1   No third-party provider can be accountable for taking a decision as to whether, ultimately, it is safe, prudent or permissible to engage a third party.

2   Due diligence is simply not a matter of black-and-white or right and wrong. Even if and to the extent your due diligence is reasonably effective and reliable (which you can never really be sure of), it may only tell you some factual information about the third party, which may not be correct, and it does not tell you whether there is other material information that was not available (either because it is not publicly available or has not been detected by the search engine). So, you cannot get a yes or no answer.

3   Your organization may already have a sophisticated vendor management system or supplier database. That system or database may well be integrated with SAP[2] or some other internal system that is used for other purposes, not just compliance screening. You may well want your screening tool to work seamlessly with that system, rather than creating a separate database of third parties just for compliance screening purposes.

In order to minimize reliance upon due diligence, your organization should design a risk assessment process which is designed to flush out, document and demonstrate the legitimate business justification for engaging with that particular third party for the intended purpose and on the proposed terms, as well as to flush out any 'red flags'. The box below entitled 'A sample red flag checklist' shows an example of a typical red flag and business justification checklist of this type.[3]

Finally, all risk assessments and due diligence must be refreshed periodically, or when new information comes to light. In the case of third parties, the due diligence should be repeated when the relationship is renewed.

A SAMPLE RED FLAG CHECKLIST

The following questions need to be answered in the affirmative, or with exceptions separately justified and documented, for each third party to be engaged in connection with the project, unless the third party is a supplier appointed pursuant to the organization's pre-qualification and competitive tender procedures, in which case questions 1–4 will be addressed through such procedures.

Save as separately documented and justified:

1 The third party:

  a. is qualified to perform the services required;

  b. will be paid no more than fair market value for legitimate services that we require and actually receive, in accordance with a written agreement;

  c. appears to have made full and frank disclosures in response to any questionnaire;

  d. has agreed to appropriate contractual provisions approved by the relevant territory lawyer to address bribery and other forms of corruption, and which make it clear that a right of termination exists if such provisions are breached;

  e. has successfully undergone any other corruption risk management steps prescribed by any group procedure, including due diligence where applicable.

2 There is a clear, legitimate business justification for our arrangements with the third party.

3 The third party will not be interacting with public officials in connection with the project, whether to obtain permits or approvals or otherwise.

4 No part of the compensation payable to the third party depends upon some favourable action by a public official or relevant person (eg a fee linked to obtaining a government permit or winning business).

5 The third party:

  a. has not been recommended to us by a public official or relevant person;

  b. so far as we are aware, is not connected with a public official or relevant person;

   c. has not requested and will not receive anything unusual with regard to compensation, such as:

     i. payment to another party or to a bank account in another name;

     ii. payment to a bank account located in a country other than where the services will be performed or the third party is resident;

     iii. payment in cash, vouchers or gifts;

     iv. provision for a large rebate or bonus;

     v. an additional fee to pay the 'expenses' of public officials or something similar.

Definitions:

- 'Client' means any person which is our actual or intended client, or in relation to whose project or other work we have engaged, or are contemplating engaging, a third party.

- 'Public officials' is defined in the code of conduct.

- 'Principal' means:

    o any owner, officer or director; or

    o any employee or other representative who has authority to make or influence decisions or recommendations regarding the relationship with the company.

- 'Relevant person' means any client, or any principal of any client.

Comments/explanation (justify and document exceptions here):

In summary

- The design of every compliance and ethics programme starts with an understanding of the risks.

- A programme will not be effective unless risk assessment is done at the right times and in the right ways.

- This is a sword and a shield – stakeholders expect compliance and ethics programmes to be based on a good understanding of the risks, but they also do not expect all risks to be eliminated.

- And due diligence plays a key role but is not the be-all and end-all – it is an information gathering tool to enable risk assessment to be effective.

This means conducting:

- an enterprise-wide compliance risk assessment to assess the relevant compliance risks in the sector(s) and geographies in which the organization operates, with the types of client, partner, supplier and other third party the organization works with, and given its business model(s) in order to design the programme;
- third-party compliance risk assessments before the organization engages with particular third parties;
- country compliance risk assessments before entering new countries;
- project or transaction specific risk assessments, to understand how the relevant compliance risks may materialize and are managed in a specific project or transaction.

Due diligence will play an appropriate role in the above risk assessments, some of which may be integrated into the organization's other risk management activities -e.g. how third parties are pre-qualified and how safety security and political risks are assessed before working in a new country.

Typically, an organization may need to conduct risk assessments (and, where appropriate, due diligence) at the following times or stages:

- when it has decided to design and implement a compliance and ethics programme;
- when assessing a potential move into a new market, sector or country;
- when considering a change in its business model, such as greater use of agents, distributors, joint venture partners, or outsourcing or sub-contracting;
- when it contemplates engaging with a particular joint venture partner or other third party;

- when contemplating a particular project, transaction or piece of work;
- when it wants to test or validate the implementation of the compliance and ethics programme across the business or in individual countries of business units.

Across the minefield: compliance and ethics meets real life

A question of coffee

Would you charge the company for coffee bought at the airport on a business trip, when you would normally buy yourself a coffee anyway?

Would your answer be different if you had a pass for the business class lounge, where you can get free coffee?

Held to ransom

A company is building a new state of the art factory. All permits have been obtained and construction of the plant and associated utilities is underway.

Late on in the project it's realized that one permit for a minor requirement has been overlooked. Papers for the permit are prepared in advance of a planning approval meeting – the last until the New Year. Approval at the meeting is expected to be a formality – but it is crucial.

The chair of the Planning Committee is a local politician up for re-election in June. The decision of the Committee must be unanimous, therefore their vote is key. After the planning meeting, the chair advises the company representative they will vote to approve the permit – if the company formally and publicly commits to a $5 million investment for the renovation of the local sports complex that the chair, in their political capacity, has been campaigning for.

'It's up to you'

It's an emergency. A piece of specialist equipment has broken down. You have to import a replacement fast. You're on the phone. On the other end they are asking you whether you are authorizing them to send it. You haven't checked if there are any import restrictions. 'It's now or never,' they say.
So what's your answer? Yes, or no?

Your manager won't promote a colleague. They think it's because the manager doesn't like them. You agree.
Anything you think you should do?

Your company is recruiting for a new office manager and your brother's looking for a new post. It's not in the department or office where you work.
Alright to recommend him?

You've just learned that one of our business partners has been fixing prices. They're a vital part of a huge contract we're trying to win, and what they've been doing has nothing to do with that.
Silence is golden?

Notes

1 https://www.business-anti-corruption.com [accessed 24.02.19].
2 Systeme, Anwendungen, Produkte in der Datenverarbeitung (Systems, Applications and Products for Data Processing).
3 Reproduced by kind permission of Subsea 7.

08

Code of conduct and policies

'Twas brillig, and the slithy toves
Did gyre and gimble in the wabe:
All mimsy were the borogoves,
And the mome raths outgrabe.

LEWIS CARROLL, 'JABBERWOCKY'[1]

In this chapter we look at why a code of conduct matters, how to go about constructing it and making it live in your organization, the sorts of areas it might cover, and what other policies might be needed to underpin it.

We the people

We the People of the United States, in order to form a more perfect Union, establish Justice, insure domestic Tranquillity, provide for the common defence, promote the general Welfare, and secure the Blessings of Liberty to ourselves and our Posterity, do ordain and establish this Constitution for the United States of America.

PREAMBLE TO THE UNITED STATES CONSTITUTION, 1787[2]

We heard recently that a surprisingly small percentage of practising lawyers in the United States have read their country's Constitution. Yet it is the cornerstone document that, ultimately, provides the foundation for all of the laws in the United States. It also happens to be beautifully written.

Which makes you wonder how many people have actually read their organization's code of conduct from cover to cover?

No doubt some compliance officers will say that they have a written statement confirming that all of their organization's employees have read the code and, moreover, agreed that they understand it and will comply with it! But somehow we suspect that's rather far from the real truth of the matter, not least because in trying to be precise about what they mean, some codes still end up talking to people like this:

> Any reference to a specific statute includes any statutory extension or modification, amendment or re-enactment of such statute and any regulations or orders made under such statute, and any general reference to 'statute' or 'statutes' includes any regulations or orders made under such statute or statutes.

(Are you still awake?)

To be fair, these days more and more people who write codes are trying really hard to change this sort of language. But even when they succeed, there is still the problem that essentially this is our, the organization's, code, and we expect you, the employee, to follow and obey it.

Us and you. Our rules. Your obedience.

Compare this to how the American Constitution makes it absolutely clear at the outset that it is speaking in the voice of everyone: We the People...

When the original authors drafted those words, they were insisting that the ultimate guardians of the rights and liberties of Americans were... Americans. And for a long time after, the Constitution was indeed widely read, known and discussed across the country. Why? Because the words were about framing the values, principles and rules of a society that people wished to live in, and were prepared to defend.

What we are going to explore in this chapter are the two big challenges of a code of conduct:

1 How to clearly set out the values, principles and rules that tell everyone how they should and should not behave.

2 And how to get people doing it and defending it.

Of course, a code cannot solve this second problem on its own. But it can become a core part of activities, discussion, storytelling, incentives and recognition that do.

Leave your code in a dry document in a drawer, or in web pages on a dedicated website, and that is where it will stay, gathering dust and as few visits as people can possibly get away with. Bring it out and get people to play with it, explore it, think about it, discuss it, value it and see it valued, and a code of conduct can become the heartbeat of an organization's culture – the voice of We the People.

What is a code – and what is it for?

'A book of rules'

Here's what Wikipedia has to say:

> A code of conduct is a set of rules outlining the social norms and religious rules and responsibilities of, or proper practices for, an individual, party or organization. Related concepts include ethical, honour, moral codes and religious laws.[3]

Defining the 'rules' by which an organization will operate is certainly an important part of a code. So let's look at this aspect for a moment.

Some people argue quite compellingly, albeit somewhat tongue in cheek, that codes of conduct have had their day. If we accept that compliance is failing for many of the reasons discussed in this book, including the length, detail and turgid tone of policies and the fact that many employees are motivated not by obedience to policy but by culture, values and incentives, surely even a code of conduct that follows the above approach is unnecessary or, in any case, ineffectual.

Despite the stress we place on ethics and culture in this book, this is not a point of view we share. To explain why, let's briefly look at another kind of code...

Out on the roads, drivers in the UK need to know the Highway Code if they are to drive safely and avoid doing harm to others and themselves. This includes how to drive with courtesy and care – but it isn't just limited to that. It has to go on to clearly define the 'rules of the road' so everyone knows what to do at, for example, a round-about – and does it.

In the jargon of London black cab drivers learning the Knowledge, 'Comply roundabout.'

It is the same for a code of conduct. A core part of its purpose is to establish the rules everyone will follow as they try to navigate through the day-to-day challenges of their work. Without knowing those rules, and what to do and not do in specific situations, there are liable to be smash-ups.

Why rules alone won't work

But the parallel between a Highway Code and a code of conduct only goes so far. On the highway there can be no ambiguity: the rules are black and white (or red, amber and green). In business, on the other hand, people must exercise judgement and make decisions about how to act in all sorts of situations, and sometimes the rules can seem open to doubt, interpretation – or deliberate manipulation. After all, in the human realm, there are always exceptions to every rule...

That is why, as well as setting out the rules, a code of conduct also needs to establish the underlying principles – the values and ethics – that inform and shape those rules and explain the intention behind them. So when the rules run dry or don't fit, the principle is always there to guide you, or to help others intervene.

Why principles alone won't work

On their own, those principles won't always work either. There is too big a distance between their generality and the way they could be interpreted or bypassed within the specifics of certain situations. Rules without principles don't work. Nor do principles without rules. You need both, and the policies contained in a code of conduct are designed to make those rules, and the principles – the values and reasons – behind them, clear to everyone.

So what's the point of a code of conduct?

Any organization that wishes to be respected and trusted wants its people, and all those who work with it, to always behave legally, with integrity and with respect for others. To express the things it stands for, it will probably work out and define its own set of values, and expect its people to do their work by following them. To do that it will go on to explain and explore the ethical behaviours it expects, and the sorts of behaviours it will not tolerate, and what it will not stand for. And it will assess the general and particular risks it faces, and work out policies that clearly tell people about those risks, and explain what they should, and should not do to avoid them – in other words, how they should conduct themselves.

Why it's special – and why it matters

The code of conduct is the umbrella – under it sit all other policies, procedures and controls. As far as possible, it should be a one-stop shop or *vade mecum*.

Where it can be said simply and clearly and without ambiguity – it can be said in the code and left in the code.

Where it cannot, without cluttering up the code, then it needs to form a separate policy or process. This allows the point to be expanded in the right way and with enough context for it to be properly understood, enough structure to be followed and precise enough to be enforced.

The code should attempt to inform the reader about, and direct them to, any relevant supporting policies or guidance.

The beginning, not the end

As the ancient Japanese proverb has it, 'Beginning is easy, continuing hard.' On the face of it, the answer may seem simple – get everyone to read, know and understand their organization's code, and that's pretty much the whole problem of compliance sorted. Except – that's a little like saying to those who hate broccoli, 'Eat broccoli, it's good for you!' and expecting them to do it.

With the best will in the world, it is very hard to motivate employees to read the organization's code, less still its policies. For a start, most employees simply do not have the time or bandwidth to read the number of policies that most organizations have and, on the face it, expect their employees to read. This is a factor both of the number of policies and also their length and the way in which they are written.

Hence the prevailing view that the best and most realistic chance of ensuring that your policies are understood and embedded is to take the approach:

> if we can only get everybody here to read one document, let's make
> it this one and let's try to cover everything we can in it, while at the
> same time making it short enough, comprehensible and engaging
> enough to assist with this goal and to maximize the chances of people
> understanding it.

Which means finding a balance between covering everything in a one-stop shop and not making it so long and turgid as to be self-defeating.

That's what most organizations do, and where most organizations pretty much leave it. Internal policies – tick. External statement – tick. But if a code is to be an effective part of effective compliance and ethics, drafting and shaping this document or app or website in a readable and engaging way is only the start. It's what you then do with it – how you make it visible on everyone's radar, bring it to life as part of your culture, make it resonant and relevant to the issues people face, and the things they care about – that matters. (See the next chapter.)

A code of conduct will only succeed when it is not just being read, but being lived.

How to create an effective code of conduct

The problem with precision

There is no greater impediment to the advancement of knowledge than the ambiguity of words.
THOMAS REID, *ESSAYS ON THE INTELLECTUAL POWERS OF MAN*, 1785

Of course, precision matters. It is one of the few forms of defence against unscrupulous manipulation of ambiguity.

But the trouble is, it is a very poor form of defence.

As virtually any legal document will demonstrate, the pursuit of precision often leaves equally important things behind – things like clarity, simplicity, transparency of language, tone of voice. Indeed, precision is often so wrapped up in its own objectives, the result is a form of opaque verbal pedantry that entirely fails to connect to or interest anyone.

Or, to put it another way, a code of conduct can be so obsessed with shaping formulae that can be defended if and when the regulators come calling, that it forgets the very people it is supposed to be speaking to – the people who will be living the code and who can prevent that from ever happening.

Yes, precision matters. But if there is any one thing we would stress above all else it is this:

> The most important principle when constructing a code of conduct is to think about your audience. Ask how you can reach them, touch them, connect to them, make them take notice, make them remember – make them care.

For most organizations this means pretty much a total re-think. The task becomes less about 'How can we be punctilious in the way we define our policies?' and a whole lot more about 'How can we bring who we are and what we stand for alive?'

As well as clear definitions, a successful code should also involve great storytelling. And if you don't have the storytelling skills, you need to go to people who do:

If the value or the rule or the principle or the law matters – then make it matter to me!

If you accept this, we suggest you are also accepting a very different process in the way you will go about creating your code. To take just one example, you won't just be formulating a hair-splitting document behind closed doors with a cabal of lawyers and specialists. Rather, you will constantly be thinking of how best to get your message across. You may even find yourself working alongside your audience, asking them at each stage to contribute, test and assess how effectively what you are doing is landing with them.

An interactive guide

Think of your code as an interactive guide – where all the organization's values, principles and purpose, its legal obligations and the behaviours it stands for and expects from everyone who works for it or with it, are all brought together in one place for easy access, and brought to life for clear understanding.

A place where people can go to check things when they are not sure. Get help and advice with any problems, ethical dilemmas or decisions they are facing. Find out where more details and specific policies are kept. Find the support they need.

A place, too, that provides a point of departure for exploring and discussing important issues. Sharing stories and finding out what others have done in similar situations. Creating rewards and recognition and incentives.

A place that ties together all the ethical and cultural and business activities of an organization.

An encouraging and empowering and friendly place!

A well-written and constructed code brings clarity and simplicity to issues that can otherwise be difficult and complex. But it is only the start of a wider process that will ultimately bring effective compliance. That will involve training, communication and education (which we deal with in the next chapter). Working with others to integrate the code into all areas of the business – until it occupies a place at the very heart of your organization. And finding ways to continue making the code matter.

Construction principles

A code of conduct reflects, expresses and represents the organization it belongs to. So every code will be different. However, all good codes will have some basic things in common. Here are some simple guidelines.

Do make sure your code:

- hangs off, and is soaked in, the values of the organization;
- has an inclusive and human tone of voice ('person to person', not 'authority dictating to subject');
- is readable – using simple common language (short sentences are good, complex sentences carrying a layered cargo of sub-clauses are bad). Test it with your audience!
- clearly defines and explains the concepts and terms it uses;
- reflects how the organization works, rather than being built around generic statements;
- is relevant to people (it's the job of the code to make them understand, take notice and care);
- brings important issues to life with examples and stories;
- gives clear guidelines for when people find themselves in a situation where they're not sure what to do;
- is relevant to your organization and sector;
- is visible and present in all aspects of your organization – it is the one common and constant face of the organization that will likely outlast most of the executives. So give it the prominence it deserves. For example:
  - use pictures;
  - get people involved;
  - tell stories;

- o think about different applications, media and communication opportunities;
- o make it accessible electronically;
- o harness social media;
- o link it to incentives, recognition and awards.
- is as short as possible!

Don'ts:

- Don't just copy and paste or outsource – your code must carry the DNA of your organization.
- Don't command or order, instruct or tell – it is not about finger-pointing at each employee or contractor.
- Don't go overboard, it will lose the reader.
- Don't be too vague. People need to clearly know and understand the organization's policies and how they are to be followed. What's more, those policies may need to be enforced as part of a disciplinary process.
- Don't imagine that once you've written your code the job is done – it's only just started!

What should it cover?

A code of conduct will include a range of compliance and ethics areas that together cover the kind of organization concerned, its activities, the places in the world where it operates and its values.

As a general rule we believe you should attempt as far as practicable to put all necessary policy wording in the code or equivalent overarching, highest level policy document. If it is too detailed or too lengthy to fit in that document, it may well be that you are trying to say too much, and that people will never read, retain or comply with it.

A code usually won't be able to include all the details of all the policies it refers to, but it should always provide clear information about where a particular policy can be located, along with easy access to it.

After all, if you can't find the policy, how can you be held to it?

It's also important that policies align with each other, so they speak consistently, don't contradict each other, and there are no gaps where critical issues have not been addressed. Where there is a gap, the organization's culture of compliance and ethics – its values and what it stands for – should in part fill it with the notion that people will do the right thing. This includes actively seeking advice on what to do.

Corporate policies

> **Policy:** A course or principle of action adopted or proposed by a government, party, business, or individual, etc.[4]

When we think of policies from a compliance perspective, rightly or wrongly we tend to think of a set of rules or principles of conduct that staff and others to whom the policy applies should follow or apply in a particular area.

Let's take the example of anti-bribery and follow it through.

A company may have a policy not to tolerate or permit bribery, but people working in and for the business are expected to follow some rules or apply some principles in order to adhere to that policy themselves, or to help ensure that the company adheres to it. In the simplest terms, a clear policy can be as high-level as: 'Do not lie, cheat or steal.' Or: 'Treat everyone honestly, fairly and with respect'.

When it comes to a compliance policy, then in the case of an anti-bribery programme, the policy may be as simple as: 'Thou shalt not bribe' or 'We shall not bribe.' To this, many may say: 'I don't remember what a bribe is' and others may feel that 'Sometimes it's obvious what a bribe is, but other times it is not so clear' or wonder, 'Does this include really small bribes?'

Certainly there can sometimes be ambiguity, although it is often overplayed. In reality, if people understand that the intention is genuinely to avoid all forms of bribery and to help combat corruption, and that the overarching policy of acting honestly, fairly, ethically and with integrity should be applied in all situations, then the number of situations in which people cannot work out what is the right thing to do is significantly reduced.

But the point is, people do have to work it out, and they can be motivated to work it out in many different ways.

The fact is, anti-bribery is a relatively complex area, and anti-bribery law especially so. There is therefore no doubt that a high-level anti-bribery policy statement (probably in the code of conduct itself, but this can be debated) and some supporting detail is warranted, even though much of what you need to say may be contained in a high-level code of conduct.

How much detail should a code provide?

As a general rule, although one of the main goals of a compliance and ethics programme is to ensure that people comply with the law, it is neither practical nor necessarily desirable to attempt to teach people exactly what the law says. It is helpful to give a high-level overview, and an organization has a duty to help ensure that people working in or for it do not, while performing what they believe to be their duties, unwittingly commit criminal offences. Also, for many people, a desire not to break the law is an important motivation. For many others, the motivation will be different, and an effective policy needs to speak to these different types.

Let's run this with our anti-bribery example.

ISO 37001[5] contains a useful, very broad definition of bribery with which most can agree:

> offering, promising, giving, accepting or soliciting of an undue advantage of any value (which could be financial or non-financial), directly or indirectly, and irrespective of location(s), in violation of applicable law, as an inducement or reward for a person acting or refraining from acting in relation to the performance of that person's duties[6]

(This and other international standards are referenced on pages 102–07.)

So, adapting this, a reasonably high-level anti-bribery compliance policy statement may say something like:

AN EXAMPLE OF AN ANTI-BRIBERY COMPLIANCE POLICY

Our company will not tolerate bribery in any form. Bribery is a criminal offence in most countries in which we operate, and we always do business in accordance with the law. We will never ask you to break the law – indeed we insist that you do not – and no one can ask or demand that you act unlawfully. If anyone tries, please tell us straightaway and we will support you!

But this is not just about law. Bribery causes significant damage to society and people. None of us want our organization or anyone who works in or for it to contribute to that damage. Indeed, we wish to play our part in helping to combat corruption and the harm it does.

So, what is bribery? In the most basic terms, bribery is where someone offers, provides, seeks or accepts some benefit with the intention that whoever receives the bribe can then be induced to perform their duty improperly. The recipient is often a public official, but it is possible to bribe officers or employees of private organizations. Our policy does not make any distinction, no matter who is involved or what the local law is – bribery is never acceptable.

A bribe may be a very large sum of money to help win a large contract, or it may be a small amount paid to a public official to induce him or her to perform his/her duty properly, ie to perform some service that the payer is already entitled to receive but that is being withheld subject to payment of the bribe. Once again, our policy makes no distinction: these so-called facilitating payments are prohibited and are never ever acceptable, even in the few countries where they are not a criminal offence.

We are not offering this as a model anti-bribery policy but rather aim to highlight what the organization is trying to say in its policy, explicitly or implicitly. Accuracy, clarity, brevity and expertise are all part of the mix. But so is plain language.

It is also possible to imagine a code that has been contributed to or even in part written by employees for employees, each of whom become a signatory to that code.

Equally, to bring the policy to life, a code might also point to, or integrate, stories about the harm bribery and corruption can do to societies, and the fallout a bribery scandal can bring to companies and their employees.

'Never mind the supplier's own code – make them comply with ours'

As part of their compliance programmes, some organizations and even whole sectors have adopted the practice of requiring their suppliers and contractors to comply with the client organization's code of conduct. This is viewed as a convenient and, in many respects, more accessible and engaging way of spelling out the legal and compliance obligations that the supplier or contractor is required to accept, instead of or in addition to the 'thou shalt comply with all applicable laws' clause in the contract between the two parties.

This approach has some merits, but when you think about it, it is hard enough to motivate and require your own staff to read and comply with your own code of conduct, and you may well only be successful if you create a code of conduct that your staff can relate to, engage with and take pride in upholding. Think how much harder it is to motivate a supplier or contractor to comply with your (their client company's) code of conduct!

By making it a contractual requirement, are you also requiring the supplier or contractor to train some or all of its own staff? If not, what is the point?

The 'compliance with applicable laws (including [any you choose to highlight in particular])' is important as a contractual requirement, and disclosing and highlighting the importance of your code of conduct may be a good way of convincing the supplier or contractor that you are serious about it. If one or two senior people at the supplier or contractor actually read your code of conduct, they may well also perceive that your approach is ethics- and values-based, and this may motivate them to engage and comply.

But you probably need all of the supplier's or contractor's staff, or at least a certain number of its key decision-makers, to act in accordance with your code of conduct, and this will not happen unless they read it and are required to comply with it – which, as we have seen, requires the whole compliance and ethics programme, training, buy-in, sanctions, incentives, etc.

Then consider that the supplier or contractor, almost by definition, has multiple customers attempting to require it to comply with their code of conduct too.

And then consider that many suppliers and contractors will have their own code of conduct, and they probably have their work cut out ensuring their staff comply with that.

By the way, if your organization is requiring a supplier or contractor to comply with your code of conduct, you may receive the response: 'Hold on, we have our own code of conduct which we hold dear and which, if you care to read it, you will see is compatible with yours.' This is actually a better response than, 'Of course, where do we sign?' and, we would say, your organization is receiving more assurance about the likelihood of the supplier or contractor complying, or acting in an ethical and trustworthy way.

Many organizations attempt to address the above issues by creating a short-form code of conduct for suppliers. This at least reduces the length and volume of requirements that the supplier or contractor is expected to read, and can focus on those risks that are most relevant; and a well drafted code of conduct for suppliers should contain introductory language that makes the supplier more likely to take it seriously. For example, here is the introduction to Subsea 7's three-page code of conduct for suppliers:

EXCERPT FROM SUBSEA 7 CODE OF CONDUCT FOR SUPPLIERS

Our code of conduct for suppliers sets out the key principles of ethical conduct that you (as our supplier) agree must be upheld when working with us (Subsea 7). It has been written in a way that we believe is most relevant to you and the interactions between our two organizations. It complements the full Subsea 7 code of conduct, where you can find more guidance, should you need it.

When an organization asks you to comply with its code of conduct, it can seem like an imposition – we know, having been on the receiving end of such requests ourselves. You may well have your own code of conduct, which you and your employees are committed to upholding. Also, such requests don't take into account the fact that an organization's behaviours are, ultimately, driven by its values and culture, not just by contractual undertakings – even though honouring such commitments is extremely important.

We trust you to uphold your contractual commitments with us, and we get assurance from your ability to demonstrate that you have your own code of conduct that sets out equivalent standards and which is embedded within your organization.

Our values of safety, integrity, sustainability, innovation, performance and collaboration underpin everything we do, including whom we choose to do business with and how our two organizations work together. We don't ask you to share our values, just to respect them.

That being said, just as we won't compromise on safety when we work with you, we consider that honesty, fairness and integrity are universal values, and we wish them to characterize the way in which our two organizations do business together.

We require these standards of you, but you can also expect them of us, and we ask that you tell us if anyone is failing to uphold them.

Please ensure that all your staff and subcontractors who are involved in your supply of goods or services to Subsea 7 operate to standards at least as high as those set out in this code of conduct for suppliers.

Thank you.

Some common but problematic policy areas

While each code of conduct is particular to the organization it belongs to, most will have to deal with common issues of conduct and areas of risk. Here we cover some of the trickier ones and pick out a few policies in areas we suspect our readers will be particularly interested. But bear in mind that, depending on what kind of organization it is, and the kind of business it is engaged in, there will be other areas, such as boycott, export controls, human rights and records management.

Gifts and hospitality

When the UK Bribery Act was going through its consultation period before coming into force in July 2011, anyone would have thought that it was all about gifts and hospitality. Indeed, much of the very active discussion seemed centred around the notion that perfectly legitimate business activities were being criminalized and that UK plc would grind to a halt. The topic of gifts and hospitality dominated the many seminars about the law coming into force, what it would mean, what organizations would need to do, etc.

Instead, this time could have been much better spent focusing on some of the more difficult aspects and areas of greater exposure for many organizations.

Are gifts and hospitality really the biggest risk you face? If so, by all means make that one of your main areas of focus, but if you have identified other risks that are higher and harder to manage, such as facilitation payments or bribery to win work, or sanctions, or competition law, then it is probably better to focus on them. Indeed, too much focus on the low-hanging fruit of gifts and hospitality can discredit your efforts to address other areas of conduct where there may be true dishonest or criminal intent.

The giving of gifts or hospitality by or to business partners, clients, suppliers or joint venture partners is a fairly common, legitimate business activity in many if not most sectors, and it is not unlawful. However, a gift or hospitality *can* be a bribe, just as any payment, benefit or advantage offered to someone can be a bribe, if it is excessive, if it is made with a corrupt intent or as a quid pro quo, or if it makes the recipient feel unduly obligated.

This is a difficult area: it's natural for most people to feel a sense of obligation if they accept a gift or hospitality above a certain value – some would even consider it discourteous and even immoral not to feel obligated. However, if as a decision-making manager of an organization you accept a gift or hospitality from a supplier, this can be problematic. After all, a sense of obligation can lead you to want to reciprocate. So many would argue that you should not accept hospitality above a modest value if you have no intention of ever awarding work to the supplier. But this is not a hard and fast rule, nor is it intended as a crusade against gifts and hospitality.

In any case gifts can be a little harder and at the same time a little easier – there is less justification for offering or accepting gifts, save as an expression of gratitude or a cultural courtesy – but it can be harder to refuse without causing offence.

On the other hand, a business meal is a recognized and effective way of enabling a business discussion that can help foster a better relationship and understanding between two organizations, and establish the goods or services that they need or can provide and whether they are good people to work with. Most people would rather be at home with their family than going out to dinner with a supplier, unless the dinner were either (i) genuinely useful from a business perspective or (ii) a really lavish treat, in which case you are back into potential excessiveness.

Rather like conflicts of interest, gifts and hospitality can also be a surrogate for, or provide a window into, the organization's compliance and ethics programme and culture. If there is a culture of giving and receiving gifts and hospitality, then even if a relatively small percentage may be excessively generous or disproportionate, and even if a smaller percentage still is offered or accepted with any corrupt, dishonest or improper intent, it may be significant. In this context, think of New York Mayor Giuliani's policy of zero tolerance of graffiti, which led to a significant reduction in more serious crime in NYC.

Different approaches

A HIGH-LEVEL APPROACH

So an organization may very likely need a clear policy on gifts and hospitality. It can be a simple, high-level policy of the type that can be included in a code of conduct, if it simply states: 'We will not offer or accept any gifts or hospitality.' Indeed, some organizations take this approach, simply to make life clearer and simpler and to avoid pitfalls, and perhaps to prevent this topic from distracting people from the more important aspects of compliance risk.

ADDING MORE DETAIL

Alternatively, it could say 'We will not offer or accept any gifts or hospitality if they are, or might reasonably be perceived to be, excessive in value or frequency or something that might induce the recipient to reciprocate by improperly performing his or her duty or function. We will not solicit gifts or hospitality.'

INCLUDING SPECIFICS

However, if the desire is to include any wrinkles in such policy (eg to exclude items branded with the logo of the donating organization, chocolates, etc, which can be and are shared with the recipient's colleagues, or items below a certain value), then a separate policy will probably be needed – not least because such mean, quibbling details have no place in a hopefully inspiring code of conduct.

Most well-managed organizations will control expenditure on gifts and hospitality that their employees may wish to offer, in the same way as they control all expenditure. For example, you won't be reimbursed by the organization for any gift or hospitality you've given unless you have received prior approval and/or you submit a valid receipt for an expense that is regarded as valid, is judged to have been reasonably and necessarily incurred and/or falls within certain limits.

Your organization may decide to have separate limits for gifts and hospitality and to require that they need prior approval in some or all cases. However, broadly speaking, if you already have reasonably rigorous expenses reimbursement policies, the gifts and hospitality policy is primarily about transparency. And when it comes to gifts and hospitality that you accept, i.e. where you are not spending the organization's money and seeking reimbursement, the organization may never be aware of what you have accepted unless you disclose it (or unless a colleague reports it).

So you could have a principled, high-level gifts and hospitality policy that simply states:

Any gift or hospitality that you offer or accept must be disclosed on a register (which is accessible to the organization's management). You must also comply with any applicable expenses reimbursement policies.

If you are comfortable disclosing what you have offered or accepted, we are confident that in 99 cases out of 100 you will make a sensible decision. Are you happy disclosing the relevant gift or hospitality to your manager, to the Compliance and Ethics function, to internal audit? Would you be happy disclosing it to a newspaper?

TIP

If an organization is investigated by a prosecutor for bribery, there is a very good chance that the prosecutor will ask to see details of all gifts and hospitality provided to public officials. If your organization chooses to set a *de minimis* threshold, below which items do not need to be registered, then it would be sensible not to apply that threshold when a public official is the recipient, but rather ask that all gifts and hospitality involving public officials be registered.

Facilitation payments

Facilitation payments (or facilitating payments, to use the strict term used in the US Foreign Corrupt Practices Act) are a US invention. The draughtsmen or policymakers behind the Act wished to criminalize bribery of foreign public officials. They attempted to give the Act as much extraterritorial jurisdiction as they could, in order to maximize its effect and, the cynic would say, to help ensure that non-US competitors were on a level playing field with US companies.

However, they also realized that the law could paralyse business and trade, unless they made an exception for 'petty bribery', ie the frequent, small amounts often solicited by poorly paid public officials who, if you did not pay them, would not perform their duty properly, in a timely fashion, or at all.

In many ways, this carve-out was sensible, as it concentrated the law and prosecutorial efforts on grander bribery, ie bribes paid with corrupt intent to obtain business or an advantage in doing business and which involve inducing the recipient to perform a duty improperly. However, the United States is one of only a few jurisdictions which make this distinction, and even under the Foreign Corrupt Practices Act the carve-out applies only if:

1 the payment is not unlawful under local law; and

2 the amount is modest and the frequency low.

In practice, this carve-out has created an unintended loophole, whereby such payments by companies are often (i) by no means as low as the lawmakers intended and/or (ii) a systematic practice. Moreover, the carve-out causes confusion and means that a disproportionate amount of effort goes into explaining how to deal with these types of situations.

Most organizations nowadays make no distinction between facilitation payments and other types of bribery, partly because the former are unlawful in most countries and in most circumstances, and partly because an anti-bribery policy cannot be truly credible or effective, and indeed cannot be ethics- and values-based, if it permits such exceptions.

THE CORROSIVE CONSEQUENCES OF FACILITATION PAYMENTS

Facilitation payments are difficult for employees because, unlike 'normal' types of bribery in which the recipient is induced to perform a duty improperly, with a facilitation payment the payer is trying to induce the wretch to do what he/she is already supposed to do.

The fact is, so-called facilitation payments are a major contributor to endemic, low-level corruption. They create a culture and practice that is extremely difficult to break. And people on low incomes can be obliged to spend a significant proportion of their annual income to access services to which they are already entitled.

At one company, if rightly or wrongly you decide that you have no option but to make a facilitation payment, the policy requires you to report this to the CEO. This is a difficult balance to strike: such a reporting requirement, indeed any adverse consequences of a facilitation payment policy, may simply drive reporting underground: people will conclude that there is no point trying to submit an expenses reimbursement claim if they will have to tie themselves in knots trying to come up with a legitimate justification for the payment, and indeed when they do not have a receipt.

However, in many cases a facilitation payment is a small amount which a well-paid employee, and the typical expat, will be able to afford out of her own pocket. On the other hand, the goal of this policy is laudable and, if the culture is right, can be effective: if you are willing to defend your decision to the CEO, then the chances are they will agree that you did your best and had little option, and they and the company will stand by you.

Many enlightened companies will recognize the importance of playing their part in combating corruption, and that it is hypocritical and unsustainable to have a policy that states, 'We shall not pay bribes – unless the amounts are small and infrequent and the recipients are public officials.'

They also recognize that this risk is one of the hardest to manage, both for the company and for its employees: if you are on your own in a strange country it can be very intimidating to be faced by any public official demanding a facilitation payment, and it takes skill and experience to resist successfully.

Enlightened companies stand by their employees and do not hang them out to dry by simply saying 'Here is our policy, you deal with it.' Organizations can and should make it clear that the employee has a defence if his safety or liberty is under threat; in practice, an organization may well recognize that an employee may feel forced to pay, not only if there is a threat of physical harm or loss of liberty, but also for fear of some other adverse effect to the employee's personal or family well-being or peace of mind. In the latter case, there may not be a defence at law, strictly speaking; but an organization may recognize that it should support its employees in this situation.

The other aspect of facilitation payments is that the organization should have in place policies and procedures to ensure that the situation is not compounded by failing to account properly for the facilitation payment. If, rightly or wrongly, an employee makes a facilitation payment, whether or not they have a defence in the eyes of the law or under the organization's policy, the organization risks committing a books and records or false accounting offence if it does not account for the payment properly. Some organizations have a 'facilitation payments' cost code for that reason. They should also ensure that the finance and Compliance and Ethics function have a full record of the circumstances in which the payment was made.

And don't forget that, if the organization is non-compliant, then the payment is being made to induce the public official to overlook this fact, ie to perform their duty improperly and obtain a benefit for the organization to which it is not entitled. So this situation should be analysed rather differently.

Theoretically, if an organization discovers that a facilitation payment has been made in circumstances where there is no safety or liberty defence, the organization may feel that it should consider self-reporting to the relevant regulatory or prosecutorial authority. But in practice an organization may well decide that a modest payment and non-systemic breach of this kind does not warrant self-reporting. This is a very difficult area, and it is beyond the scope of this book to provide advice or opinions in this regard.

AN INSPECTOR CALLS

A manager of an organization's office in a country where bribes are customary arrives at work one hot, July day to find that the electricity has been cut off. There is no air conditioning and the computers do not work.

The manager discovers that an inspector paid a visit and determined that the electrical supply was unsafe or did not comply with regulations (they were not completely clear). The inspector said that the electricity must be disconnected until the problems have been addressed. This would take at least two to three weeks.

It is pretty clear that the electricity supply will be promptly reconnected if a bribe is paid to the public official.

The manager does not believe there is any safety or regulatory fault with the connection. In other words, this is a 'shake-down'. So there's a decision to make: either pay the reprobate a bribe or send the employees home for two or three weeks and the organization will suffer significant cost, disruption and probably losses – all because you're not willing to pay £50 or £100.

In this situation what would you do? Would your answer be different if in fact your electrical supply really were unsafe or defective? What do you think should take precedence here – the imperatives of your compliance code or your business? Or would you say it's better just to push this sort of problem out to a third party?

One of us once asked a partner at a blue-chip accounting firm with offices around the world how on earth they manage such problems. Their answer was that they use an agent to manage all of their offices and properties so they do not have to confront these issues themselves...

Conflicts of interest

One of us used to work for an Anglo-Swedish company, and perceived that the Swedish approach to bribery always started with: *Where is the conflict of interest?*

This is a good point. When you think about it, there is always a conflict of interest where bribery is involved. The bribe payer is trying to induce the bribe recipient to put his interests (and it is normally a he – *discuss*) ahead of those of the organization that he serves.

Bribery of public officials is perceived as being more common than bribery of people who work for a private organization, but clearly those conflicts of interest can still exist and be exploited. For example, if you work for a private organization and your job is to:

- certify that a contractor has performed its work properly and is entitled to payment; or
- prescribe drugs for patients whose costs are reimbursed by your employer,

you could be improperly induced to give that certification or write that prescription. You would be putting your interests, or those of others, ahead of the interests of the organization that you serve, which could end up paying for defective work, or a prescription that is unnecessary, or unnecessarily expensive.

An effective compliance and ethics programme will almost certainly include a policy requirement that any potential conflicts of interest should be disclosed and appropriately managed. Such a policy will make it clear that there is nothing inherently wrong with having interests that may conflict with your employer's.

However, if you or a family member or personal or business associate has an interest that could conflict with those of the organization, the best way to manage the potential conflict is to make sure that you have been transparent. In many cases, that transparency is sufficient, but in some cases the manager or others to whom you have made the disclosure may need to agree with you further steps to manage the conflict of interest or to avoid a potential conflict of interest crystallising. For example, if you work in procurement and a family member works for a potential supplier of the organization, it should be agreed that you will not be involved in any decision-making regarding the potential award of work to the supplier or the management of any contract with that supplier.

A conflict of interest can occur in many different ways, and it may be a state of affairs, or it may arise in the context of or be applicable to a particular project or transaction, or to an aspect of someone's work.

Examples include:

- financial or ownership interest (eg you have a significant shareholding in a client company, or your father earns a commission for work referred to a consultant);

- management or decision-making role (eg. your brother is a director of a supplier, or your spouse is a procurement manager at a client);

- public service (eg you work in construction and your daughter is a councillor involved in town planning);

- volunteer work (eg you work in oil and gas or pharmaceuticals and you volunteer part-time for an anti-hydrocarbon or, as the case may be, an anti-animal testing lobbying group);

- outside employment (eg you are seeking approval to work in your spare time in a business of a similar nature to your own work for your employer).

Conflicts of interest are also relevant to understanding and assessing the risks that may be associated with dealings and links with public officials – see below.

Dealings and links with public officials

In this area there is, on the face of it, more clarity – which is also supported almost universally by the law. Employees and those who represent the organization should refuse all requests for payments and benefits to be provided to public officials that are not legitimate, published government levies or fees.

That includes never engaging public officials to provide services outside of their normal function, and never offering gifts and hospitality to a public official without appropriate authorization.

What the above sections on gifts and hospitality, and conflicts of interest, and the following sections on political, charitable and community support, commercial sponsorship and lobbying have in common is this: great care must be taken to ensure that direct or indirect benefits are not conferred on public officials or client representatives as a quid pro quo, with a corrupt or dishonest intent, or so as to create an undue obligation or conflict of interest.

The link between these various aspects, as well as associated pitfalls and appropriate guidance, should be clearly explained in the organization's policies, and additional procedures may be needed if this type of activity is key to, or common in, the organization's business model. Common examples include:

- offering or agreeing to provide employment, an agreement for services or work experience to a public official or client representative, or one of their relatives or other personal associates;
- providing political, charitable or community support, or commercial sponsorship, when there is a possible link to a public official or client representative;

- entering into an agreement with a person (organization or individual) because of their connections with public officials or clients.

As a general principle, such situations can be managed by ensuring that any such interests or connections are disclosed and appropriately managed, and that the organization has a policy or other guidance to employees to the effect that:

- The organization generally only offers or agrees to provide employment, an agreement for services or work experience to people on merit and pursuant to a competitive process, and not because of any such connections. If it is because of such connections, it must ensure that they will not be leveraged improperly or unethically.

- The organization does not provide charitable or community support or commercial sponsorship at the request of, or in order to curry favour with, a public official or client representative or as a direct or indirect incentive or reward to a public official or client representative for the award of work or of any advantage in doing business

- To the extent appropriate the organization conducts due diligence to ensure it has all relevant information to enable it to identify and assess any connections, interests or influences described above and to ascertain where any such support will go and how it will be used.

- An appropriate red flag checklist should be consulted before entering into any such arrangement, as in the example provided by Subsea 7 below.

RED FLAG CHECKLIST

The following checklist should be used when the organization is considering:

- engaging an individual as an officer, employee or contractor, or for work experience; or

- providing charitable or community support or commercial sponsorship.

In this checklist, references to:

- 'the beneficiary' mean the charity, community or other organization or person that would receive the support or sponsorship in question;
- 'the individual' include any company through which he/she provides services; and
- 'relevant person' mean a public official or client representative, or one of their relatives or other personal associates

1   As far as we are aware, having made appropriate enquiries, including of the person at our organization proposing the engagement of this individual or the provision of the support or sponsorship:

   a. Is the individual or beneficiary a relevant person or an organization connected to a relevant person?

   b. Has the individual or beneficiary been recommended to us by a relevant person?

   c. Are we considering engaging this individual, or providing support or sponsorship to the beneficiary:

      i.   because of the individual's or beneficiary's connections with, or ability to influence, a relevant person;

      ii. to curry favour with a relevant person; or

      iii. so that a relevant person may stand to benefit personally (eg through some hidden financial or ownership interest or reputational enhancement)?

   d. Does a relevant person stand to benefit personally?

   e. Are there any potential conflicts of interest between:

      i.   the individual and their role at our organization, on the one hand, and their personal interests or associations; or

      ii. the beneficiary, or its interests, connections or charitable or community goals, and the work of our organization?

2   Will the individual be engaged or, as the case may be, will the support or sponsorship be provided on merit, and not because of any such connections or influence?

3 Has the individual been asked to declare any potential conflicts of interest between their role at our organization and their personal interests or associations?

4 Is there a legal obligation to provide charitable or community support? If so, is the requirement to provide support of a particular type or to a particular beneficiary, or do we have discretion to make our own choices?

5 If the individual or beneficiary is a personal associate of someone at our organization, has that person declared that connection and abstained from the decision-making process?

6 Have we undertaken any due diligence and follow-up reasonably necessary to ensure:

   a. we have all relevant information to enable us to identify and assess any connections, interests or influences described above; and

   b. that the charitable or community support is used in the way we intend?

If the answer to any of the above questions raises any red flags, the matter should be discussed with the relevant compliance officer, who will agree a way to proceed that is compliant and ethical.

Dealings and links with representatives of the organization's customers

As we've explained in the section 'Conflicts of interest' (page 188), most if not all of what we say above regarding public officials applies to dealings with representatives of your organization's customers, regardless of whether they are considered public officials.

Community engagement, charitable donations and political contributions

Charitable and community donations and support are a legitimate corporate activity, but they can also be a form of disguised bribery or the conduit whereby, with or without the donor's knowledge, money is channelled to corrupt public officials. For that reason, great care needs to be taken with such activities.

The key principle for employees to understand is that they must be sure that the intended recipient is what it purports to be and does actually receive the money and spend it in the manner intended, and that such contributions are not provided as an inducement or reward for any improper conduct.

There is also an emotional element that can be exploited. If it appears that it's for a 'good cause' people may naturally want to agree to the request. But just because it's 'for charity' doesn't automatically make it okay. Normally charitable and community donations are made voluntarily and proactively, and not at the request of some other person. Corporate donations of this type should be made in accordance with the organization's community engagement and charitable giving goals and strategy.

If a client or public official requests that the organization make a charitable or community donation, this should be viewed as a red flag. It does not mean that the donation cannot be made, but it does mean that it must be carefully reviewed and any corruption risks specifically considered.

The same is true when there is a local legal requirement to make such a contribution – just because it is a legal requirement does not necessarily mean that the identified recipient of, and intended use for, the donation are legitimate.

As far as political contributions are concerned, this is quite culturally- and country-specific, and political contributions are often subject to strict laws. Many countries prohibit corporate contributions or donations to political parties or to any organizations, think-tanks, academic institutions or charities closely associated with a political party or cause. Where permitted, if an organization makes them, clearly great care must be taken to ensure they do not act as a form of bribery. Moreover, care should be taken to ensure that no charitable or community support amounts to disguised or unintentional political support.

Commercial sponsorship

It is legitimate and reasonable for an organization to provide commercial or corporate sponsorship, but it can raise similar issues to charitable or community support. If the money or other benefits are provided not as a philanthropic gift but in anticipation of legitimate benefits in return, such as advertising, profile-raising, services or marketing opportunities, it should be considered commercial sponsorship. The compliance justification lies in the fact that the value of the sponsorship has been assessed commercially as providing legitimate anticipated benefits of equal value in return, rather than an expectation of some non-transparent, potentially improper benefits.

The story of 'The sponsored swim' is a good example of how to look at sponsorship and charitable or community support as a risk and policy area, and how to train effectively:

THE SPONSORED SWIM

Your organization (Ethico) is working on a large project for an important client, Universal Hydro Technologies (UHT). One of UHT's senior managers, Tomas, contacts your project team with a request: he and a few of his colleagues are doing a sponsored swim in aid of a well-known local charity in the area where the project is based. They are just looking for some sponsorship.

Tomas stresses that this is an entirely personal endeavour, not a UHT initiative, and that his connection with his employer (your client) is a completely separate matter. He is looking for corporate sponsors. He asks you if Ethico is willing to make a contribution – perhaps £1,000.

There is clearly no corrupt or dishonest intent here, but agreeing to this request risks breaching various provisions of the codes of conduct of both Ethico and, very likely, UHT (conflicts of interest, gifts and hospitality, charitable donations and community engagement). If you look at any good code of conduct, it very likely requires its staff to avoid conflicts of interest, not to solicit gifts or hospitality, and not to make charitable or community donations at the request of a client or public official. You might need to explain to Tomas that Ethico's policies prevent you from agreeing to his request and that UHT would probably do the same in a similar situation.

Offering to sponsor Tomas yourself instead of asking Ethico to do so could also be the wrong solution, unless you personally really feel strongly that you wish to support the charity. A useful analogy is this: if you wished to provide a gift or hospitality that was not approved by Ethico or exceeded any limits in Ethico's policy, you could not get around this by paying for the gift or hospitality yourself.

It may feel wrong to turn down a request for charity. But would your answer be different if Ethico were currently bidding for another project for UHT? Or if it was likely to bid in the near future? Would Ethico only sponsor Tomas and his colleagues to avoid upsetting an important client? How would this look to one of Ethico's competitors, if they became aware of it, especially if Tomas asked them too and they declined?

This sponsorship risks mixing business with pleasure. Be very careful about asking for personal sponsorship from someone with whom you have primarily a business relationship, not a personal one. Would you ask Tomas to sponsor you? If you ask a supplier to sponsor you, is it fair? How easy is it for them to say no?

If Ethico wants to make a contribution to the same charity of its own volition, consistent with its own charitable and community goals, that is another matter.[7]

Care should be taken to ensure that any commercial sponsorship does not create a conflict of interest or inappropriate sense of obligation or indebtedness, and that it is not provided as a direct or indirect incentive or reward to a public official or client representative for the award of work or of any advantage in doing business.

Lobbying

'Lobbying' can be defined as trying to persuade a politician, some other public official, the government or an official group that a particular thing should or should not happen or that a law or rule should be changed or promulgated to give the organization or industry represented by the lobbyist an advantage.

Care should be taken to understand when the organization's staff or third parties may be engaged in lobbying on the organization's behalf. This should be part of the risk assessment, but even if the organization does not engage in lobbying or government affairs frequently or in the formal sense, guidance may be needed to sensitise employees to the risks that they may be engaged in ad hoc lobbying, or that what they are doing could amount to or be construed as lobbying.

In terms of minimum policy requirements, any lobbying activity undertaken on behalf of an organization should be in accordance with local laws and the organization's code of conduct, including the zero tolerance of bribery and corruption. Individuals or entities engaged in lobbying activities on behalf of the organization (including third parties) should be considered as high-risk and must:

- have appropriate, senior authorization to do so;

- be registered in the relevant country where applicable;

- undergo an appropriate risk assessment (including screening or other due diligence as may be necessary to gather the information necessary to understand and manage the risk);

- agree to strict anti-corruption representations, warranties and undertakings;

- conduct themselves in a way that conforms with all applicable laws, the organization's code of conduct, and with honesty, integrity and transparency in all dealings with governments, their agencies and representatives. In particular, they should be transparent about whom they represent and what their agenda is.

Dealings with business partners

As we have already seen, third-party risks are among the hardest for an organization to manage. The organization needs to set out clearly in its policies its expectations around the engagement of, and conduct by, business partners and other third parties. These expectations need to be made clear to employees and those third parties.

Broadly speaking, those expectations should be that:

- Care must be taken to ensure that the organization only works with third parties (clients, partners, suppliers, sub-contractors, agents and consultants) that operate to the same ethical standards;

- In particular, such third parties do not engage in bribery or corruption or other unethical business conduct on the organization's behalf or in its name, and that they are not the conduit for corrupt proceeds or self-enrichment – even when local laws require that the organization work with local partners.

The compliance risks with third parties are managed by a range of procedures and controls that are discussed in more detail in Chapter 11. This includes risk assessment, red flag checklists, due diligence and procurement procedures.

Other policy areas

Your risk assessment determines what compliance risks you face and therefore what you need to include in your policies and what areas might need specific policies or even procedures in order to ensure sufficient awareness and to manage those risks adequately.

In addition to the 'problematic' ones we have explored in this Chapter, you will probably want to cover the following compliance risks too:

- sanctions and export controls;
- competition/anti-trust law;
- data protection and privacy;
- information security;
- human rights and modern slavery;
- anti-money-laundering;
- anti-fraud (including false claims);
- tax evasion;
- discrimination;
- bullying and harassment.

You may choose to have separate policies for each of these activities, or it may be adequate and indeed more effective to include them in the code of conduct and/or one or more other overarching policies.

Such overarching policies can be very useful, as you can use them to pull together, summarize and/or draw attention to all relevant and related policies. You can explain how conflicts of interest, gifts and hospitality, lobbying, etc. can all be relevant to forms of bribery, and then set out specific guidance on those areas not already adequately covered in the policies already mentioned.

When there's a conflict between your minimum standards and local culture or laws

The first of these conflicts is quite a common dilemma, the second less so. What do you do if, having set the policy bar for your organization at a certain level and committed to upholding it wherever your organization operates, you find that local culture or law expects or requires a lower standard?

It is hardly credible or sustainable for an organization to say: 'We will not pay bribes – except in country X, where they are commonplace', or 'We will treat everyone fairly and with respect – except in country Y, where different castes of people are treated differently.' This will undermine the compliance and ethics programme, as well as being inherently unjust and hypocritical. It is quite common for people to say that bribery is part of the culture in a country, and that it is disrespectful and culturally imperialist to insist on a no-bribes policy, or that granting a sub-contract to a company owned by a close relative is not a conflict of interest but the prudent way to ensure you deal only with trustworthy sub-contractors.

What if your policy states that you will only deal with suppliers whose standards are consistent with your own, and yet you wish to work and appoint suppliers in a country with a poor human rights record? If local laws in a country set a lower bar than your organization's code of conduct, then usually there is no reason why you cannot operate to the higher standard, although you may come across cultural objections such as the examples above. But we recall a colleague who described the difficulty for his international company working in South Africa during apartheid. Their code prohibited discrimination, but local laws effectively required it in some respects.

This is not the place to provide definitive answers to the above challenges, although in most cases answers that are both practical and ethical do exist. Rather, our aim is simply to highlight the fact that such challenges will arise, and the organization's programme, Compliance and Ethics function and leaders will need to anticipate and find ways of dealing with them.

Across the minefield: compliance and ethics meets real life

A conscience-free lunch

Some years ago, I was having lunch with three colleagues. All four were managers and three were roughly the same seniority, the fourth being one or two grades lower. The meal was a low-key celebration of a successful transaction on which we had all worked. It was not an official, company-sanctioned celebration event. When the bill arrived, all four of us assumed and suggested that we would split the bill four ways.

Then I suggested that the executive who was a direct or indirect line manager of two of the managers present would very likely agree that it was reasonable and appropriate for the company to pay for the meal. If not, I said I was more than happy to pay my share.

The manager who reported direct to this executive said good idea, but he promptly passed the bill to his junior and said: 'You pay and claim on expenses and I will approve.' I said 'No, you can't do that.' 'Why?' asked all three of them. 'Because I am pretty sure our policies will require that the most senior person present pay the bill, so that his manager, who is not present, will be able to approve or disapprove it.' 'Oh yes, good point,' said the other three.

So the senior manager paid the bill and agreed to ascertain whether the executive (his direct manager) was happy to approve it. But these were all senior, responsible managers, two of them in functional roles that involved them more directly than, you might argue, most employees in being a good custodian of the shareholders' money. Why did it need the compliance officer to be the policy expert and conscience, even when he did not have responsibility for that particular policy?

Another kickback

A new country manager meets the MD of one of their biggest local suppliers, whose contract is due for renewal.

The current unit price under the contract is £1,500. It is hard to say what represents fair value, as the range is probably somewhere between £1,000 and £3,000.

The MD of the supplier says to the country manager: 'Renew the contract with a unit price of £2,500, and we will split the profit with you.'

'It's up to you'

It's been going on for some time – someone on your team keeps turning up late for work and you're certain they've got a real problem with alcohol. But they keep on insisting that they haven't.
What's your next move?

It wasn't your fault. You were sitting with a competitor and they went to make a phone call, and they left a document that summarized their pricing strategy.
Use what you've seen?

We did all the checks and hired a supplier. They've become vital to the project, which is now in a critical phase. Then we discover they have been seriously mistreating their employees.
How would you handle it?

You've just been asked by a supplier if you'd like to go the final of a football match. You'd love to, but you know that their contract is due for renewal.
Should you refuse?

Notes

1 L Carroll (1871) *Through the Looking-Glass, and What Alice Found There.*
2 See Library of Congress: www.loc.gov/item/48034353/ [accessed 24.02.19].

3 https://en.wikipedia.org>wiki>Code of Conduct [accessed 24.02.19].

4 *The Oxford English Reference Dictionary* (1996), 2nd edn, p 1120.

5 BS ISO 37001:2016.

6 Permission to reproduce extracts from British Standards is granted by BSI Standards Limited (BSI). No other use of this material is permitted. British Standards can be obtained in PDF or hard copy formats from the BSI online shop: www.bsigroup.com/Shop [accessed 24.02.19].

7 Reproduced by kind permission from a Subsea 7 training scenario.

09

Communication, education and training

In this chapter we look at how everyone in the organization needs to be educated on its compliance and ethics policies, why such policies and the issues they address matter, and how you can go about bringing them to life.

La grande illusion

It has often been observed that perhaps the biggest challenge with communication is the notion that it has in fact taken place. You've identified compliance risks. Commitments have been agreed. Policies written. The code of conduct exists. Now you need to get it into the hearts and minds of all the people who need to know and live it and make sure they understand it. So how do you do that?

As the title of this chapter suggests, you now need to develop a well-thought-through programme of communication, education and training to communicate your ethical stance, core policy commitments and your code of conduct, raise awareness and thereby gain buy-in, educate people on why it's important (for example, explaining the damage done by corruption), and train people on how to apply the code and other policies.

What's more, you have to communicate all this to everyone who needs to be aware of it – not just those who must comply (most obviously employees, but potentially also suppliers, subcontractors joint venture partners, consultants and intermediaries) but also those who are looking for assurance that the organization is committed to ensuring compliance with law and ethical business conduct (eg clients, investors and other stakeholders).

But there's a danger that comes with this: the illusion that, because everyone who needs to has gone through all the required education and training – look, you've even got all the data to prove it – the organization now has effective compliance and ethics in place. That's not how it works. There are many reasons for that, but here's just one that we've assembled from a number of different employee complaints:

> 'Every year it's the same. The managers say we all have to complete the compliance e-learning stuff, but we don't even have enough time to do our jobs anyway, and they expect us to do their training in our time! People resent that. So they usually do it with a negative frame of mind at the last possible minute and just try to get it over with.'

There is often a huge gap between the good intentions mapped out by training or described in company communication, and the cultural reality on the ground. It's not until everyone sees that the values and principles their organization says it stands for are things that their leadership, managers, team members and staff all really do care about that compliance comes alive.

The usual answer to that familiar old question of how you eat an elephant is, 'One mouthful at a time.' But actually, there's a much better answer: 'Get everybody to take a share.'

Compliance is a social animal, but it needs time to soak into the social fabric, and an organization needs to be able to know how well it's done that. Measuring the numbers of people who have completed the annual e-learning won't tell you. You need to be able to measure the impact it had on awareness and attitudes, and the extent to which it is being lived and how healthy your culture really is.

Communication versus education and training

'Tell me and I forget, teach me and I may remember, involve me and I learn.'

FROM THE XUNZI WRITINGS OF XUN KUANG, 3RD CENTURY BCE

Communication is essentially about *raising awareness*. Placing an idea, concept – or policy principle – into the minds of people so it is something that they are conscious of, even if they don't understand it or know what to do with it. Education and training are somewhat different. They are all about getting someone to understand the purpose of something, why it is important, what to do with it and what difference it makes to them and to others.

Creating awareness

At the very least, or to start with, you need to raise awareness of the existence, content and reasons for the organization's high-level compliance and ethics principles and of the relevant policies and procedures. The more clear, engaging and self-explanatory they are, the less you will need to train people on a policy or procedure, but you will always need to make sure those who need to know have read and understood it or will follow it. However, to the extent that the policies and procedures contain detail and are helping to explain and navigate complex areas of law, operations or important ethical principles, employees and others will need to be trained on them to ensure a sufficient level of understanding.

An awareness-raising campaign or initiative may be global or local, and the risks they are designed to address may be more prevalent in some places or for certain roles than others. Not all policies are global. Some may be very specific to an activity, office or region. But making sure people from outside the region become aware of that policy when they need to be can also be important.

Training versus education

It is axiomatic that training is not the same as education. For example, you might attend your local rugby club on a Wednesday evening before a match on Saturday for training on skills, tactics and formations; but were you to spend a year in New Zealand playing with aspiring All Blacks, that would be a rugby education.

When you apply this distinction in the area of compliance and ethics the difference becomes quite clear and relevant:

- **Compliance training:** Teaches people specific skills or content, so that, for example, they know what the policy says and practice how to apply it.

- **Compliance education:** For compliance and ethics to become part of the culture, people need to be educated more broadly on the context and the raison d'être, and thus be able to think and act for themselves, guided by better education.

For many people and in many cases, practical training will often cover both these requirements, but it's important to point out that some people, by virtue of their learning style, personality or role, need to know all the theory and science, or the why; some don't and simply want to know what they have to do and how to do it.

Some people like to place a great emphasis on that distinction between 'training' and 'education'. Training is more practical, teaching people how to apply a particular policy. Education, in contrast, helps them to understand why that policy matters, so they can think and act for themselves. However, in practice the two mostly work together.

Making training land with your audience

This is not a book about best practice teaching methods, and there are many great resources out there to help you create effective training. However, whatever you do, what matters most is that it helps your audience to understand the 'what' and the 'how'. If you can also explain the 'why' and get people to care – and to see that the organization cares too – they are more likely to remember it and to apply it properly.

Here we give just a few examples of how you can think about doing that.

Target leaders and management first

If the management is already on board before training sessions with staff begin, they can become part of those sessions, demonstrating how they care by nodding from the sidelines, giving anecdotes, asking questions and giving answers, even delivering part of the training to show this is business need, not just a compliance function.

Active and interested management presence tells a big story. But so does absence. It is a bad sign if members of management find reasons why they don't need to attend. Just as we discussed within 'top-level commitment', if managers find reasons not to participate in the messaging and its delivery then others will follow suit.

Find ways to bring the issues to life

For example, to help raise and maintain awareness and stimulate thought, discussion and buy-in, you might develop thought-provoking ice breakers like this:

HOW DO YOU DEFINE INTEGRITY?

When you are walking your dog at night... and he does his business on the pavement or on someone's property... do you clear it up?

   Even when nobody is watching?

   How do you define integrity?

   Doing the right thing – even when nobody is looking.

But it is also a good idea to get people more deeply involved in exploring the grey areas around an important issue. Indeed, it's possible to create interactive scenarios and even games that get people increasingly involved in just how difficult some situations can be.

Use real-life dilemmas and values moments

We give many examples of these in the 'Across the minefield' sections that end each chapter in Part Two of this book. However, it's not just about the examples you choose but the way in which you engage people in the real-life problems that compliance and ethics is all about!

In our own experience, one of the most effective training and education sessions was to get a leadership team to develop its own compliance and ethics dilemmas in a workshop, present them at the end, vote on the best ones, then fine-tune and publish the most useful for use by everyone across the company. The education came not from hearing and remembering the 'correct answer' to a dilemma but in thinking them up in the first place, realizing where the dilemma might lie, having the discussion about possible answers, and of course the competitive element.

Training examples

EXAMPLE 1: 'THEFT WITH A DIFFERENCE'

One of our favourite examples of a good training dilemma or 'values moment' is a really simple one.

A newspaper story published in the *Daily Mail*, 27 December 2017, revealed that UK supermarkets were losing more than £3 billion per year[1] to what you might call 'theft – but with a difference'. Many UK supermarkets allow customers to use their own scanner as they go around, to avoid having to queue at the end and empty and repack their bags.

To a large extent this is an honesty system, although customers are subject to random checks, so their bags might be unpacked and scanned once in a blue moon. There came a time when it dawned on supermarkets that they were selling vast quantities of carrots and yet their stocks of carrots were not dwindling; and conversely they were always running out of avocados, despite relatively modest sales.

To their (and our) amazement, supermarkets discovered that this system was being abused on a grand scale! People had worked out that they could scan a cheap item, such as a bag of carrots, and put an equivalent weight of avocados in their trolley. Other shoppers proudly admitted that, when the automated check-out machine asked them how many new plastic bags they had used, they avoided the charge of 5 pence per bag by lying.

Ten or 15 minutes discussing this story is a real eye-opener, both for compliance officers and those being trained.

First, it says a lot about human nature and the challenges that a compliance and ethics programme has to overcome: people will lie, steal or breach a policy, and they will justify it to themselves or not even view it as a breach. The supermarket customers were committing theft, but they were convincing themselves that it was something else, something less, in some cases simply something clever. Yet, if they were willing to do what they did, why not simply put a bag of avocados in the trolley and not pay anything for them? The answer lies partly in their perception of whether they would get caught and would have a good excuse (which tells us that a lot of people are dishonest, if they think they can get away with it) and partly in their willingness and ability to convince themselves that it somehow wasn't the same as stealing.

Second, this story and others like it can also engage an audience very quickly and deeply. Suddenly, honesty, ethics, integrity and even compliance become interesting, people compete to provide insights and to demonstrate that they wouldn't dream of doing such a thing. Before you know it they will be thinking up other examples and applying basic, personal values to analyse them. When faced with this story and others like it, most people will conclude that you cannot really justify dishonest or illegal behaviour, even if you would like to. It is reassuring to see how many conclude that honesty is the best policy.

Try doing the same thing with this even simpler example: 'You receive the bill in a restaurant, and you notice you have been undercharged. Do you tell your waiter?'

EXAMPLE 2: INTEGRITY MOMENT – REQUEST FOR A FAVOUR WITH A CV

This example takes a real-life case and gets people to climb in and get involved in 'being there' and understanding the challenges and in-the-moment state of mind involved.

Scenario:

- Our rig was being demobilized and exported out of country. This is normally done on the basis of paperwork, but on this occasion a customs officer was sent to do an inspection.

- On board the rig, the process went smoothly and the officer was OK. He merely asked to see one item listed on the exportation documents.

- Just before checking the item, the customs officer took our employee (David) to one side and told him that his son was looking for a trainee position. He asked if he could send a CV.

- David did not promise anything but told the officer he could send the CV.

- The inspection was completed, and the customs officer was extremely quick in issuing his final report in the afternoon. He cleared the rig the same day, which is not so usual.

- Very quickly after issuing the report, the customs officer called David to tell him he would send his son's CV.

- David felt a bit afraid and unsure of himself, not least because there will be more rigs to clear in the near future…

Questions:

- How would you have felt?
- How would have you reacted?
- Do you think David did the right thing?

What happened next?

- David's manager, Marie, congratulated him on the successful demobilization of the rig very few days after the exportation.
- Marie felt David was looking for help and advice.

- David told her the story. He looked happy to have shared it with her – it was like a weight off his shoulders
- Marie felt a bit 'stuck', so she informed the compliance officer and the regional manager.
- A few days later the customs officer's son sent his CV. He had completed university and was looking for real position, for which he might genuinely be qualified.
- The customs officer tried to call David again.
- David and the compliance officer agreed the wording of an email, which David sent to the customs officer's son, explaining that HR has a specific site and process for advertising and filling vacant positions at the company.
- David felt very relieved.

Discussion:

- All David did was agree to receive a CV. When asked, he had to decide quickly how to react, without causing offence or prejudicing the relationship with the customs officer and the smooth process.
- He did not have time to seek advice, and the best answer did not occur to him in the heat of the moment. Would you have answered with the following response: 'I would be happy to ask our HR department what is the process for applying for jobs.'
- He sensed that the request was problematic, but he couldn't quite put his finger on it.
- Later he understood that the customs officer was possibly trying to take advantage of the situation, and that it was important that his grant of clearance for the rig was not, and could not be seen to have been, in return for the offer or promise of some personal advantage or benefit.
- The customs officer never openly requested a job for his son, but by his attitude/behaviour it appeared he was trying to link the clearance of the rig to a job opportunity for his son.
- Such requests are often deliberately subtle, so that they can be deniable.

EXAMPLE 3. USING COMPLIANCE DILEMMAS FOR IN-PERSON TRAINING

You can also use more nuanced 'compliancy' dilemmas in a similar way as an effective, in-person training tool. Here is a nice example of how to do this.

Scenario – 'A social dinner invitation':

- You are approached by a colleague whose wife has arranged a dinner for the two of them with another couple (her friend and her husband).
- The dinner is purely social and private – but by coincidence, it turns out the husband of the friend works for a client on whose tender your company is currently working.

Questions:

Your colleague has the following questions:

- Am I OK to attend the dinner and claim it on expenses?
- Is the current tender a problem?
- If so, can I put another client's name on the expenses claim?
- Alternatively, can we split the bill and I claim half on expenses?

How would you answer? Which parts of your code of conduct and other policies are relevant?

Discussion:

- You should obviously refer to guidance regarding offering hospitality in your code of conduct and gifts and hospitality policy, but you should also consider your policies regarding expenses and the proper use of company money.
- If the meal is purely social and private, and you and your spouse were already planning to attend and pay, why would you think of charging the company?
- Would the expense be reasonably and necessarily incurred in connection with your work?

- The current tender is an issue, but not if the meal is genuinely a private matter and each couple is paying their share.
- If it were otherwise reasonable to charge the company but there is a current tender involving the client, then:
  - changing the name of the client would not be acceptable – in fact it would be deceitful;
  - paying for the client and his wife but only charging the company half would not be a solution;
  - splitting the bill and claiming your half on expenses would be OK, but it comes back to that first question: would you feel comfortable charging the company for something you were going to do anyway?

What does your policy say?

The company's code of conduct and gifts and hospitality policy has the following provisions that may be helpful when you are confronted by a dilemma such as this...

Later in this chapter we also explore the use of such values moments for communicating about the organization's values, ethics and compliance to its clients. And in the 'Across the minefield' sections of this book you will find many such scenarios, stories and dilemmas that you may want to use or adapt.

Turn employees into communicators and teachers

So often training is something done to people, but it can also be something done by people – and participation can be positively, as well as negatively, incentivized. For example, creating a film competition in which employees are invited to make their own short films around key issues using their own scripts and cast.

A similar idea is often used very effectively in health and safety programmes when employees are asked to send in photos of safety risks they have encountered not just on the shop floor but in their lives outside work. The best photos are given prizes and selected for community discussion.

Work with what you have

For most organizations, as with much of their compliance and ethics programme, the approach to training and education is constrained and dictated by resources and practicalities. This is understandable, but necessity can also be the mother of invention. If you dared to do something different, might you achieve more? Could you do something less, such as compliance and ethics quizzes on a smartphone app, that actually achieves greater employee engagement than a 'full compliance training module'?

Don't forget the story about the woodcutter who takes time out to sharpen their axe and thus is able to be more efficient and effective and achieve far more than the much more muscly competitors, who are simply trying to chop as hard and fast as possible.

How effective is your training, and are you wasting your time? Are you doing it to tick a box and be able to show to prosecutors, regulators and other stakeholders that everyone did their compliance training? Never mind the quality, feel the breadth. Haven't we said that several times about compliance programmes?

Be useful and convenient

Often, training asks people to go to it, but it can also go where people are. For example, providing convenient guidance and tools to staff at the coalface, like an app to help you deal with a facilitation payment demand or to remind you of gift and hospitality limits. And when it comes to communication, it can also push out content for easy consumption – stories, commentary on a case in the news, discussion around an issue highlighted each month... and so on.

On your time – or ours?

A big issue in many organizations is the sense among employees that they are being asked to give up their own time to train. Some organizations get over this by integrating learning into the business agenda, so it becomes a regular part of meetings, team briefings and other key business events. Others make learning part of their 'Make a difference day' or corporate social responsibility events in which employees get involved in community projects. Still others incentivize learning with rewards or prizes.

The key is to try to replace any resentment and cynicism with positive reasons and benefits. Training is part of your personal and professional development, and you get it for free! It also enables staff to take ownership of the ship and make it the best vessel afloat!

Making e-learning more effective

Compliance training is an area that has seen significant advances. Online training has been adopted by many organizations due to its obvious benefits: convenience of delivery, consistency of content and message, trackability, electronic reminders, and so on. There are a great many providers of e-learning content and platforms, offering a range of off-the-shelf, tailored or hybrid modules covering many compliance risks and different approaches to compliance.

Those that can be fully or partly tailored are likely to be far more relevant, engaging and effective, as they can adopt the organization's language, tone and branding and be tailored to particular sectors and risks. For example, one company's e-learning programme combines messages with film footage, making it as watchable as YouTube, and allowing it to be completed on the phone. Another used audio that a pharmaceutical sales representative could listen to in the car and which mimicked a radio discussion programme.

E-learning is certainly a good place to start for an organization seeking to kick-start its compliance and ethics programme and get some key, consistent messages and training out to a large audience as quickly as possible. But as we have seen there are also disadvantages and dangers – not least in the potential for giving an organization false readings and a false sense of security.

Some of the obvious disadvantages of e-learning, by contrast to in-person training, is that you cannot gauge the level of audience understanding, buy-in and knowledge gaps, you cannot explore areas of greater interest or need that the audience might bring to your attention, and you miss the opportunity to share and explore stories and dilemmas with them.

Measuring effectiveness

To mitigate this danger, it's important to try to measure effectiveness, or what difference the e-learning has made, and not mere completion rates or even pass marks.

For example:

- Carry out a full, or sample, before-and-after survey that assesses changes in knowledge and attitude among all participants or a representative sample.
- Look for visible signals of change, such as an increase in whistle-blowing or questions about the programme.
- Invite people to participate in blogs, internet discussions about topics covered in the e-learning.
- It's also worthwhile pointing out that one very good way of knowing how far people have adopted compliance and ethics is to measure the degree of resentment they express towards any learning requirements made of them.

Communication

... with third parties

Compliance doctrine places a great emphasis on 'training' third parties or those for whose conduct and actions the organization may be held responsible – especially if they are considered high risk. This topic is discussed also under procedures and controls, but bear in mind that it is just as much about communication as training. Are you really going to train the supplier, and most of its key members of staff, on your uniquely effective (in your view) code of conduct? And just how effective is that going to be when they have so many other clients seeking to do the same thing?

In our view the answer lies much more in how convincingly and clearly you engage with the third party, or to put it more figuratively, getting the third party in a 'bear hug':

> 'You know our standards and commitments. They are essentially the same as yours, which is why we have chosen to work with you and trust you. So we just want to make sure both parties are aligned and clear about how important this is. Moreover, you the supplier can play a key role in helping us to spot and navigate the compliance and ethics risks we may face. You folks know much more about this than we do. This is your country and your area of expertise.'

... with consortium and joint venture partners

What we've just said about other third parties holds true here, but the message and communication goals with consortium and joint venture partners are somewhat different.

In Chapter 14 we talk about the importance and difficulty of implementing a compliance and ethics programme in a joint venture company. For that reason, the communication with any joint venture (JV) partner(s) goes much further than it does with suppliers, sub-contractors and even agents and intermediaries. It is not just about mutual expectations of how the partners should conduct themselves in a compliant way when working together, but also about the need to implement a compliance and ethics programme in the JV itself.

There needs to be a clear meeting of minds and attention to sufficient detail in discussions, and any eventual JV agreement regarding:

- what that programme will look like;
- how it will be implemented;
- which individual working in the JV will take responsibility as full- or part-time compliance officer;
- and which of the partners' existing programmes will be used or copied (normally, it makes sense to agree to use whichever partner's policy or procedure is stricter).

Just as important as all this detail is the need to agree to speak with one voice to the JV management team, just as parents need to speak with one voice to children, even if they disagree on something behind the scenes.

To a certain extent, the same is true of consortia, by which we mean a non-incorporated alliance of the type sometimes formed between two or more contractors for purposes of one bid, project or framework agreement with a client. If a consortium is limited in time and scope in this way, then implementing a compliance and ethics programme within it may have a very different and less formal meaning, but it is still just as important to have a shared understanding about compliance, of the expected standards and conduct of the consortium and its members, and of what policies and procedures will be followed in the course of the consortium's work.

...with clients, investors and other stakeholders

An enlightened, sophisticated client or other stakeholder will not trust you much based on what you say, but on what you do and your track record. Nonetheless, it is important and worthwhile to communicate clearly to such stakeholders what your values and compliance and ethics programme are all about and how important they are. This builds your credibility and shows that you know what you are talking about. It may also reduce the risk of the client treating you unfairly or dishonestly, eg if you are bidding for work and they are tempted to reveal your price to another bidder.

Also, stakeholders may give you credit for your compliance and ethics, but only if they are aware of it from your communications, including publicly available policies and other documents, and key performance indicators (KPIs). If the organization has a reputation for being ethical and honest, it may receive the benefit of the doubt in times of crisis (such as a product recall), which can give it a breathing space in which to act and start to recover.

The more you communicate your commitments to more parties, the more feedback you will get and the more you will feel obliged, but also able, to stand by those commitments.

Imagine this: you use a values moment (such as the one we give in 'What's the problem?' below) at the start of a meeting with a client. Might not your client think differently about you, and perhaps treat you differently, after that? This example demonstrates to your client that you put its interest first and can be trusted to look out for them. But if you explain to the client that you use this example and others like it to train your own staff, it should make the client think: 'This is an organization that is serious about embedding its values, and that wants its people to take an ethics- and principles-based approach to business conduct. I ask them periodically to complete a due diligence questionnaire and provide loads of information about their policies, procedures and controls, but actually this insight into their culture tells me a lot more about how I can trust them.'

WHAT'S THE PROBLEM?

Our client wants to award a contract to us – but they can only do so pursuant to a competitive tender process. So at least one more bidder is needed.

Our bid manager Paolo suggests we contact RelCo, a related company in which we are a stakeholder. Paolo's idea is that RelCo might be willing to submit a bid. We could make sure they know what price to bid to avoid winning.

It is clear that RelCo would have no intention of winning the work, but the client wants to award us the work in any case.

So what's the problem?

Discussion:

- You could infer that the intention or effect of the 'phoney bid' would be to mislead the client about the truly competitive nature of the tender process.

- Surely it doesn't make any difference if the request comes from the client?

- But if the client needs to demonstrate that it has received a certain number of bids, this implies that the client is not able to waive its own procedure.

- This should make us suspect that some ultimate client or owner, who is entitled to rely on those procedures, is being defrauded.

- This 'phoney bid' would most likely breach competition/anti-trust law (in the European Economic Area, it's considered a form of bid rigging known as cover pricing), and it would very likely breach fraud laws in many countries.

- But it's not really that difficult: it would be dishonest, untrustworthy and not the sort of behaviour with which we wish to be associated. Look at it this way – think carefully before putting that 'clever' idea into action, even if you think it's the only way to get the job done:

  o Would you be happy reading about it in the newspaper?

  o If not, then it's probably not as clever as you first thought.[2]

Collective action – including communication with governments, ministries, local communities, NGOs, embassies

Logic and best practice demand that an organization that is serious about reducing corruption and certain other forms of non-compliance should seek to participate in appropriate collective action initiatives. As in many places in this book, we are using anti-bribery/anti-corruption as the example, as it is an especially relevant focus for collective action.

Collective action means finding ways to collaborate (subject to applicable competition and anti-trust laws, of course) with competitors and peers in the same sector and across sectors, with clients, suppliers and subcontractors within sectors, as well as with external advisers and stakeholders, not-for-profit organizations and ultimately with governments. The goals of such collaboration should be to share and enhance best practice, leverage the profile and influence of large, blue chip organizations and a combined voice, raise the profile of anti-corruption efforts and, not least, find ways of tackling the demand side of bribery and corruption.

Such collective action can and should play an important role in:

- actually reducing the risks; and
- convincing stakeholders that your organization is serious about compliance and ethics.

Much of the focus of this book and of prosecutorial and regulatory efforts is to discourage, prevent and punish bribery by bribe payers, ie the suppliers of bribes. In practice, efforts could be significantly more efficient and effective if ways can be found to tackle the demand side by discouraging and punishing those that demand or solicit bribes or engage in other forms of corruption, and by reducing the opportunities and incentives for them to do so. This is in part the goal and focus of collective action.

International anti-corruption efforts at an intergovernmental and non-governmental organization (NGO) level recognize the importance of tackling the demand side. Very modest progress has been made in some respects:

- Helping to make anti-bribery/anti-corruption a mark of progress, fairness and respect in a developing country and reducing the sense that it is a new form of colonialism.

- Recognizing the need to tackle money-laundering, ie by trying to make it difficult for people to spend the proceeds of their crime, eg by creating public registers of the salaries of public officials and by trying to strengthen anti-money-laundering laws and procedures.

- We once attended a very interesting talk given by the head of one of Transparency International's Chapters. She described a business environment that sounded a complete nightmare from an ethics and anti-corruption perspective and comprehensively discouraged all attendees from wanting to do business in that country. When we asked what we could do to help, she said that we should stop allowing corrupt public officials to buy houses and boats in London, New York and Geneva and to pay private school fees in the United Kingdom and elsewhere.

- The US and French authorities have made some progress in using civil powers to confiscate assets reasonably believed to have been acquired with the proceeds of crime; and the United Kingdom utilized a new 'unexplained wealth order' for the first time in 2018.

There are many good examples of collective action efforts. Here are just a few:

- Organizations can provide funds or other corporate support to NGOs such as Transparency International (which is global) or the Institute of Business Ethics (to give a UK example). Such organizations have credibility and, very often, their voice and actions can reach farther and have more influence over national and international lawmakers when it comes to business ethics than individual companies, trade associations and (depending on your point of view) lobbyists.

- Trade associations and organizations like the International Chambers of Commerce can perform a similar role and deserve corporate support for the same reason.

- Companies can work with the types of organization mentioned in the preceding two bullets to ensure that they have a good understanding of the challenges faced by business, and that guidance and standards issued by them are fit for purpose and relevant in the real business world. Working with national and international standards organizations to develop anti-bribery compliance standards is a good example of this.

- The Global Infrastructure Anti-Corruption Centre (GIACC) publishes a compliance programme for governments, as well as ones for funders and project owners.[3]

- At a very simple level, if all companies working in a particular sector or location present a consistent, united front when resisting demands for bribes and facilitation payments, then they are more likely to succeed and bring an end to such demands.

Always remember...

Even though we are required to be compliant in our places of work, the fact is people are human. They will naturally migrate towards those who have been helpful and pleasant to them and give a good service or who are recommended enough times by people they trust, and shy away from those who have not given a good service either directly or according to word of mouth. This is a human trait and compliance needs to recognize and tap into it if it is truly to succeed.

Clearly a communication or training programme that is viewed as irritating, confusing or boring will be discussed in that way, and can have the opposite of the intended effect, undermining the whole programme.

So remember who your audience is. Communication is *not* about ticking boxes for the regulators – it is about making compliance come alive for employees and colleagues you are trying to reach.

Across the minefield: compliance and ethics meets real life

A mere inconvenience

A contractor wants to provide lavish hospitality to the senior managers of its client, but is prevented by both companies' gifts and hospitality policies.

It decides it would be very clever to award a very large 'bonus' to one of its senior managers, on the understanding that they use it to buy a yacht, with which they will entertain the client's managers.

Double whammy

You are investigating new allegations that some of your supply chain team are involved in a kick-back and bid-rigging scheme. Suspicions have been swirling for years, fuelled by the fact those allegedly involved always have the latest hand-held devices, go on good holidays and own expensive cars. The manager is known as the

'Godfather' and at face value their lifestyle is beyond the means of their salary. Despite audits, no proof has been found.

After a recent 'tip-off', which again fuels your determination to get to the bottom of this, you engage a team of investigators who come recommended as thorough and reputable. The investigators review all the material and do some basic research.

At an update and investigation strategy meeting, the investigators report that their review of material and basic research does not reveal any inappropriate behaviour on the part of the identified persons. They add, however, that they also pursued some additional lines of enquiry that have revealed some interesting and potentially incriminating financial activities and behaviour.

Naturally you are interested and ask to know more. The investigators explain they are unwilling to give details unless we agree to acknowledge that these sources are unofficial, and information is obtained on a 'don't ask how' basis.

'It's up to you'

A colleague's been going through a really difficult divorce and you've just learned that they've been falsifying expenses. They beg you not to say anything and promise it won't happen again.
Let it go?

This way we'll make sure the environment is protected, but it's really expensive.
Find something cheaper?

There's a panic. A colleague is on holiday and out of touch, and your team has to get hold of information that is on their computer. One of the team say they think they know the colleague's password.
Try it?

You learn that there's someone on another team who has just joined the company and has 'inside' knowledge of how a government department you're in negotiations with assesses bids.
OK to find out what they know?

Notes

1   https://www.dailymail.co.uk/news/article-5215073/Shoppers-steal-3-2bn-self-service-tills-year.html [accessed 18.02.19].

2   Reproduced with the permission of Subsea 7 from training content.

3   http://www.giaccentre.org/governments.php [accessed 17.02.19].

10

Whistle-blowing hotline and speak-up culture

In this chapter we look at how whistle-blowing is a vital part of effective compliance and ethics, helping an organization to uphold its code, take its own pulse, and get authentic and highly valuable feedback on areas where it needs to improve. However, there are many challenges to be overcome if a whistle-blowing policy is to succeed.

The importance of whistle-blowing

The world is a dangerous place not because of those who do evil, but because of those who look on and do nothing.

ALBERT EINSTEIN, 1953[1]

In the previous chapter we made the point that effective communication should be two-way. While there are many other channels through which an organization can get feedback, the most important is what is commonly called a 'whistle-blowing' or 'speak-up' channel.

For a compliance and ethics programme to be credible and effective – and for any organization to ensure it is always doing as it wishes to do – it needs to encourage and make it easy for people to come forward, if they believe the organization or people working in or for it are failing to uphold the organization's stated ethical commitments and policies. This means having a whistle-blowing policy that explains how and why employees and others should do this, how whistle-blowers will be protected, how allegations will be investigated, and what the organization will do if the allegations are substantiated (eg sanctions for wrongdoers and enhancements to policies, procedures and training).

It also means providing a variety of different channels in the hope that a whistle-blower will feel sufficiently comfortable with at least one of those channels to come forward. Those channels include making people aware that they can raise their concerns with their manager, with a more senior manager, with the HR, Legal or Compliance and Ethics functions, with group head office or, if none of those channels is acceptable, via an independent, external whistle-blowing helpline managed on behalf of the organization. By such means, the organization can get feedback on its compliance and ethics programme, and learn about possible breaches, especially from employees and ex-employees, but also from suppliers, business partners, members of the public and all other stakeholders.

We never cease to be surprised by the central importance of the whistle-blowing channels and policy to a credible and effective compliance and ethics programme. They are one of the fundamentals of a compliance and ethics programme, irrespective of what compliance risks you are managing, and even before you consider what additional procedures and controls may be necessary or desirable to manage those risks. It is hugely important. And yet the hotline is consistently an issue. A colleague recently told us that while they have tens of thousands of employees, they only have a small handful of calls.

The challenge is how to integrate a whistle-blowing hotline, and its use, into the DNA of the company.

The problem with whistle-blowing

A big part of the problem can be found by going to any thesaurus and taking a look at the company 'whistle-blowing' keeps. You'll find words like these:

Inform, betray, incriminate, denounce, blab, tell on, squeal, rat, blow the whistle on, sell down the river, split, grass, snitch, stitch up, shop, dob in.

The simple fact is, whistle-blowing is definitely not one of the preferred ways to win friends and influence people. It still carries a massive negative charge. It's not just that the whistle-blower may be seen as 'villain' or 'traitor', or viewed through a particular cultural lens. It's also that throughout history whistle-blowers have generally had, and been seen to have had, a rough time of it.

In recent years there have been signs that this may be changing. Think, for example, of those who have courageously spoken out about doping in sport, in the 'Me Too' campaign, exposed data misuse and corruption at the heart of governments and the banking system, told their stories of childhood abuse and named their abusers, held their own companies to account for the health or environmental harms they have caused. What's more, social media can and frequently does amplify stories of criminal or unethical behaviour, helping to expose rogue institutions, groups or individuals.

Nevertheless, it will usually take enormous courage and determination to stand up and speak out about something you have witnessed that you know is wrong, and no whistle-blowing helpline can possibly be effective unless it understands this.

Think what it takes for someone to speak up...

Of course, there will always be false alarms, fake calls, reports based on malice or bad faith, trolls and trivialities. But let's imagine that you are an employee who is genuinely concerned about unethical or illegal behaviour...

SPEAKING UP

To speak up is an act of trust not just in the good intentions of those to whom you speak, but their power to protect you.

They say, 'We will protect and support you.' But will they?

> Can they really protect you from the retaliation or quiet vengeance of the individual or group you are calling out, or the interests of the organization whose integrity you are calling into question?
>
> When push comes to shove, will they be on your side, or the side that holds all the power?
>
> You risk the opprobrium and hostility of your colleagues. The security and trajectory of your career. The reputation of a 'troublemaker' that will follow you down the years. A future without references, cast in shadows. Immense pressures and strains placed on the relationships you care about most. Social isolation and possible mental health issues. A life as an outcast.
>
> Can you – should you – trust those who say they have the power to ensure your life will not take such a course if you speak up?

The importance of creating a process people can trust

For those who are considering reporting a breach of their organization's code of conduct, it is a whole lot easier to do nothing, turn away, stay silent, and keep any whistle firmly in their pocket. It's not worth the bother...

If people are to take the risk of speaking up, they must be sure that the process you offer them really is trustworthy, reliable and clear. So before you open any whistle-blowing channels, your entire process needs to be very carefully thought through and fully in place. This requires:

- **Experience:** If you do not have someone in-house who is experienced in whistle-blowing procedures, it is essential that you bring such expertise in.

- **Training, trialling and testing:** Before your procedures work in the real world, they must be rigorously tested, and those who will be responsible for dealing with real cases must be extensively trained. Poor training of managers who may have to deal with real cases can and does undermine trust in the process and any willingness to speak up.

- **The clear backing and commitment of the senior leadership** to support the process and protect those who have the courage to protect the organization by speaking up against abuses of the code.
- **The provision for anonymity,** despite the problems that can come with this. We discuss this further in a moment.

Not just the words, but the values, intentions and promises of your organization are on trial. What you do consistently, or fail to do once, will determine the trust or lack of it that people will place in the whistle-blowing process – and the commitment the company has to its code of conduct.

Regional and cultural differences

As in many things, the United Kingdom stands roughly halfway between the United States and the rest of Europe when it comes to its whistle-blowing culture.

For reasons we have outlined above, until quite recently, and maybe even today, establishing a whistle-blowing policy and culture within a commercial organization in the United Kingdom would still be quite counter-cultural and involve overcoming various perceptions and cultural obstacles to do with 'grassing' and telling tales, and many of those unpleasant words listed near the start of this chapter.

Many countries in the rest of Europe have an even stronger objection to the concept of whistle-blowing, especially anonymous whistle-blowing. This is for important, very valid historical reasons we should understand and respect, based as they are on some very unpleasant history involving *collaborateurs* and the *Stasi*.

Yet for the last 10 or 15 years, organizations with a listing in the United States have had to implement compliance and ethics programmes that included a whistle-blowing policy and channel and made explicit provision for anonymous whistle-blowing.

As stricter anti-bribery laws have been implemented in more countries, including France, Brazil, Mexico and Chile, and as the international consensus has crystallized around what constitutes compliance and ethics programme best practice, the important role of a whistle-blowing policy and channels for employees and others to raise concerns about unethical conduct has become clearer and less controversial.

For example, this is what the International Organization for Standardization (ISO) has to say on the matter:

FROM ISO 37001 (ANTI-BRIBERY MANAGEMENT SYSTEMS)[2]

The organization shall implement procedures which:

1 encourage and enable persons to report in good faith or on the basis of a reasonable belief attempted, suspected and actual bribery, or any violation of or weakness in the anti-bribery management system, to the anti-bribery compliance function or to appropriate personnel (either directly or through an appropriate third party);

2 except to the extent required to progress an investigation, require that the organization treats reports confidentially, so as to protect the identity of the reporter and of others involved or referenced in the report;

3 allow anonymous reporting;

4 prohibit retaliation, and protect those making reports from retaliation, after they have in good faith, or on the basis of a reasonable belief, raised or reported a concern about attempted, actual or suspected bribery or violation of the anti-bribery policy or the anti-bribery management system;

5 enable personnel to receive advice from an appropriate person on what to do if faced with a concern or situation which could involve bribery.

The organization shall ensure that all personnel are aware of the reporting procedures and are able to use them, and are aware of their rights and protections under the procedures.

It does not necessarily make it any easier to implement such a policy and channels and to embed them in the culture of an organization – both within senior management and within the broader employee population.

ONE SIZE DOES NOT FIT ALL

From a practical standpoint, it is unsafe to assume that the programme you have in place in the United States or United Kingdom can be applied to other jurisdictions. European countries in particular have data protection requirements that vary in application from jurisdiction to jurisdiction. Likewise, there may be requirements to collaborate with and obtain approval from a works council or employee delegate or register the hotline with regulatory bodies.

It is not that hotlines are discouraged. In fact, the law generally encourages or requires them. Much of the concern lies with protecting privacy and data, as well as a general dislike for anonymous tip-offs, for reasons embedded in recent history.

The fact is, whistle-blowing is one of the best ways of finding out whether your policies, procedures and controls are being complied with. And if you're serious about upholding your code of conduct, you should be willing to invite others to tell you if you are failing to do so. Internal audit functions are quite good at identifying weaknesses or failures in an organization's system of internal controls, especially financial and procurement controls, but statistics show that internal audit detects only a small percentage of breaches of the organization's code of conduct.

In any case, a prosecutor or regulator will not find an organization's compliance and ethics programme credible if it does not include a whistle-blowing policy and whistle-blowing channels that the organization is genuinely committed to promoting and embedding.

Anonymity

As stated already a whistle-blowing policy and channels should also cater for anonymous whistle-blowing. In many countries whistle-blowers are entitled to legal protection against retaliation, but it is well known, and confirmed again and again by these writers' own experience, that people will be much less likely to come forward and raise concerns if they have to identify themselves.

Additionally, information disclosed by a whistle-blower is confidential provided that it does not impede an investigation. In the event of fraud, a police investigation may follow and the whistle-blower may be asked to give evidence in court. For this reason, a number of whistle-blowers prefer to remain anonymous even though this may make it more difficult to follow up their allegations.

Having overseen hundreds of whistle-blowing cases over the last 10 years, Andrew would probably choose to be anonymous if he were a whistle-blower. It is the rational choice. No matter how ethical the organization and no matter how committed it is to protecting whistle-blowers, taking their concerns seriously and investigating and remediating cases, a whistle-blower needs to be satisfied as to the credibility of the person or team who will be investigating his/her concerns and the procedure they will follow, before revealing his/her identity.

But anonymity brings difficulties with it...

When a compliance officer receives an anonymous whistle-blowing allegation, the fact that it is anonymous makes it harder to assess the credibility of the allegations, especially if there is no means of communicating with the anonymous whistle-blower. Nevertheless, an organization needs to learn that the decision to be anonymous does not in and of itself reduce or undermine the credibility or good faith of the whistle-blower. The compliance officer needs to convince the whistle-blower of the integrity and competence of the people and processes by which the allegations will be investigated and the whistle-blower protected.

In an ideal world, the whistle-blower also needs to understand that it can be very hard to understand allegations properly and design a suitable investigation which has a reasonable chance of success, if the whistle-blower, as is almost always the case, has provided incomplete or unclear information.

However, if the compliance officer is able to communicate with the whistle-blower, eg via the helpline provider or an anonymous email address, not only can the compliance officer complete the gaps in his or her understanding and assess the nature of the evidence, but the whistle-blower can also assess the credibility of the compliance officer.

Dealing with anonymous whistle-blowers and assessing their good faith

In the first one to three years of implementation of an organization's whistle-blowing helpline, management teams at each level, including the most senior level, will have to come to terms with their first troubling case, perhaps against a valued member of a management team, brought by an anonymous whistle-blower.

The typical reaction of many managers when they face their first anonymous case is to complain that the whistle-blower is acting in bad faith, that it is cowardly and unfair to make anonymous allegations and that the organization should not feel under any duty to investigate. However, as explained above, raising concerns anonymously is not in and of itself an example of bad faith, but a rational and reasonable way to behave that should be respected and sympathized with. Forty to 60 per cent of whistle-blowing allegations are likely to be anonymous (depending on country, sector and other cultural factors), and an organization cannot afford to ignore or forego anonymous allegations as a rich source of valuable information, if it wishes even to scratch the surface of the unethical conduct that may be going on within.

An organization should not attempt to identify an anonymous whistle-blower, but it is natural and reasonable to try to work out who it might be when attempting to assess the credibility and reliability of the whistle-blower and of any evidence he/she has produced or may be able to produce.

Although the whistle-blower is entitled to protection if acting in good faith or on the basis of a reasonable belief, and the organization very likely needs to commit to investigate all such allegations, it is sensible to have a caveat that they will only be investigated if the organization believes an investigation is warranted or could be designed and conducted in a way that has a reasonable chance of success on the basis of the information known to the organization.

This needs to be very carefully communicated if it is not to be viewed as a 'get out clause' that puts people off. Our advice is, as always, to seek the understanding and involvement of your audience. Be clear and transparent. Explain the challenges. Explore the issues. Get people to experience things from that side of the fence. Regularly elect front-line staff onto the investigation team. Stress co-ownership – this is the process we have to help us all be who we want to be.

It should also be pointed out that if the organization declines or fails to investigate allegations promptly, effectively or at all and, as far as reasonably practicable, to provide feedback to the whistle-blower, it runs the risk that the whistle-blower may bring allegations to the attention of a third party, including a prosecutor or regulator. This is another good reason to have a whistle-blowing policy and helpline in the first place.

Investigation and remediation of whistle-blowing cases

It is important that an organization has procedures for investigating and remediating whistle-blowing allegations, and we examine these in more detail in Chapter 12. One of the key ways of ensuring that your organization's whistle-blowing policy and procedures are credible and trusted is to investigate and remediate effectively and professionally and, as far as possible, to raise awareness of the fact that you have done so, so everyone becomes increasingly trustful of the integrity of the process.

We have seen how it takes a mixture of courage and determination for a whistle-blower to raise their head above the parapet and bring concerns to the attention of senior management or the Compliance and Ethics function. Aside from concerns about retaliation and future career prospects, they are likely to have genuine doubts about whether it is even worth bothering. If the organization can repay the whistle-blower's confidence, or the suspension of their scepticism, and do a good job of getting to the bottom of their concerns, taking decisive steps to punish wrongdoing, keeping their identity and involvement confidential, and protecting them against any retaliation, then they will realize that it was indeed worthwhile.

Even more importantly, other potential whistle-blowers are much more likely to come forward in the future.

What types of cases should be regarded or treated as 'whistle-blowing'?

Whistle-blowing laws in most countries tend to categorize and protect whistle-blowers who raise concerns about serious illegality or matters having a significant environmental or safety impact. To be protected, whistle-blowers normally have to be acting in good faith or at least on the basis of a reasonable belief that their suspicions are true.

For example, the UK Public Interest Disclosure Act protects people who make a disclosure that they reasonably believe shows a criminal offence, a failure to comply with legal obligations, a miscarriage of justice, danger to the health and safety of employees, damage to the environment, or the hiding of information which would show any of the above actions. In the United Kingdom the requirement used to be that the whistle-blower must be acting 'in good faith', but it is now a 'reasonable belief' standard. As seen earlier, ISO 37001 refers to protection against retaliation for those making reports in good faith *or* on the basis of a reasonable belief.

In drafting a whistle-blowing policy, an organization will have to have regard to applicable local laws in terms of whether it must or should protect whistle-blowers who raise concerns on the basis of a reasonable belief, even if they are not acting in good faith.

In practice, if the organization truly wants to encourage whistle-blowers to come forward, it may well decide that it needs to offer the wider protection.

And in any case, an organization can receive very useful and important information from a whistle-blower who is not acting in good faith: a disgruntled former employee with a grudge against her corrupt former manager; or a supplier who contacts you and says: 'We accepted the need to pay your procurement manager a 5 per cent kickback each year if we were to remain on the preferred supplier list, but when he started to ask for 10 per cent we felt that was going too far.'

Similarly, in terms of the types of cases that should be in scope, an organization is likely to decide that it wants to hear about any allegations or suspicions of unethical conduct, perhaps defined as a breach of any part of its code of conduct.

Why use an external whistle-blowing helpline?

In theory, there is no reason why an organization should not provide and manage adequate whistle-blowing channels that are purely internal, such as an email address or telephone number by which the whistle-blower can contact the chief ethics and compliance officer, the head of internal audit, or even the chair of an Ethics Committee. In practice, the decision whether to use an external provider will depend on a variety of factors, such as:

- how many people are employed by the organization;
- how many cases are anticipated;[3]
- what resources and skills the organization has to handle emails and, especially, calls (Different external providers can offer good call-handling skills, whether by using operators with humanities degrees and good listening skills, or by using people with investigations experience who know what type of information should ideally be extracted from the caller in order to give the organization the best chance of being able to investigate the concerns effectively. The organization will need to decide which approach is best suited to its purpose and culture.);
- whether the helpline should be available 24/7/365;
- whether the helpline is also intended as an advice line, or a line that can be contacted for instant guidance;
- whether the organization believes its staff are more likely to come forward if they can contact an independent, external provider;

- whether an internal or external helpline can provide an adequate line of communication with an anonymous whistle-blower (see discussion earlier in this chapter).

Externally administered helplines are not particularly expensive, so even an SME with very modest resources may well find that it is more cost-effective and resource-efficient to use an external provider.

External providers should have the resources, expertise and experience to handle lots of cases efficiently and professionally, and in a way that inspires confidence in whistle-blowers who communicate with them by telephone, email or via the internet. If your organization is likely to have a lot of cases, you may wish to make use of the case management system that some providers also offer. If you only have one or two dozen cases per year, you should be able to manage them with a spreadsheet.

The independence of external whistle-blowing helpline providers

This is not a major point, but in providing full and helpful disclosure to potential whistle-blowers about the process, their protection, what will happen to their disclosure and what they are getting themselves into generally, it is appropriate to explain clearly that an external whistle-blowing helpline provider is, in most cases, not truly independent. (The same is true of the chief ethics and compliance officer or others internally to whom the whistle-blower may communicate concerns.)

The external helpline provider is usually contracted to and paid by the organization, and their role is normally to receive allegations (whether by telephone, email, via the internet or through some other means), remove anything that may identify the whistle-blower if he/she has expressed a desire to be anonymous, and communicate the allegations promptly to the organization (normally to a senior independent or quasi-independent officer or manager, such as the chief ethics and compliance officer, internal audit director or chair of the Audit Committee). The terms of the contract with the organization and the external helpline provider's professionalism, expertise and processes should provide a reasonable level of assurance regarding protection of the whistle-blower's identity or confidentiality.

We hasten to add that we know of no examples from our own experience of a helpline provider revealing the identity of a whistle-blower or breaching a whistle-blower's trust, and we would be extremely surprised if any reputable, professional, self-respecting helpline provider would do so.

Making it live and work

Encouraging people to speak up is not easy. But over time it is possible to develop the vital trust required.

A useful parallel is a 'neighbourhood watch' scheme in which neighbours come together and agree to watch out for each other and work together to keep each other safe. Often such schemes start out very tentatively, particularly in unsafe neighbourhoods where on the one hand people fear retaliation from others if it becomes known that they have reported drug-dealing, violence or other crimes, and on the other hand they are suspicious of the police and authority. However, over time as neighbours join together to protect and support something they increasingly view as 'theirs', such schemes can become remarkably effective.

Within an organization there are specific things that will help to make a whistle-blowing policy effective and successful.

Branding

What's in a name?

As we've already discussed, the very word 'whistle-blowing' has a certain amount of stigma attached to it. In seeking to encourage as many people to come forward as possible, an organization should think carefully what to call its policy and helpline and those who raise concerns.

Many people have a fair idea about whistle-blowing and whistle-blowing protections, although there are a lot of misconceptions, so whistle-blowing is a useful term for many. However, many organizations and helpline providers prefer to use a term such as 'speak up' and talk of fostering a 'speak-up' culture, on the basis that this is much more likely to encourage people to come forward.

Of course, the name does not matter if there is nothing else in place to earth the process positively rather than negatively.

Making it visible and familiar

Probably more than most things, whistle-blowing channels need great – and authentic – marketing. There are of course many ways to do this, and many channels through which it can be done, but here are some base lines:

- Communicating in a clear, friendly voice – and ideally through the voices of employees – will help. Using formal legalese won't.
- Create a strong visual presence along with effective messaging to give whistle-blowing its own 'brand identity'. As an example, one of the best posters we have seen showed a basket of beautiful, shiny green apples with one rotten one nestling in the middle. The text of the poster simply said: 'Don't let one bad apple spoil it for everyone', followed by an invitation to speak up (Figure 10.1).
- Place branded materials where people will easily and regularly see and read them in the workplace and online.

The importance of communicating success

If faith and trust in the whistle-blowing process are to be developed, an organization must find ways of communicating its success in investigating and addressing whistle-blowing concerns and protecting whistle-blowers. The difficulty is that to a large extent it needs to do so by talking about real cases (so people recognize the authenticity

FIGURE 10.1   One bad apple

SOURCE   Reproduced by kind permission of InTouch, an Expolink Group company

of the stories), but without revealing inappropriate detail about whistle-blowers, wrongdoers and case facts.

This is not always as hard as it seems: most organizations will have a grapevine. It may not be wholly reliable and there will be misinformation, but when an individual leaves an organization abruptly or under some sort of shadow, employees tend to notice and talk about it, and they tend to think they know why the person left. Their information may not be very accurate, but if people think a whistle-blower raised concerns and the organization did something about it, this is likely to embolden other whistle-blowers and reinforce the credibility of the organization's whistle-blowing policy and process.

There are also many other ways to confirm that the organization has a positive attitude towards anyone who is prepared to stand up for its values. For example:

- Communicating the results of investigations on a no-names basis. This should always be done with precision – but it can also be done in a way that makes each case clear, accessible and engaging! After all, these are 'stories about us and how we stand up for what we believe' and they provide the organization with a transparent opportunity to show everyone how it will uphold its code and the law.

- Consistently visible support from the CEO and senior leadership that demonstrates their determination to support the code and those who stand up to do so.

- Visibly transparent reporting by the leadership team when a case has revealed a weakness in the company's code or culture. It is possible to speak honestly about this, what the company has learned and how it will respond, without breaking any confidentiality.

- In some cases where confidentiality is no longer an issue for a whistle-blower, it is even possible to consider recognition or reward for their actions and the positive impact they have had on the organization. *However, it is vital no pressure is placed on a whistle-blower to do this.*

- If, once it has been resolved, a 'beacon' case can be used as a story example, and if the participants are willing to contribute on the basis that certain information will be withheld, this can throw light on the whole process.

- Pulling current and past stories in from elsewhere and asking for views.

- Inviting individuals who have been involved in significant cases outside the organization to speak or be interviewed.

It is even possible to rethink whistle-blowing within the wider context of feedback:

THE REVAMPED HOTLINE

At a round table event a few years ago, one chief compliance officer explained they had completely revamped the hotline and marketed it as a 'speak-up' line designed to attract comments of all types, whether compliance, ethics or feedback on the working environment.

Their efforts transformed the hotline completely and the number of calls escalated dramatically.

They recognized that the change might not necessarily yield more calls of a whistle-blower type. However, what it did was give them insight into some of the cultural dynamics and issues that they could work on. The branding also meant that they had to ensure they kept their side of the bargain by following up on the calls.

Their hope was for a more positive association with the hotline or speak-up line that would then make people more likely to call if they either knew, or suspected, something inappropriate was occurring. Undoubtedly the increased number of calls put pressure on the resources of the Compliance and HR functions, but the benefits and value to the organization overall made this extra burden more than worthwhile.

The characteristics of a speak-up culture

A speak-up culture actively encourages people to let the organization know if it is failing to live up to its code, or if others are failing it.

This is actually part of the goal – the destination for effective compliance and ethics. And that is precisely why it is the result of having many different things in place:

- The whistle-blowing policy and channels are familiar, and clearly and visibly branded.
- There is consistently visible and, ideally, conspicuous support from the CEO and senior leadership (not just in a letter that fronts the code).
- The policy is also reinforced by a culture in which speaking up is clearly encouraged and valued.
- The organization is consistently seen to listen respond and protect.
- The organization takes the time to communicate success.
- People see the code of conduct as their code of conduct, and the values and principles it speaks up for as their values and principles, so speaking up becomes something everyone views in a positive light.

None of these things will succeed on their own – they must work together if a whistle-blowing policy is to succeed, and become part of 'We the People'.

Across the minefield: compliance and ethics meets real life

Avoidance tactics

A boss I worked for in the past, who reported to the chief executive, used to leave the Christmas party early and give me the bill to pay, so that she could approve the bill rather than have the chief executive scrutinize and potentially criticize her expenses claim.

More double standards

While conducting a visitor on a field trip to site operations, the site manager referred to several landowners who were complaining their land was contaminated. The site manager explained the steps he was taking and that they were in line with generally accepted local practices and had been approved at the highest levels of the company for years. He was planning to push back on the landowners and fight any claims they made.

The visitor was familiar with how the business conducts similar operations in other countries where there are strict procedures, regulations and penalties concerning the use, handling, containing and off-site destruction of the very same products in discussion. However, while recognizing this may be standard practice locally, the visitor was nonetheless horrified to see the company allowing obviously sub-standard practices here while at the same time adopting the highest standards in other jurisdictions.

The approach fundamentally contradicted the company's – and the visitor's – values of applying the highest standards across all its business operations.

'It's up to you'

You're looking for quotations from contractors to perform home improvements. They are all costly, but one contractor offers to perform the work for cash, without charging VAT, thus potentially saving you 20 per cent of the price.

What would your values tell you to do – and why?

One of your colleagues has made some really nasty homophobic comments on their Facebook page. They include comments about members of their team.

Do they have the right to say what they want?

One of your company's joint venture companies is submitting a tender. Your JV partner asks you if your company can submit a bid too, even if you have no intention of winning.

That OK? Does it make any difference if someone from the client asks you to do it?

You've taken over an important project and have just learned that your predecessor made sure everything would run smoothly by paying a select group of local government officials small but regular cash sums. If you don't continue the 'tradition' you know you're in for serious problems.

What are you going to do?

Notes

1 Albert Einstein, *Conversations avec Pablo Casals*, 30 March 1953 (translated by Robert I Fitzhenry).

2 BS ISO 37001:2016.

3 Benchmarking data are hard to come by and vary greatly across sectors, geographies and cultures, but it could be anywhere between 3 and 18 cases per 1,000 employees per year, and some would argue that an effective whistle-blowing culture will encourage case numbers in at least the middle of that range.

11

Procedures and controls

In this chapter we explain how, taking into account the right policies, effectively written and communicated/trained, the organization can then assess whether the relevant compliance risk is adequately managed, or whether it can and should be reduced further through procedures and controls.

What are 'procedures and controls', and what are they for?

People tend to talk about 'values-based compliance' or 'rules-based compliance'. However, at a further extreme than rules-based compliance is procedures-based compliance. By this we mean that, if the organization does not have an effective values-based compliance and ethics programme and its people cannot even be trusted or persuaded to comply with the rules, then theoretically it is possible to develop a programme based, as far as possible, on procedures and controls for every transaction and operation.

Such an organization does not rely on employees being guided by their values and on their being aware of, understanding and being obedient to a policy when taking actions that could entail compliance risks; instead, it attempts to impose a high degree of bureaucracy, so that various procedures, controls and approvals have to be navigated.

We are exaggerating to illustrate the point, but it is important to understand that procedures, processes and controls are different from policies and that they have a role to play in every compliance and ethics programme, wherever your programme is on the spectrum between values-based and procedures-based.

A very simple example of this is a financial control designed to manage expenditure on, say, meals and hospitality:

- Even if an organization does not have a gifts and hospitality policy designed to address any associated compliance risks, it can have (and is likely to have) a procedure whereby any expenditure incurred by an employee on the organization's behalf has to be approved by that employee's line manager (either in advance or after the event), then approved by the Finance function.

- Both approvers will be checking whether the expenditure is reasonably and necessarily incurred in connection with the organization's business and falls within relevant permitted categories and financial limits. The Finance function may approve all transactions or just some, but this is a detail that we can explore further later.

Other examples include:

- Accounting controls can prevent any payment being made without the recipient being cleared by using software to verify whether the recipient is a politically exposed or connected person or on the specially designated persons lists.

- Whether the person requesting the appointment of a supplier has done any due diligence or has any concept of the importance of verifying the recipient of the payment, the system will ultimately control whether the payment is, or is not, made.

Identifying where procedures are necessary

When performing a risk assessment as the first step in designing its compliance and ethics programme, an organization may decide that certain activities or transactions are so high risk that they can only be conducted via a procedure.

In any case, in practice a well-managed organization will have a range of procedures and controls by which it ensures efficient and effective management and operations, custodianship of its shareholders' assets, and reliable books and records and reporting.

Such procedures and controls can and should form part of the compliance and ethics programme. In many cases they will be directly suited to managing a particular compliance risk or a particular aspect thereof, and by utilizing or leveraging them one can reduce the need for additional or duplicative bureaucracy.

How procedures can help

One way of looking at procedures and controls is to think of them as what you need to have in addition to your policies and training, or when you want to make sure that your compliance programme operates in the way you intend.

If you have, say, a policy that every new employee will be given a copy of the code of conduct and is required to undertake online training within two weeks of joining, then a procedure is a way of making sure this happens.

If intelligently designed, procedures can:

- prevent employees and other people working in or for the organization from doing something they're not supposed to do, or doing it in an unapproved way;

and

- help people navigate an actual transaction that is permissible but inherently complicated and full of pitfalls.

Let's take another example:

- In the pharmaceutical sector a certain type of clinical study may be ethical and permissible, provided it is conducted within strict parameters and in accordance with certain strict criteria. A standard operating procedure may provide guidance and information about whether and how such an activity is permissible.

But...

- Some compliance and ethics programme doctrine, and some organizations categorize/group procedures and controls along with policies. However, normally people will be trained on an organization's policies, whereas the procedures and controls do not usually require training in order to ensure that people become aware of and understand them. Rather, if the person does not follow the prescribed procedure, they will not be able to effect the desired transaction or operation, and if they do something in breach of a policy or procedure, the control should pick it up.

Again, an example will help to illustrate this:

- In reviewing expenses and reimbursement claims, the Finance function identifies expenditure in an unapproved category or in excess of prescribed limits.
- The control may catch the breach before the transaction can occur, or before any harm has been done or, at worst, in time for the Business, Compliance or one of the other relevant functions to address the problem.

So it is certainly worth distinguishing between on the one hand, policies, and on the other hand, procedures and controls. Both should be kept to a reasonable minimum in order to avoid excessive and counterproductive bureaucracy and the perception thereof.

Policies need to capture the key principles of acceptable conduct and, as far as possible, be written in an engaging way. They should be sufficiently few in number and sufficiently short to enable the organization to train all relevant people to understand and comply with them.

Procedures and controls do not need to be designed in accordance with the same principles, but from an effective compliance and ethics programme perspective they should still be kept as simple and comprehensible as possible and not be allowed to proliferate unduly, or else the business will not be sufficiently agile, and staff will not take, or will not feel trusted to take, responsibility.

Of course, an organization may choose to design and implement a plethora of complex procedures and controls in order to satisfy its other needs, over and above its compliance needs.

Types of procedure and controls

While not an exhaustive list, the following represent perhaps the most common and important types of procedures and controls.

HR procedures for:

- vetting and screening of employees before recruiting them for high-risk roles, including following up of references and checking qualifications and, where appropriate, criminal records;
- values-based interview questions to help ensure that the right type of employee is identified and attracted;
- induction procedures to ensure that new employees receive copies of, and training on the appropriate policies;
- setting values-based objectives and rewarding performance that helps to uphold those values (see our further discussion of this in Chapter 13);
- disclosing, approving and recording potential conflicts of interest;
- ensuring that bonus/incentive schemes contain appropriate checks and balances to mitigate non-compliance incentives or other unintended incentives;
- ensuring that employment contracts include the right to dismiss an employee summarily for material breach of the code or any other policy;
- maintaining appropriate disciplinary procedures to sanction employees in accordance with local law.

Financial controls to ensure:

- segregation of duties between individuals with ability to initiate and approve a transaction;

- appropriate delegated authorities for, inter alia, entering into contracts, payment approvals, cheque signatories;
- dual signature required for cheques/payments, invoices, contracts etc;
- appropriate supporting documentation to be attached to payment approvals and cheques/payment requests;
- gifts and hospitality and other expenses reimbursement approval procedures;
- reconciliation of key accounts (bank, supplier, accounts receivable, etc);
- limits on level of petty cash floats and their use.

Tendering/client/commercial controls, including for:

- identifying and assessing any compliance risks associated with potential clients or customers;
- approving the commercial and other terms of any bids or tenders;
- approving applications for variations, extensions of time and payment (to help manage the risk of false claims).

Procedures for assessing the compliance risks associated with:

- a project or tender, or a move into a new market or sector or country;
- and for ensuring that such risk assessments take place.

Procurement/supply chain management procedures for:

- pre-qualifying suppliers/vendors/subcontractors by ensuring that they are valid, legitimate organizations manifestly qualified to provide the relevant goods or services;
- due diligence procedures to obtain information to assess the suppliers' suitability and any risks they may present;
- as far as reasonably practicable, using only pre-approved preferred suppliers;

- as a matter of principle, as far as reasonably practicable, ensuring that supply contracts are awarded pursuant to a competitive tender including at least three bidders;

- elevating any exceptions to the above principle for approval at a more senior level;

- ensuring that a person recommending a supplier is different from a person approving its appointment and, if possible, that a third person approves any payments to a supplier;

- approving work performed by a supplier, and approving any applications from a supplier for payment by the organization, in order to help manage the risks of false claims and conflicts of interest;

- auditing suppliers from a technical, quality, safety and ethics standpoint.

Procedures for approving and monitoring high risk third parties – such as commercial agents, joint venture partners and certain types of consultant:

- Over and above the applicable procurement procedures outlined above, such procedures may also include additional or deeper due diligence procedures (discussed elsewhere) as well as procedures for ensuring that relevant managers understand and accept their accountability for any compliance risks associated with such third parties and are able to understand, and demonstrate that they understand the associated compliance risks.

- Such procedures may include a business justification procedure and, potentially, the requirement for the appointment to be approved by a more senior or independent officer, committee or body.

Contracting procedures:

- For example, to ensure that contracts with suppliers and other relevant third parties (including those discussed above) contain appropriate clauses requiring compliance with applicable law and ethical business conduct principles or obligations.

The dreaded compliance clause

It is widely agreed that the writer, Jonathan Coe, has written the longest sentence in the English language (13,955 words, in his novel *The Rotters' Club*). Other contenders might be James Joyce (in the final chapter of *Ulysses*) and, more recently... the dreaded compliance clause.

It's symptomatic of so much that is wrong with compliance. What started out as a one- or two-sentence 'Thou shalt comply with all applicable laws' clause has now become a complex and contentious clause or series of clauses, sometimes extending to three or four pages, and about as interwoven as the Gordian Knot. We have seen memoranda of understanding in which the anti-bribery/anti-corruption compliance and business ethics clause is the longest of all clauses and accounts for almost half the document!

In part, the reason for this is understandable but not laudable. Organizations want to be able to demonstrate to a regulator or prosecutor (and indeed to the relevant third party) how important compliance and ethics is to them. They judge that, the longer, more explicit and more onerous the clause, the more likely it is that the third party will take note of it and comply with it and, even if it does not, that the prosecutor or regulator will be impressed by it.

They also take the view that a mere compliance-with-the-law clause may not alert the third party to particular laws or types of laws (and ethical business conduct expectations) with which they are concerned, such as anti-bribery, human rights, data protection, health and safety, and so on. So they gradually add each of these specific topics to the list.

They then go further, to some extent for laudable reasons. Rather than expecting or requiring the third party to be or become an expert on all applicable laws or indeed on specific examples such as the US Foreign

Corrupt Practices Act, 1977 (FCPA)[1] or the UK Bribery Act 2010,[2] they seek to spell out in relative layman's terms what they really mean:

> Thou shalt comply with all applicable anti-bribery laws, including without limitation the US FCPA or the UK Bribery Act and local anti-bribery laws in country X. For the avoidance of doubt, this means that thou shalt ensure that no bribe or other improper payment or benefit is given, offered, solicited or accepted as an inducement or reward for someone to perform a duty improperly, whether that person is a public official or otherwise. Also, thou shalt ensure that no person associated with you shall give, offer, solicit or accept etc as aforesaid.

Such clauses become longer and longer, and more and more complex. Yet who within the relevant third party will actually read them? And who within the relevant third party actually needs to be aware of and take steps to ensure compliance with them?

Admittedly, it should be practicable for an organization to communicate to its relevant staff that a contract that it has signed with a client or other third party contains anti-bribery or compliance obligations that must be strictly complied with. That communication could include any specifics that may go above and beyond what the relevant staff are already familiar with.

But consider for a moment another common feature of these clauses...

Some organizations require their suppliers to comply with the client organization's code of conduct and anti-bribery policy, and that the supplier's own suppliers and subcontractors also so comply.

Again, the thinking behind this approach is commendable and understandable in certain respects: the first organization's code of conduct hopefully sets out the compliance and ethics expectations in a clear and engaging way, so what better way of making clear to the supplier or other third party exactly what the organization's expectations are? However, if you consider how difficult it is for an organization to embed its own code of conduct, what are the chances of the supplier having the resources and strategies likely to enable it successfully to embed the client's code of conduct in the supplier organization? Moreover, the supplier may well have its own code of conduct that it holds dear and which it is manfully attempting to embed, and it probably has many other customers and clients seeking to require compliance with their codes of conduct.

And that's not all. Such clauses can unwittingly or unfairly impose a stricter obligation than the relevant law. When you consider the above examples, the US FCPA or the UK Bribery Act may not actually apply to the supplier in the country in which it will perform the contract, or at all – even though one or both of those laws may apply to the client that is seeking to contract with the supplier.

There is a good chance that the supplier will be subject to local anti-bribery laws, which may to all intents and purposes be as strict as or broadly comparable with those two laws. If there are differences between the scope of the relevant laws, they are likely to be at a level of detail that is not strictly relevant to the client organization's desire to manage the compliance risk. It is these differences between different local laws or the different level of profile or enforcement in different countries that prompts the organization to seek to be much more explicit in its anti-bribery or compliance-with-the-law clause.

But let's just consider the above requirements for the supplier to ensure that no person associated with it pays a bribe.

The UK Bribery Act is generally considered to be one of the strictest anti-bribery laws in the world, and it holds organizations to a very high standard: they will be strictly, criminally liable if they fail to prevent bribery by persons associated with them, eg suppliers and subcontractors as well as, perhaps more obviously, agents and intermediaries. However, they have a defence at law if they can show that they did all that they reasonably could to prevent bribery by such persons. This is the so-called 'adequate procedures' or 'compliance programme' defence discussed elsewhere. In other words, the organization's obligation at law is to have in place a compliance programme designed and implemented in accordance with international best practice to prevent bribery by associated persons.

And yet the absolute obligation under a compliance clause to ensure that no such bribery takes place, or to represent and warrant that no such bribery has taken place, goes beyond even the strict UK Bribery Act and means that the organization could be liable contractually, even if it has the world's best anti-bribery compliance programme and breaches no laws itself.

Sometimes the above outcome is not the intention of those who designed the client organization's anti-bribery policy or its contractual anti-bribery clauses, but they may like the chilling effect that it has on the supplier or subcontractor. They calculate that the more frightened the supplier is of breaching the clause, the more likely it is to go to great lengths to ensure compliance with the clause. In many cases, such an approach is also consistent with the desire of those at the top of the food chain to push the compliance risk down the supply chain, at least as far as those major contractors and suppliers with deep enough pockets to satisfy a prosecutor. But is it fair, and is it effective?

In the oil and gas sector, safety has long been approached as a shared challenge, with organizations up and down the supply chain, from international oil companies downwards, working together with a very high degree of transparency to share best practice, information about accidents and near misses, and lessons learned, all with the shared goal of actually improving safety performance and reducing death and injury. This contrasts with the above approach to some areas of compliance, notably anti-bribery/anti-corruption and, to a certain extent, what we are seeing with human rights clauses. With anti-bribery /anti-corruption, the priority has been to push the risks down the supply chain if at all possible, and to hope to be able to demonstrate that one's compliance programme is defensible, rather than focusing on what will ultimately minimize non-compliance.

Some key procedures and controls specific to compliance and ethics

Due diligence

One of the key areas of procedures to manage supplier and other high-risk third-party compliance risks is due diligence. This should be part of the procedure for pre-qualifying and approving a supplier or other third party and, as far as possible, should be embedded in such procedure. It is discussed in more detail in Chapter 7.

Gift and hospitality procedures

An organization is likely to need to put in place procedures for approving and registering gifts and hospitality offered, accepted or declined. Its expenses approval and reimbursement procedures may adequately cover that which is given by the organization or its staff to third parties, but approvals are obtained retrospectively, whereas it may be prudent to require prior approval for some gifts and hospitality, eg above a certain value or to public officials. Further, anything received from third parties will be invisible, unless recorded in a register or, in extremis, noted and reported by a colleague.

Table 11.1 is an illustrative example of how an organization might choose to set approval and registration thresholds.

TABLE 11.1 Gift and hospitality approval thresholds

Gift and hospitality approval thresholds			
Registration and pre-approval requirements	Most types of gift or hospitality		Special types of gift or hospitality
	Gifts	Hospitality	
Record on the register	> $30	> $60	Any gift or hospitality provided to a public official
Manager pre-approval	> $100	> $250	
VP pre-approval	> $250	> $750	Any travel or accommodation, if the value exceeds $60 Any hospitality with a personal companion

(continued)

TABLE 11.1 (*Continued*)

Registration and pre-approval requirements	Gift and hospitality approval thresholds		Special types of gift or hospitality
	Most types of gift or hospitality		
	Gifts	Hospitality	
SVP or EVP pre-approval	N/A		Any travel or accommodation, if the value exceeds $250 Any hospitality with a personal companion, if the combined value exceeds $500
Commercial or operations director and CECO pre-approval	N/A		Any gift or hospitality provided to a public official

Definitions and notes:

1. Hospitality includes meals, refreshments, entertainment, travel and accommodation.
2. Dollar limits are per person, unless otherwise stated.
3. An officer or employee of a national or state-owned company is normally considered to be a public official. Guidance from the compliance function should be obtained before offering gifts or hospitality to such people.
4. Accommodation means hotel or other overnight accommodation.
5. Hospitality with a personal companion means any hospitality with an accompanying spouse, partner or other family member, personal friend or associate.
6. Vice president, senior vice president or executive vice president or approval is required in accordance with the above requirements when hospitality *includes* some travel or accommodation, as well as when travel or accommodation is offered *without* other hospitality.
7. Requirements are cumulative, so eg hospitality whose value exceeds $750 requires registration, manager pre-approval and VP pre-approval.

SOURCE Reproduced with the kind permission of Subsea 7

Having a register

Here you can see how quite a few concepts and nuances need to be communicated. It is probably for this reason that most organizations decide they need to have clear definitions of acceptability and financial thresholds.

Regardless of how much the organization's policies are defined and prescriptive, a register should be one feature of the organization's approach to this area. The idea of a register is to encourage transparency and to enable lighter touch procedures and approval limits as a quid pro quo.

'If you are willing to disclose accurately what you offered or accepted, nine times out of 10 you are likely to make good decisions about acceptability. In return, we have increased the thresholds above which you require management approval.'

Conflicts of interest procedures

It may be desirable for an organization to put in place procedures requiring that any potential conflicts of interest be recorded on a register, as well as disclosed in accordance with the relevant policy. The organization may also need to put in place procedures for managing such conflicts of interest, for example for someone to abstain from procurement decision-making.

When you consider both these examples, you will see that it is possible for an organization not to have such procedures but merely to rely on its gift and hospitality and conflicts of interest policies, or indeed on even higher level, principles-based policies. In other words:

1 Do you need a procedure to ensure that people comply with those policies?

Or:

2 To guide them through how best to comply, would you put all your efforts into raising awareness and understanding of the policies and trust people to comply with them, whilst recognizing that they may not have the bandwidth to absorb and deal with yet another procedure? And punish those who do not comply?

In our experience, employees find conflicts of interest difficult to understand and recognize. In any case, the purpose of a register is to make sure that employees can prove that a potential conflict was appropriately disclosed and that no further risk mitigation steps were agreed with their manager, or that such steps were agreed, documented and complied with.

Let's take the example of an internal investigation focused on a manager's close relationship with the owner of a key supplier:

- The manager insists that everybody knew about his close relationship, and that he therefore does not need to produce evidence of how and when it was disclosed, to whom and in what detail.

- He also insists that the company has suffered no loss as a result of the close relationship.

In fact, this is very hard to prove, and it is preferable for an organization to be able to say: 'The onus is on you to make the disclosure and to show that you did so. It is not for us to try to prove that a loss was suffered by the company. It should be enough for us to show that you never disclosed the conflict of interest, and as a result you were in breach of your employment contract.'

In the case of gift and hospitality policies, procedures and registers, a principles-based policy, like the example examined in Chapter 8 (page 184), ought to suffice. Unfortunately, no prosecutor or auditor is likely to be enlightened enough to consider such an approach adequate. So a reinforcing procedure will likely be necessary too. But this serves to highlight a tension between effective, realistic compliance and defensible compliance.

Across the minefield: compliance and ethics meets real life

The laundry

An audit of a State-owned enterprise (SoE) identified some payments missing the proper financial paper trail and approvals. On making further enquiries, it was determined there was a high likelihood the payments were improper.

The persons interviewed stated that the payments, and their purpose, had been approved at the highest levels. Further investigation confirmed this was indeed the case.

However, the executives, who had authorized the payments, claimed that the authorization followed an instruction to make the payment by the majority shareholder – the State. So the State was investigating an SoE that had made an allegedly improper payment following instruction by the State.

Initially the State denied all knowledge. It was only when proceedings were threatened against the corporate individuals that the State admitted that it had indeed given instructions for the payments be made.

The two dealers

To buy a car, I went to two dealers and asked them to give me their best price.

One of the two dealers simply said, 'Look, rather than my giving you a price, I promise you I can match the other guy's price.' 'No good,' said I. 'It would be unfair. I asked the other guy to give me his best price, and if it is the cheaper of the two, I will go with him.'

People can be genuinely surprised if you take this stance, but I think that's because they are used to unprincipled wheeling and dealing and don't expect those basic, old-fashioned standards to be taken seriously nowadays.

'It's up to you'

Your customer is about to award you the contract but insists that you pull the environment programme that was a key part of your responsible bid. If you don't agree they'll almost certainly go with someone else.
How are you going to handle this one?

You've sent a highly confidential email to the wrong person.
What now?

You're in a hotel waiting to pitch for a big new contract and you just happen to meet one of the team you'll be pitching to. You have a couple of drinks together, and without meaning to they tell you something that you shouldn't know, that will give you quite an advantage. 'Whoops!' they say, 'Shouldn't have said that! Let's just forget that happened, shall we?'
Should you? Can you?

It's late. You're all tired. But the deadline has already passed. If you all work overnight you'll get the job done. The team wants to go for it, but you think it's just not safe – there are too many risks. Everyone else disagrees.
If they're willing, is it okay?

Notes

1 Foreign Corrupt Practices Act of 1977, as amended, 15 U.S.C. §§ 78dd-1, et seq.
2 The Bribery Act 2010, https://www.legislation.gov.uk/ukpga/2010/23/contents [accessed 24.02.19].

12

Investigations, remediation and enforcement

Having explained the importance of the whistle-blowing policy in Chapter 10, in this chapter we examine the importance of having good, effective, fair and consistent procedures for investigating reports or suspicions that the compliance and ethics policies or procedures are not being complied with and for remediating breaches discovered.

This is where culture meets compliance, in the sense that there needs to be a just but firm process for sanctioning non-compliance. We want this to be about culture and values, but policies must be upheld and, if you breach them, there must be consequences and disincentives for non-compliance.

When the need for an investigation arises

We have seen how, if you really wish to make sure your compliance and ethics programme is as effective as possible, you need to seek out, obtain and utilize any and all feedback and other insights into its effectiveness you reasonably can. This may include comments about what works or what does not work, what's confusing or poorly understood, what is too bureaucratic or clunky, and what is effective but will ultimately be circumvented because it is too difficult or time-consuming and makes the business inefficient and insufficiently agile.

'Feedback' may also take the shape of allegations, suspicions or reports of breaches or failures of, and weaknesses in the programme – including what are very broadly known as whistle-blowing cases.

They include not just information brought to the organization's attention by an internal or external whistle-blower, via an internal or external whistle-blowing channel, but also breaches, control failures or weaknesses that are detected by internal audit or by compliance monitoring, or that a manager observes or suspects. If this kind of feedback informs you that the organization or certain people who work in or for it appear not to be complying with your compliance and ethics programme, then you need to get to the bottom of it.

You may have discovered an individual who may need to be removed from the company; or you may have discovered a broader problem with the culture, or it may simply be that the relevant policy or procedure is poorly understood, too complicated and time-consuming, or simply does not work. Whatever it is, you need to understand the facts and decide what remedial action is necessary.

The importance of enforcement

Sometimes, inaction says a whole lot more than action.

As we have already said, if you want people to take your compliance and ethics policies and commitment seriously, they need to see that you are both willing and determined to uphold them, and that you do so. By acting clearly, fairly and determinedly, people will see both 'stick' and 'carrot': the potential downside for them of failing to comply, and that the organization really does care about, and will uphold, its code

There is another important consideration: whistle-blowing and other such feedback are some of the few signs the organization may receive that something may be amiss. As we have explored elsewhere, legal and reputational damage are very likely to occur if the organization, or people working in or for it, behave unethically, or if unethical conduct or culture is not detected and nipped in the bud. Even someone who is cynical about compliance and ethics will probably recognize that one of the benefits of having a credible whistle-blowing policy and process is that it reduces the chances of the whistle-blower bringing their concerns to the attention of a prosecutor, regulator or other third party or stakeholder.

When should an organization self-report?

Whistle-blowing or other such feedback may be the first or only sign that something has gone wrong or is going wrong within the organization, and the organization needs to get to the bottom of it to be able to judge whether it has a problem that it should report to relevant authorities, be they regulators or prosecutors.

There is an awful lot of discussion about whether and when an organization should report itself to a prosecutor, such as the US Department of Justice or the UK Serious Fraud Office. There is no easy answer to this, and we have found that it does not help if one stands back and applies normal ethical or moral behaviour principles.

Imagine you have discovered that your organization or someone who works in or for it has done something illegal.

- Does your experience, or do your normal ethical or moral principles, tell you whether you should inform on the organization or that person?

- Should you tell the police if your son is shoplifting? What if your daughter has broken the speed limit when driving?

- Would or should you report yourself for breaking the speed limit, and do you set a higher or lower bar for yourself?

- What if your spouse committed a murder, or some other far less heinous crime?

The problem is, there's no parallel that can really help you decide whether it is right and proper to report your organization or an employee or other person.

And it can be equally unhelpful to consider what sort of criminal offence or other conduct would or should disqualify an employee from working in your organization. For example:

- If an employee is convicted of a hate crime, but it is not associated with their work and is in a purely personal capacity, the chances are you may not have a policy that has been breached. You may or may not have any clear right to dismiss the employee in accordance with the contract of employment or your employee handbook.

- What if the conviction is for an affray, eg getting into a fight in a public place? Does the conduct have to be relevant to the employee's work or their fitness to work for the organization?

- What do you do if you do not have a clear contractual right to terminate, but you wish to terminate the employment?

All three of us agree that none of these considerations helped us arrive at a clear policy as to whether and when it is right to report an employee to the police or an organization to a prosecutor or regulator.

If someone within the organization has done something unethical or illegal, you may well be very clear in your mind that the organization is responsible for that conduct, but do you then believe it should be held criminally culpable? Rightly or wrongly, this dilemma is usually resolved in a more practical way: organizations make a judgement – you might say a cynical judgement – about the likelihood of the relevant prosecutor or regulator finding out about the misconduct if the organization does not self-report; and the benefit, if any, that the organization expects to receive as a result of coming forward voluntarily.

This book is not the place, and the authors are not sufficiently expert, to advise whether and when it is right, desirable or even obligatory for an organization to self-report. All such cases are extremely fact-specific. What is easier to say is:

1 If you conduct a prompt, effective internal investigation, you will be in possession of as many of the facts as possible in order to make a well-informed decision.

And:

2 If you bury your head in the sand and choose not to find out the facts:

 a. the organization is vulnerable to the authorities finding out through some other means, in which case the consequences for the organization may be far more severe;

 b. the organization may therefore have breached its duty to its stakeholders; and

 c. you will not know whether there is an ongoing problem or even, if the misconduct was in the past, whether those involved continue in responsible roles and could be putting the organization at risk.

What is clear is that it is useful and important to investigate credible concerns that the organization or certain people may be behaving in an illegal, unethical or non-compliant manner. None of your employees, your other stakeholders, or indeed the prosecutor or regulator will consider your compliance and ethics programme to be credible if you fail to do so. What's more, you will not be able to identify and remediate weaknesses or gaps in your programme, or issues with organizational culture or its education and training.

So, an effective compliance and ethics programme needs to include appropriate procedures, resources and skills for conducting effective investigations, for sanctioning appropriately those who have breached the organization's policies, and to remedy any weaknesses or gaps in the programme.

In rare cases the investigations team may reasonably conclude that investigation of an incident is either impractical or unwarranted. For example:

- There may be insufficient information for an investigation to be designed that has a reasonable chance of uncovering the necessary details of the incident.

- Or there may be reasonable grounds for believing that the allegation is made neither in good faith nor on the basis of a reasonable belief.

Any grievances relating to an individual's employment (eg working practices, health and safety, fair treatment or terms and conditions of employment) should be dealt with through the relevant HR grievance procedures or provisions.

Being fair, consistent and even-handed

It is really important that sanctions for breach of the organization's policies are consistent and fair, whether across geographies and functions, or up and down the management chain. In other words, a valued senior manager should not be let off more lightly – indeed should arguably face stricter sanction – than the more junior manager or employee. And the sanction for breach of a particular policy in the United States should be the same in France or India.

To achieve this fairness and consistency, it may well be necessary or desirable to have some sort of tariff or framework, so everyone is dealt with fairly in a manner appropriate to the violation, and as consistently as practicable, across different countries and business areas. There should be a 'disciplinary principle' that certain serious violations generally warrant dismissal. Examples might include bribery, fraud and other criminal conduct involving dishonesty or otherwise directly relevant to the employee's work for the organization.

However, it is not possible to be prescriptive, and in our view it may not be appropriate for the level of sanction to be determined by the damage caused to the organization by the breach. If someone behaved dishonestly or fraudulently, that should be viewed as a serious disciplinary offence, regardless of whether it costs the organization £150 for an expense that was dishonestly claimed, or a lot more as a result of a civil or criminal action being brought against the organization.

But we have jumped ahead by talking about disciplinary principles and ranges of sanctions.

The key principle here is to make sure that fair and effective investigations take place in the first place, following which senior management at least have the information to take well-informed, hopefully sensible and enlightened decisions regarding the consequences for individuals and, potentially, for the organization.

Having the right skills and guidance

Those involved in internal investigations should have the right combination of skills, independence, understanding of the business and of the relevant control framework and policies, as well as seniority or at least gravitas. On a more practical level, they need to acquire an understanding of different types of evidence and how to obtain them, including hardcopy documents, emails and other electronic data, and witness testimony and interviews.

An investigations team or function, even in the most modest sense of the word, that will be deployed or trained to conduct investigations should have the appropriate mix of the above qualities and skills. They are unlikely to be found in one person or function, whether Compliance, Legal, Audit, HR or Security.

If the organization has the budget and the volume of cases to justify recruiting one or more specialists, the skills may be found in a professional fraud investigator. They may also be found in the person of a former police detective, who is likely to have the interview skills, investigation planning, and evidence weighing and preservation skills and experience, but who may have much to learn about corporate politics and an inquisitorial approach.

Many organizations do not have the budget or the number of cases to justify a dedicated internal investigations resource. The few that do can take a much more considered approach. Most organizations will have to rely on people rolling up their sleeves and applying some broadly applicable skills and experience from their role in Legal, Compliance, HR, Audit or Security.

The organization will need to provide guidance or training for people who are, or are likely to be, involved in internal investigations, and a practical procedure that can be followed by people who may only be involved occasionally, as well as by management who are trying to assess the facts that have been discovered and reported and the limitations in the evidence and in the investigative steps.

Managing investigations: some good practice guidance

How to *conduct* fair, efficient and effective investigations is a complex, specialist area, and any organization implementing a compliance and ethics programme would be well advised to seek expert help, either from external advisors or by hiring an experienced investigator, who can:

- help design appropriate procedures and governance;

- provide specialist advice in areas such as preservation of evidence, protection of rights of those accused of criminality, and when to refer something to the police or prosecutors;
- provide training on some or all of the above; and
- conduct any large, complex or sensitive investigation.

However, for many organizations, paying for external investigations advice or services or to hire a specialist investigator may be neither affordable nor feasible, save when the risks clearly justify the costs.

All that being said, organizations with limited resources or wishing or needing to start small and take incremental steps should not be unduly intimidated – much can be achieved in practice through common sense, designing a clear, just process, and sticking to it. There are some basic principles regarding sound, effective conduct of internal investigations that an organization should follow and set out in guidance and training for those who will be involved.

Some basic principles

If an organization is faced with allegations or suspicions of misconduct, whether by employees or others working for them, that could imply criminal or significant civil liability or reputational risk for the organization, it should most probably engage outside legal counsel – if and to the extent that legal privilege may be an important consideration – and/or other specialist investigators.

It is important to start off in the right way, in terms of preserving evidence, obtaining and preserving legal privilege (if available), and retaining and preventing the destruction or amendment of hard copy and electronic records, including emails.

Subject to the above, here are some key factors and areas of guidance to consider and address in the design and implementation of the investigations aspects of an effective compliance and ethics programme. They fall under three broad headings:

1 There should be an appropriate governance framework and procedure that ensures the right people and processes are informed, consulted, involved or engaged.

2 Those who are likely to become involved in internal investigations should receive training and guidance on the conduct of investigations: the what, the why and the how.

3 Those who become involved in specific cases – whether as whistle-blowers, witnesses or suspects – should receive guidance on:

a. what to expect;

b. what their rights are; and

c. how their rights will be respected and protected.

In the case of suspects, the timing of such guidance will depend on when they may reasonably be informed of the investigation without 'tipping them off' or otherwise compromising the evidence or independent conduct of the investigation.

REPORTING AN EMPLOYEE TO THE POLICE

When an investigation reveals that an employee may have committed a criminal offence, the organization will usually first consider whether such conduct may result in criminal liability for the organization itself and what self-reporting obligations or considerations may need to be considered.

Subject to such considerations, the organization may consider it has a societal duty to report suspected criminal conduct to the police, or it may not be able to prove the criminal conduct or any self-enrichment without police powers (such as access to bank account details). So it may decide to refer the case to the police.

In practice, the police may be indifferent to or uninterested in cases involving potential criminal conduct by an employee against a corporate, such as theft or procurement fraud, unless there is compelling, conveniently compiled evidence of self-enrichment by the employee. Yet it can be very hard for a company to find such evidence without access to bank accounts and other police powers.

Having the right people involved in internal investigations

When designing the governance and procedures for investigations, or at the latest when faced with its first internal investigation, the organization should identify the appropriate people or categories of people who should be involved. Even a small organization will have to find the right people to call upon if the need for an investigation arrives, despite the fact that they may only be called upon for a small percentage of their time and will not be full-time or specialist investigators.

However, there is a real factor in play here: even a mid-cap, listed company with, say, 5,000 employees, may not be able to justify hiring one full-time, specialist investigator. A large organization might have that luxury and, above a certain size, a few organizations may be able to justify and afford a team of investigators who can then offer a broader mix of skills and experience, the capacity to handle more than one investigation at the time, and even specialize in, and have responsibility for different regions. But most organizations will have to use people from other functions and provide appropriate training and guidance. Typically, this will mean lawyers, compliance officers, HR managers, internal auditors and perhaps people from the Finance or Procurement functions who have familiarity with the relevant procedures and controls that may be looked at as part of the investigation.

A note on the role of HR

The role of HR deserves special mention. HR managers often have some of the key skills and experience that are relevant, especially as regards interviewing employees. And if the investigation relates to a potential breach of employment practices (eg bullying, harassment or discrimination), the HR function will be subject-matter experts and owners of some of the relevant policies and procedures.

However, an investigation interview is very different from a job interview – or even a disciplinary discussion. Moreover, the purpose of a compliance and ethics investigation is to ascertain the facts. It is then for line management, with appropriate HR support, to decide whether disciplinary action is required and to conduct any disciplinary procedures. For that reason, it is important to ensure that any HR manager involved in an internal investigation is not only independent but is not the same person who will need to conduct any subsequent disciplinary hearing or appeal.

Ensuring the investigation is independent

It is essential that investigations be conducted in a way that is independent, preserves confidentiality as far as possible, respects and protects any whistle-blower's identity or anonymity and the right not to be retaliated against, respects and protects the rights of all others involved, and is generally just and reasonable. Above all, innocence should be presumed and whistle-blowers protected.

Independence is partly a matter of character, partly role or function and partly facts. In other words, someone with the perfect qualities may not be independent, if they are being asked to investigate their own team, function or business unit, or someone with whom they have a personal relationship.

The investigation should be tasked, resourced and skilled to establish:

- what happened;
- who was involved;
- what policies and procedures were breached;
- why it happened; and
- what was the motivation for it.

Reporting the findings of fact

A fact-finding report should then be presented to appropriate managers, so they can decide whether those involved should face any disciplinary procedure, and whether any other remedial steps should be taken. Ideally, the fact-finding report should also contain recommendations for any policy or control enhancements or lessons learned about the compliance and ethics programme.

Depending on the seriousness of the allegations and of the findings, the recipient(s) of the report may be the direct or indirect manager of the person(s) investigated, or more senior manager or steering group.

Disciplinary proceedings

Normally, if an individual is to face disciplinary proceedings, that is a decision for their direct line manager. However, if the findings have broader ramifications for the organization or its compliance and ethics programme, it will be appropriate for a more senior manager or steering group to have some say, at least in the broader remedial actions and certainly in any decision about whether reporting the organization or any individual externally is necessary or desirable. Moreover, the direct line manager may not be independent enough to assess and accept the implied criticism of her people or business unit.

Governance procedure

The governance procedure should specify which people or roles should have what degree of involvement in which types of investigation, and what more or less prescriptive procedures they should follow. It is useful to apply a 'RACI' matrix approach:

- Which people or roles should be responsible?
- Which should be accountable?
- Who needs to be consulted (and might need to provide consent or approval)?
- Who merely needs to be informed?

(All consistent with good governance and a need-to-know principle.)

The procedure can be flexible, and for most organizations (including SMEs), resource and other constraints mean that it will need to be. It can and should be adapted so it is reasonable and proportional to:

- the organization;
- the seriousness of the allegations or suspicions being investigated; and
- the risks to the organization.

Handling whistle-blowing and other reports

Ideally, any whistle-blowing allegations or other reports or suspicions of a compliance and ethics breach by employees or others working for the organization (including agents and other third parties), whether received via channels provided by an external helpline provider or through internal channels (such as an email address or telephone helpline) should be received and triaged by the chief ethics and compliance officer.

They should then be investigated by a person or team as close to the relevant business unit or function as is reasonable, and consistent with ensuring independence and protecting confidentiality or anonymity. This is partly to ensure the business units maintain accountability for compliance and ethics, but more practically to ensure the investigator/investigations team have a good working knowledge of the business unit and its control environment. Typically, this means investigations are conducted by people one level above the business unit being investigated, but it may be possible and consistent with the above principles for senior managers of a business unit to conduct the investigation, if only junior managers or other staff members are implicated.

When triaging reports, the chief ethics and compliance officer can also assess the potential significance of the case. In other words, if the allegations or suspicions are substantiated, what are the potential legal, reputational, financial, management or cultural consequences for the organization? Is a senior manager or a management team under suspicion, which might lead to disruptive departures and business interruption and succession issues? Could there be significant harm to the organization?

An illustrative list of the types of case that are likely to be considered significant or material in this sense is provided in the following box. Such cases may warrant:

- the engagement of outside counsel or other specialist investigators;
- greater urgency and resources;
- head office leadership or oversight of the investigation; and
- more planning for eventual outcomes.

SIGNIFICANT CASES

Cases likely to be considered as 'serious' include any alleged incident:

- of retaliation against a whistle-blower;
- involving a member of a senior management team;
- involving more than one business unit or function;
- that could prompt significant media attention or reputational harm for the organization;
- involving potential criminal or significant civil liability;
- involving a significant breakdown in accounting systems or internal accounting controls;
- that could result in (1) suspension or debarment by a government or development bank, (2) loss of any licence or other government authorization or privilege;
- suggesting obstruction of justice or interference with an investigation;
- suggesting a pattern of significant non-compliance;
- that could affect the organization's share price or stock exchange rules compliance (if the organization is listed);
- that could lead to de-listing from, or suspension of trading on, a stock exchange.

Note: The list is not meant to be exhaustive, and there may also be occasions when a routine matter develops into a serious one. If in doubt, err on the side of caution and categorize as serious.

Preparing an investigation plan

It is sensible for the investigations governance and procedure to require that an investigator or investigations team prepare a plan for their investigation.

Depending on the organization's resources, it may not be realistic to be too prescriptive about this requirement or about what should be included in any such plan, but it is nonetheless helpful for investigators to understand the merits of a plan. It should keep them focused on:

- the allegations and emerging evidence;
- what they need to prove and how; and
- reasonable timelines.

It is important to remind investigators of the benefits of returning repeatedly to the allegations and to the steps taken and evidence established thus far. Otherwise it is easy to lose sight of details of the allegations.

Conversely, the allegations can often be understood better or differently if they are revisited after some modest investigative steps. This in turn can lead to amendments to the investigation plan and timelines.

Ensuring the process is just

As a matter of just process, it is important that anyone accused of non-compliance should be told of the allegations against them and given an opportunity to provide their version of events and to answer accusations.

However, it is also important to plan and execute an investigation so that, as far as possible, discreet steps are first taken that may independently corroborate or disprove allegations and facts, before they are presented to the accused. Ideally this may be through electronic or hard copy documentary evidence, and all other things being equal, initial steps should prioritize potential sources of such evidence. But do not forget that witness testimony is also evidence, even though it may not amount to conveniently clear proof but has to be weighed against other testimony, including that of the accused.

(It's also really important to note that the term 'accused' is by no means the perfect term. It does not really seem suitable to most internal investigations, and we use it for convenience. Most of the time, what we really mean is the person against whom allegations have been made or about whom suspicions have arisen.)

Nevertheless, all too often inexperienced or impatient investigators jump straight in and present the allegations to the 'accused'. Not only may this alert the person under investigation to the existence and possibly the identity of any whistle-blower, but it may also enable them to reject the accusations in a way that, at least initially, seems credible. Subsequently they may then be able to tamper with evidence and/or prepare a story that is consistent with the allegations and evidence available, as they now understand them.

Making decisions based on the evidence

It is important that management understand that most investigations will not result in cast iron proof but, rather, a balance of evidence pointing towards the allegations being substantiated or unsubstantiated. This means management probably having to make a decision based on its judgement of the evidence.

One of the best ways to help navigate this difficulty is to ascertain facts and details as far as possible before interviewing the person under investigation. It is often the contradictions between their otherwise credible denial, and the facts and details already uncovered by the investigator, that will lead to the investigator – and ultimately to the management decision-makers – deciding whether, on the balance of probability, the 'accused' did in fact behave in the way alleged.

And remember, this is a balance of probability test! The organization is trying to decide whether the alleged non-compliance took place and, if it believes on the balance of probability that it did, it should normally feel justified in taking remedial action accordingly. Indeed, its compliance and ethics programme may not be viewed as credible in the eyes of employees, regulators or prosecutors, if they do not. This may not be totally or conveniently consistent with the evidence or proof required in order to dismiss or otherwise sanction an employee in accordance with their contract of employment and applicable employment law.

An employment tribunal, or its equivalent in many jurisdictions, may or may not set the same standard when deciding whether an organization's dismissal of an employee is fair, lawful and otherwise justified. But in any case, the organization needs to have the strength of its convictions and act upon its reasonable, considered belief – even if it may have to enter into a compromise with the employee, when it believes the employee is dishonest or untrustworthy but cannot provide it to the legal standard required to dismiss the employee summarily.

External resources

External specialist forensic or IT assistance may be required when:

- it is necessary or desirable to engage in the capture, processing and review of emails or other electronic data;
- there are third parties involved;
- there is a particular need for the perceived independence brought by a third party;
- for example, a fraud appears very complex and is of an unfamiliar nature to in-house specialists.

Remedial action and sanctions

As mentioned already, it is important that everyone is dealt with fairly and in a manner appropriate to the violation, and that any remedial action is as transparent and consistent as practicable across different territories and business areas, subject always to local law.

It may be helpful to consider the following disciplinary principles that can or should help determine the seriousness of the breach and the appropriateness of a more or less serious sanction:

- awareness of relevant policy;
- intent (careless, reckless or intentional);
- motive (self-enrichment, business benefit, other);
- cooperation and responsiveness;
- repeat or first-time offender;
- seniority;
- scope and impact of breach.

It may also be helpful to have in mind the following range of sanctions, listed in descending order of seriousness:

- report to the police;
- termination of employment;
- resignation;
- demotion;
- final written warning;
- written warning;
- oral warning;
- salary or bonus reduction;
- coaching;
- re-training.

The investigator's perspective and the pitfalls to beware

To finish, it is helpful to consider investigations and the associated organization dynamic, issues, tensions and pitfalls from the perspective of an experienced investigator. For this, we turn to someone with far more expertise than we have on this matter, and cite directly from Crawford Robinson, Head of Investigations, British American Tobacco, and Chief Operating Officer of the Association of Corporate Investigators:[1]

The interactions of employees with their colleagues, management and/or external stakeholders can create business success or failure. On many occasions, success and failure are not mutually exclusive: a business can be 'successful' but inappropriate in the way it, its employees or external agents have conducted themselves. Hence, for any business, people are not only the most important asset but also the one asset that can let it down most. The unpredictability of employee behaviours is what keeps the investigator at work.

Today's highly regulated operating environment lends even more importance to the way in which investigations are conducted. Human resources, legal and security practitioners, compliance officers and information security professionals are increasingly faced with the need to conduct thorough and rigorous investigations to help business demonstrate both internally and externally that it behaves responsibly in all its activities.

Complainants making allegations quite rightly have an expectation that an investigation will be handled objectively, fairly and with the utmost professionalism. Those who are the subject of an investigation have justifiably similar expectations, as should the entire organization. For this, they will look to the investigator, and to achieve that the investigator must go far beyond the application of their technical skill to those often understated and nuanced 'softer' attributes – emotional intelligence, sound judgement and the ability to deal with and manage ambiguity are just a few.

The five 'dos'

1 **Get to know the senior managers before an investigation:** Personal knowledge and direct experience with senior managers such as the Legal Counsel, Human Resources, Finance, Audit, Business Unit heads, Security and others will be helpful in most circumstances, allowing a more nuanced judgement of advice you give. Time invested in getting to know the business and its managers will pay dividends.

2 **Be well informed:** The lead investigator should be as well informed as possible. Although decisions may need to be made in compressed time frames, the lead investigator must still do the best they can to obtain all the information reasonably available in a timely way to help senior managers make the decisions that need to be made. As an advisor they must also consider whether any senior managers have conflicting interests that should be disclosed and whether those conflicts merit withdrawal from all or part of the decision-making.

3 **Share the burden:** Never base your advice on one sole perspective; there is every reason to seek legal counsel and other guidance in developing options to put to senior management. The role of the lead investigator, especially at the start of a case, can be an anxious one and you have every right and, indeed, should use business judgement, third party experts and counsel to develop and clearly understand the options before presenting them for decision. The investigator should never leave themselves in a position where as sole advisor they end up having to swallow the poison pill of the business.

4 **Keep a decision log:** It is essential to keep a written record of your prior discussions, advice and guidance given and received, presentation of the information, appraisal of the options considered and senior management deliberations. It is all too easy for decisions to be challenged afterwards as hasty, misinformed or uninformed, and we have all come across circumstances where memory is selective after the event. Although making these records should also be done in the knowledge that they may ultimately be disclosed to third parties, it is useful to have a written record of the possible risks associated with decisions and that these were considered.

5 **Act as a senior manager and leader in your role as an investigator:** Managers should be managers and investigators should be investigators – but it is your role to empathise with, understand and where appropriate lead both. You must help business managers to resist the impulse to take over and instead help them focus on working collaboratively with the investigators. You will also gain enormous respect by providing guidance and support to business efforts to address the matter in hand.

The five 'don'ts'

1 **Don't allow hasty decisions:** You will feel great pressure to act quickly. Of course, some actions such as information/evidence preservation will be vital and have to be completed within tight time constraints. However, sometimes the pressure to end discussion and make a decision will genuinely be an unnecessary and unwelcome distraction. Much of this pressure will be internal and very intense. Business pressures, personal agendas, and genuine time demands can make ending discussion and forming a decision seem the best course at the time. The experienced investigator will know how to offset this pressure and counsel that, as time passes, the quality of information tends to improve. Whereas a concern for the business may be that circumstances could change very quickly, a cool head and experienced hand will often see that the way ahead will soon become clear and the business can avoid the potential harm of ill-informed decisions. Other pressure will be external, with regulators, external auditors or third parties suggesting that some decision needs to be made immediately.

2 **Don't pretend you have a stronger position than you have:** You are a senior manager, but you are not the CEO. Don't think you have more influence than you have: if you do you may damage your ability to counsel, advise and liaise with real influence. If you do have concerns that your voice is not being listened to, there are other avenues of recourse, but belligerence is not one of them. Who you can approach, whether internal or external counsel or a member of the Audit Committee, should always be considered prudently, taking into account personal reputation, corporate impact and potential consequences for both.

3 **Don't be adversarial:** It is your responsibility to work collaboratively with the management team so that they get the right information, in good time and in sufficient but not overwhelming detail to make soundly based decisions recognizing the risks involved. Occasionally, disagreement over tactical approaches of investigation may arise, but often self-restraint may well be the order of the day if you are to achieve long-term gain. It is also worth remembering that a leader is only a leader if they have followers, and this applies both to the respect you will hold in the business and the respect you receive from your investigative colleagues in achieving demonstrable, visible and transparent progress in effectively establishing the truth.

4 **Don't blindside your line management:** There is nothing more fatal to your credibility. Make sure your manager is fully and appropriately briefed; it is your role to plan carefully and thoughtfully, giving your line manager the time and space to think through the issues. This not only increases the likelihood of the agreement and support of your manager, but in worst case scenario, 'top cover' to challenges that may arise in execution of your plan of investigation. Timing is everything, and briefing your line manager on some critical aspects of an investigation just before an imminent meeting with the CEO will never gain support for your endeavours. It is your role to consult, listen to, guide and advise your line manager and other senior managers appropriately.

5 **Don't routinely seek consensus:** Having said all the above, there will be many occasions when, aside from being regarded as a good listener and wise counsellor, you may need to be an active advocate for a particular position or point of view. Your standpoint may not always be listened to, to the extent you may expect or wish, but at least it should be respected. Only rarely should you find yourself as the Lone Ranger.

Across the minefield: compliance and ethics meets real life

Payment for healthcare

If you lived in a country in which you were forced to pay a small bribe to gain access to healthcare for your children, can you honestly say that you would not pay?

But...

Would you also pay a bribe to obtain a driving licence for yourself or for a family member?

Would you pay a bribe in order to win work or an advantage in work for your organization?

It's just not cool

When asked why he hadn't stepped in and reminded those around him that what they were doing was in direct violation of the company's code of conduct and values, the employee relied that he felt he would have been seen as 'uncool' by the others if he had done so.

'It's up to you'

We've been employing a local contractor. They're very good. Then you learn they don't employ anyone who belongs to a particular faith because most of our employees just wouldn't use them if they knew. *Now what?*

We've just received final payment for a contract. It came with a thank you letter from the client. Now someone on our team has realized we made a mistake and overcharged.
Say nothing?

You overhear a manager telling a disabled colleague that they can't apply for a certain job because they just 'wouldn't fit the bill'.
Take action? What would it be?

You go out with colleagues from one of our joint venture partners and discover both your companies work for the same client, though on different projects. The partner tells you the client is so 'tight' the only way to make money out of them is to overcharge them. They've been doing it for years.

Any of your business?

One of your team is 'bad-mouthing' their colleagues and two of the managers on social media.

Anything you can do about it?

Note

1 This article represents the personal views of the contributor and not those of British American Tobacco or the Association of Corporate Investigators.

13

Assurance and continuous improvement

In this chapter we look at how a programme should be monitored,
measured and reported on in order to answer the question, 'How
effectively – or ineffectively – is it working?'

We look at an overall approach to compliance and ethics programme
assurance; what things can and should be measured and are meaningful;
how not to be fixated about quantitative measures, when qualitative stuff
may be more valuable, even if not so satisfyingly black and white; and offer
some monitoring, auditing and measuring tools and tips.

And then we look at the need for, and how to achieve, continuous
improvement, based on the results of your assurance programme and other
feedback and insights obtained.

The need for assurance

In *Man and Superman* (1903) by George Bernard Shaw, the character
Tanner says, 'The only man who behaves sensibly is my tailor; he takes
measurements anew every time he sees me, while all the rest go on with
their old measurements and expect me to fit them.' Measurement is
vital, but it won't tell you anything about where you are now and how
you are doing unless it is a true measurement of the current situation.

A truly committed board, and indeed the management team at the
country, region or business unit level that fully understands and

accepts accountability for compliance, should be asking the chief ethics and compliance officer: 'How do I know the compliance and ethics programme is effective?' In other words, if they really understand the importance of the programme and their accountabilities, they should be seeking assurance that the programme is designed, implemented and embedded in such a way that it is truly effective and the relevant compliance risk is being adequately managed.

This is true of any risk management programme: If we don't have appropriate assurance, how can we as the board or senior managers be confident about the organization's performance, reporting and system of internal controls in order to satisfy our governance, reporting and other obligations?

Monitoring, auditing, measuring and reporting are all key to assurance: they give you the means to know if your compliance and ethics programme is appropriately designed, implemented and followed, and working effectively. The weaknesses and gaps discovered via these means, via whistle-blowing – often categorized as a form of monitoring – and via other feedback such as comments and suggestions on what doesn't work, what is clunky or too bureaucratic, what is poorly understood, should then be addressed and remediated as part of continuous improvement.

In this way you keep tabs on what's really happening and ensure that in terms of both its design and implementation the programme remains fit for purpose, is followed and enforced, and is effective.

Monitoring and auditing

What's the difference?

Let's start by clarifying two important terms. Generally speaking, monitoring is about real-time surveillance and oversight of your programme, whereas auditing is a retrospective exercise.

This may be a useful distinction when considering what different monitoring and auditing options might be available to you. However, it is important to note from the outset that each needs the other and both must be present for effective compliance and ethics to happen.

Implementing a compliance and ethics assurance framework

In relation to risk management generally and how well an organization is doing in managing its risks, it is generally recognized that there are and should be different levels of assurance or 'lines of defence'.

In other words, how do the board, senior management and other stakeholders obtain 'assurance' that the relevant policies, procedures and controls are properly implemented, followed and effective, and the relevant risk is thus being adequately managed?

There are three lines of assurance:

1 first line or management assurance;

2 second line or functional assurance;

3 third line or independent assurance, which can be divided into internal and external independent assurance.

This approach can be used for designing and implementing a compliance and ethics programme assurance framework which pulls together the various possible approaches to monitoring and auditing. It also helps the organization to spot the gaps in its programme and indeed the aspects of its programme in relation to which it has less or perhaps no assurance.

Table 13.1 sets out the Subsea 7 compliance and ethics programme assurance framework using these three lines.

There are four main elements here:

1. Management assurance

Line management, with the help of the relevant business unit compliance officer(s), self-assesses its understanding of the requirements and expectations of the compliance and ethics programme and the state of implementation of its various elements.

The business unit compliance officer, if any, is ideally a member of the relevant management team and wears a management or 'first line' hat in this situation, even though they hopefully retain a significant

TABLE 13.1 Compliance and ethics programme assurance framework

First line (management) assurance	Second line (functional) assurance	Third line (independent) assurance	
		Internal	External
Management self-assessment dashboard	Compliance and other functional monitoring	Internal audit	Good corporation, ethic intelligence, BSI, DNV, bureau veritas, etc.
• Management understands and accepts accountability for compliance and ethics • Management obtains assurance as to effective implementation of the programme within its business unit, and provides such assurance to group • Business unit compliance officer wears two hats: helping with the above but also part of the management team self-assessing and reporting upwards	• Second line (or functional) assurance provides assurance in a number of ways • Each function owns and operates controls relevant to the risks that it manages • Functional risk owners/experts design and implement procedures and controls in accordance with best practice • Those procedures and controls are formally or informally monitored and continually improved	• Internal audit performs compliance audits • Compliance function is neither sufficiently independent nor (usually) appropriately skilled to do so and, in any case, operates as a business partner, not as an auditor • Internal audit builds on and leverages its skills in traditional audit areas (financial and supply chain management controls) • Internal audit staff are trained to increase their understanding of relevant compliance risks and the compliance and ethics programme	• A third party can be used if and when desired, to provide more (or more independent) assurance about the design and/or implementation of the compliance and ethics programme • The scope of such review and/or the standard against which the organization is evaluated can be agreed with the chosen provider • The desire or need for assurance as to the design of the programme depends on the expertise of the chief ethics and compliance officer

- A dashboard translates the compliance and ethics programme into two or three dozen clear, simple implementation tests
- These tests are quantitative where possible but often necessarily qualitative
- Management team self-assesses using a RAG (or ROYG, ie red/orange/yellow/green) rating, and a brief comment explaining any items that are not green
- Priorities for further implementation are identified from among non-green items
- This dashboard is provided each year-end as part of a compliance and ethics report

- Each compliance risk has a functional risk owner/expert, who identifies appropriate measures and analytics and provides regular reports on implementation of our anti-corruption programme
- The above monitoring activities should be mapped, understood and leveraged, and enhanced if judged appropriate

- Internal audit expands the scope of its audits and/or brings a greater compliance focus to its existing scope
- An internal audit protocol can be developed, covering those elements of the management self-assessment dashboard that are quantitative or objectively ascertainable
- Audits can be thematic (ie a specific compliance audit in a high-risk business unit) or can build specific compliance focus into a broader, conventional audit

- The desire or need for more (or more independent) assurance as to the implementation of the programme depends on the independence, expertise and limitations of the internal audit team and methodologies
- The desire or need for (more) independent assurance about design and implementation may be the board's; or it may be that of an external stakeholder (eg client or investor).
- In the case of external stakeholders, only external assurance will suffice to any significant extent. However, it is arguably only worth seeking if the relevant external stakeholders will give significant credit for it

degree of independence and are also the subject matter expert who should be able to help the management team understand its accountabilities and responsibilities.

Although the management team is, in a sense, marking its own homework, a well-designed self-assessment tool, the right culture, and the right incentives and disincentives can combine to make this a credible and useful tool. For example, if management knows that the board will take a dim view of a self-assessment that proves, through subsequent audit, to have been incorrect or overly optimistic, they are much less likely to exaggerate.

More fundamentally, if the culture is such that the management team truly understands and accepts its accountability for compliance and ethics, and that it is not a failure to admit that there are areas of the programme implementation that can be improved, or that their understanding of the expectations of them are imperfect, then they are more likely to embrace this self-assessment approach.

In a self-assessment dashboard, the management team of the relevant business unit assesses how well it is has understood and implemented each element of the anti-bribery/anti-corruption compliance and ethics programme by answering some key questions and grading or rating itself accordingly.

Where possible, the questions are quantitative and objective, but some are necessarily qualitative or subjective, and they are no less valuable for that. Each answer is rated red, amber, yellow or green:

- red = not implemented;
- orange = substantial improvement required;
- yellow = some improvement desirable;
- green = properly implemented.

The organization can obviously decide how many of these 'traffic light' colours to use and how to define them. Any that are not green require a brief explanation or clarification and an identified improvement action. In this example, a few questions are risk-rating rather than implementation-rating questions: if the answer is yes, the risk rating is red or orange and the next question needs to be answered.

2. Functional assurance

Second line assurance is provided by the Compliance and Ethics function and the functions that 'own' other key policies, procedures and controls that form part of the compliance and ethics programme and the organization's business management system more broadly, eg Finance, Supply Chain Management/Procurement, HR.

Such assurance is considered to be semi-independent, as these functions are also, in a sense, 'marking their own homework'. However, each function and functional head should be largely independent of line management and answerable to the board or senior executive of the organization. They are in a position to appraise more dispassionately, and in a more informed way, how well each business unit management team understands the requirements of the compliance and ethics programme and how well they are doing at implementing it within their business unit.

In our view, it is preferable if any regional and group compliance officers are still acting as business partners rather than policemen or auditors. As such, if they have significant concerns about the compliance and ethics programme within a business unit, it is much better if they can, as far as possible, discuss the matter with the business unit management team and any local compliance officer and attempt to remedy the shortcoming, rather than simply reporting their concerns to senior management or the board with or without any advance warning to the business unit management team. In a similar way, even an independent internal auditor should make sure the management team of the business unit being audited understand the draft audit findings and had an appropriate opportunity to dispute, correct or clarify matters.

Nonetheless, the board or senior executive of the organization can and should surely take more assurance from what the second-line tells them than they take from the largely non-independent first line assurance.

There are various ways in which the Compliance and Ethics function can obtain and provide assurance. Broadly speaking this can be thought of as 'compliance monitoring'.

Clearly, the chief ethics and compliance officer will wish to design some appropriate metrics and indicators, but a lot can also be learned through monitoring visits. Such visits are somewhat like audits. Some management teams respond better if they treat them as audits; some respond better if you can convince them that the main purpose of the visit is not to find fault or to catch them out but to help them to understand what is expected of them, what good looks like, and how to remediate any gaps or weaknesses that emerge during the discussion.

Such monitoring visits can and should include an ongoing discussion and assessment of the risks, the chief ethics and compliance officer's and management's understanding thereof, and how well the business is managing them. The fitness for purpose of the compliance and ethics programme is thus continually monitored and can be improved.

3. Internal independent assurance

It is important for the board of an organization to obtain an appropriate degree of independent, third line assurance about how well the organization is doing at managing compliance risks (just like any other risks) and the state of implementation and effectiveness of the programme that has been put in place to manage those risks.

A well-managed organization with sufficient resources and critical mass would normally have an Internal Audit function that is well placed to perform this role. Some Compliance functions have their own Compliance Audit function, the idea being that auditing compliance and ethics programmes is a specialist area requiring deeper knowledge of such programmes and the risks they are designed to manage than is normally found within a conventional Internal Audit team.

While it is true to say that internal auditors tend to be comfortable with conventional internal controls and processes, rather than some of the 'softer' aspects of an effective compliance and ethics programme, in our view it is better to utilize the Internal Audit function to conduct compliance audits. Many of the key procedures and controls that they will be asked to audit will be familiar to them. Indeed, they probably form part of their normal audit scope (supply chain management procedures, financial controls, delegation of authority limits, etc).

Some aspects of a compliance and ethics programme lend themselves to conventional internal audit approaches. For example:

> Has the business unit implemented the required financial control and supply chain management procedures, and does transaction sampling provide adequate evidence of such procedures and controls being followed?

Other aspects are necessarily – indeed desirably – more qualitative. For example:

> Does the business unit demonstrate top-level commitment to compliance and ethics, and does the culture of the business unit encourage whistle-blowing?

You could say that some aspects, such as whether all relevant staff have undertaken the annual compliance training, do not need internal audit to tell you whether they are in place and healthy. For example, the chief ethics and compliance officer may be able to consult the organization's learning management system dashboard to find out what percentage of the employees in a particular business unit completed their compliance training on time, or at all. However, including this in the self-assessment dashboard helps embed local management accountability for compliance training; and including it in the scope of internal audit introduces some healthy tension into the system.

Most experienced managers in large organizations are used to internal audit, and in particular to the process by which adverse findings are agreed and reported to the board, remedial actions and timelines are agreed, and internal audit conducts a follow-up audit to check that the agreed actions and timelines have been complied with.

An enlightened manager will also understand the value of such audits to him or her, not just to the board or others seeking assurance.

4. External independent assurance

We now turn to the 'fourth line of defence' or external independent assurance.

Even if your organization has a well-resourced and skilled Internal Audit function, its board is likely to need or wish to have some more independent assurance from time to time, in the same way as external auditors provide assurance about the organization's system of internal controls and the fairness and reasonableness of its financial reporting. What's more, external stakeholders are likely to give more credit to external assurance.

When it comes to compliance and ethics programmes, clients, partners, investors, regulators and other stakeholders are increasingly looking for independent validation of what the organization claims to be its effective compliance and ethics programme. An investor will want to know that the company in which it invests is willing, able and likely to minimize the risk of a damaging compliance breach occurring by having in place an effective compliance and ethics programme that has been designed and implemented in accordance with best practice.

Similarly, if an organization has identified sub-contractors, suppliers or other third parties it intends to engage with who can present a significant compliance risk, and if it believes that risk can and should be mitigated by those third parties having a compliance and ethics programme, it will wish to gain assurance about that programme, rather than simply relying on what the third party says about it.

Some organizations use their Internal Audit function or engage external auditors to audit their major suppliers' compliance and ethics programmes. Investors and other organizations may look for independent validation by some independent, credible, perhaps accredited firm, rather in the same way that many organizations are expected to have their safety or quality management system certified to an international standard by an accredited organization.

The chief compliance officer of an international oil company (IOC) said that if he relied on the fact that one of his company's major contractors had a compliance and ethics programme that was certified to the international anti-bribery standard (ISO 37001) by an accredited or independent firm, he would not feel comfortable defending this position to a prosecutor, if his company were investigated for a potential corruption offence by that contractor. However, that IOC is probably in a very small minority of companies that have the resources and expertise to audit a contractor's compliance and ethics programme to a greater degree, and to get more assurance about that programme, than it would get from the knowledge that the contractor's programme had been certified by an accredited firm to an international standard. In any case, the key point here is that the effective implementation of a supplier's compliance and ethics programme may only partially manage the compliance risk that the client is concerned about.

Fundamentally, an organization wants and needs to know that its partners, suppliers and subcontractors are trustworthy: are you able to trust them to do all that they reasonably can to prevent corruption (or other compliance and ethics breaches) occurring?

Certification of an organization's compliance and ethics programme by an accredited firm, or an audit by a client's Internal Audit function or an external audit firm, may tell you something about the design of the programme and the extent to which it can be seen that it is being implemented and followed; but it may tell you very little about how trustworthy the organization is, and whether it can really be relied upon to conduct its business honestly, ethically and with integrity. What it will tell you is something about its ability to manage the relevant compliance risk and, arguably, its commitment to doing so.

Quantitative versus qualitative assurance

To paraphrase JRR Tolkein's *The Hobbit*, if dragons live nearby, it's always best to factor them into your plans.

Auditing and assurance methodologies can struggle when they are not working with the merely quantitative, objective, documentary evidence-based measures and indicators. How do you obtain and provide assurance about something that cannot be written down? To give you a good example:

- An assurance provider can look at a policy, determine whether the policy is well written and covers the appropriate areas, look for evidence that people have been trained on that policy, and understand how the target audience for such training were selected.

- They can then look at a sample of transactions that should have been conducted in accordance with the policy, test whether they indeed were, and examine whether the transactions did in fact follow every detail of the policy without any departures or exceptions.

But while that sounds all well and good, it doesn't always work out. Let's say the external auditor wants to understand how the organization manages the compliance risks associated with lobbying:

- Typically, the auditor will ask the organization for a copy of its lobbying policy.

- The organization may say that it does not really conduct any lobbying.

- The auditor may reply that any interaction between representatives of the organization and a public official – including employees of a state-owned company, if they are customers – may amount to lobbying, if this interaction is intended to influence policymaking in any sense.

- The organization may say, yes, but we have clear policies and training about interactions with public officials and we would expect our people to follow that guidance when doing something that may or may not technically amount to lobbying.

- The auditor may say that lobbying is a high-risk activity that requires a specific policy (even though, when you consider what a good lobbying policy should include, it is neither long nor particularly specialist).

- The organization may say, we are trying to avoid having a policy for every situation. Not only is that not possible, but the financial services and pharmaceuticals industries have demonstrated that such an approach does not work – indeed they have tested that theory to destruction.

Unless you work in a Government/Regulatory Affairs function or have a specific lobbying role for an organization, you are very unlikely to say to yourself, 'What I am now about to do is lobbying. Let me look at my organization's lobbying policy and remind myself what I must and must not do.'

Of course, if an activity that an individual or organization habitually conducts on behalf of an organization is inherently complicated or has many pitfalls, a specific policy or even procedure may be warranted.

Let's ask a different question:

- How can an auditor assess whether an organization has 'top-level commitment'?

Typically, an auditor may ask to see copies of minutes of board meetings or other meetings at which compliance and ethics was 'on the agenda'. They may ask to see high-level communications from top management about the importance of compliance and ethics. If they are really advanced they may ask to see videos.

However, the point is, there are many extraordinary, important ways in which top-level commitment can be, or fail to be demonstrated, or in which its presence or absence can be sensed by an organization's employees, but cannot be evidenced to, or detected by an auditor who does not happen to be present at the time or does not spend long enough at the organization, absorbing its culture and that top-level commitment through osmosis.

The following is a real example that illustrates this:

VISIBLE COMMITMENT FROM THE TOP

'When I conduct compliance monitoring visits to high-risk countries and, sometimes, high-risk third parties, we often try to coordinate with the chief executive or another member of the senior executive team that is visiting at the same time. We will give a joint presentation and then the senior executive will lead a discussion and question and answer session.

'It is noticeable how such an approach can and does encourage attendees to engage in the subject and raise questions direct with the senior executive, such as, "Can we be really clear, do you really mean that we must resist the demand for a facilitation payment, even if the time delay and cost consequences for the organization may be significant and quite disproportionate to the amount of payment?"

'To see and hear the chief executive or another member of the executive team answer in the affirmative is far more impressive and compelling than to hear it from the guy in the grey suit from the Compliance function.'

An independent compliance monitor

The ultimate form of monitoring or independent assurance is when an independent monitor is appointed to an organization, either by the organization itself or by a prosecutor or regulator.

When facing an investigation and potential prosecution, conviction or settlement, many organizations identify one of their key priorities as avoiding the appointment of an independent monitor. In fact, such an appointment can be an opportunity as much as a challenge, although this does depend on who chooses the monitor, what type of person or firm is chosen, and what their agreed scope of work is.

Assuming the monitor has a very good understanding of compliance and ethics programmes and of your organization's sector or business, and that they or their appointer are not determined to implement *their* programme at *your* cost, a compliance monitor can give the chief ethics and compliance officer and/or those responsible for implementing a cultural change programme an armchair ride.

We liken it to the Spenlow and Jorkins characters in Charles Dickens' novel, *David Copperfield* (1850) – Jorkins is Spenlow's fictitious business partner, and whenever Spenlow wishes to decline a customer's request, he always says, 'I would be happy to agree, but my partner Mr Jorkins would not be happy.'

It is much easier for a CECO to implement a programme and deal with any pushback, and to earn the monitor's trust, by working with the monitor collaboratively and constructively, rather than with distrust and combat.

Measurement and reporting

Another element of monitoring, assurance and continual improvement is to introduce compliance metrics and reporting.

That which gets measured (or reported) gets done, and well-designed measures can provide leading or lagging indicators of risks, weaknesses, failures or other problems happening or brewing that the programme may or may not be adequately managing.

But there's a health warning here too! Measures can also lead to perverse focus on non-priority matters, or to a tick-box compliance culture, or indeed to process taking over from culture.

Are whistle-blowing reports a 'measure'?

We've already discussed how whistle-blowing allegations and other reports or suspicions of improper conduct in breach of an organization's code of conduct are one of the main – indeed few – sources of information about whether the programme is being followed, how effective it is and whether it needs to be improved.

Most obviously, it tells you whether there is sufficient awareness and understanding of the relevant policies and procedures. One of the conclusions at the end of many internal investigations is that, whether or not the original allegation has been substantiated in whole or in part, the employees involved and probably others would benefit from refreshed training.

Whistle-blowing statistics are not a true measure, but organizations, and especially their boards and Audit Committees or equivalent, often seize upon them as being one of the few, apparently tangible measures available to them. However, in reality, they are more of a window into the compliance and ethics programme, or what is known in pharmaceuticals as a 'surrogate'. They may or may not be an indicator of something, but you cannot necessarily tell what it is.

If you have a lot of whistle-blowing reports, this may well tell you that you have been successful in promoting the various whistle-blowing channels and making people feel confident enough to use them. It may also tell you that you have real underlying problems – a submerged iceberg only partially revealed by the visible peaks that are these whistle-blowing reports.

Measuring ethical targets

For an organization's compliance and ethics programme to be assessed as 'best practice' or 'world class', it will be expected to have found a way of including ethical targets and measures in employee performance management.

This makes perfect sense in theory but is difficult to achieve in practice. Organizations will continue to need to work out how to include ethics, integrity and/or compliance in their corporate performance objectives, in the same way as they may already do for safety and may well be attempting to do for other values (such as teamwork, innovation etc.). They also need to work out how to create a sensible system of SMART (specific, measurable, attainable, relevant and timely) individual performance objectives around ethics and integrity. Such objectives should be defined proactively and measured at the end of the year against objective criteria. But how do you define something that is meaningful, measurable and not trite? Well, here are some examples:

- I agree to treat everybody with respect and not to shout at my team members.

- I agree not to offer or accept any bribes or excessive gifts or hospitality.

- I will record all potential conflicts of interest and applicable gifts and hospitality on the relevant online registers.

- I will refuse to bid for work if I am concerned that the tender process may have been subverted by corruption or anti-competitive behaviour.

- I will ensure that no facilitation payments are made, even if this results in costly delays for the company.

Those last two bullets provide a very useful illustration of how meaningful ethics objectives and incentives should do precisely what you say, ie incentivize and reward the right behaviours.

Suppose, for example, that an employee has refused a £100 facilitation payment demand at the cost of tens of thousands of pounds and a delay of several weeks when the business could not operate. As a direct result of standing up for what is right, the employee has failed to deliver the targeted results. So, when going through the performance appraisal at the end of the year, will the organization's culture and systems reward or penalize?

This tells us how important it is for the organization to be very clear that it will not pursue commercial gain at the expense of its ethical standpoint, or the law. Rewarding such behaviour is one way to make that position clear. Penalizing it would tell everyone a very different story.

The road to continuous improvement

All the activities we've looked at in this chapter are about providing insight, information and controls that allow an organization to assess the effective implementation of its compliance and ethics programme. But as we said at the start of this chapter, they are also key to achieving continuous improvement of that programme.

What's missing is a way to put these things together so you have a working continuous improvement process.

Making lessons count

How do you actually benefit from the insights and information you get? How can you make sure that any lessons learned go back into the programme to improve it, so it continues to become ever more effective? That's the purpose of continuous improvement.

Here we outline the basic principles of continuous improvement. However, always bear in mind that the objective is to create a living culture of compliance and ethics that is endorsed and supported by your people. If the lessons you learn instead are all about piling more and more policies and rules on the organization so it becomes ever more bureaucratic and stifling, the most likely outcome is that you will achieve the opposite of your goal.

Making sure the air stays fresh

Continuous improvement can mean continuously layering in more and more complexity and stifling everyone. That can and does have bad outcomes. Think which is worse – having people ignore policies that are there, or not having a policy at all. Probably the former, as it creates a general culture of 'rule breaking tolerance' which then becomes an issue when the organization needs to enforce a policy.

To counter this, regular reviews should be carried out to see if policies and procedures need updating, simplifying, re-promoting – or just deleting. This includes reviewing company policies to understand how they interact with each other, whether they connect, overlap or leave gaps, and whether they can be improved in terms of relevance of application and ease of understanding and use.

It is easy to create policies, difficult to delete them. Regular spring cleaning should be done to reorganize them, tidy them up or throw them away. As well as ensuring that you aren't piling on useless or positively counter-productive bureaucracy, this also goes a long way to ensuring that each policy or aspect of the programme is seen as relevant and useful in the minds of budget holders and the organization at large.

How much is enough?

The question 'How much is enough?' is frequently asked, but all too often by people who want to know, 'When developing our defensible programme, what minimum "adequate procedures" can we get away with in the eyes of prosecutors and regulators?'

How much is enough depends on what risks you face and whether your programme is appropriate and adequate to mitigate those risks to a reasonable degree; and how well you have embedded it. It is no good saying that you looked up guidance on this and it said you only need this much for the size of your company and the resources you have.

So the question only becomes a good question if, instead, you are asking what would be effective in truly implementing and embedding the programme. It's about recognizing that it's an ongoing process, that things can always improve, and that it is fundamentally about getting your organization's values, culture and incentives right and living, rather than how many policies and procedures you need. It's about how effective and relevant your risk assessment is, not how many suppliers you have screened.

By the same token, it is not reasonable, nor is an organization expected, to deploy unlimited time, effort and resources. If you're a big organization and your question is, 'How many compliance officers is enough?', then the answer is not 'X per 1,000 employees'. Rather, you should consider how to embed compliance as a management accountability and responsibility and how most efficiently and effectively to deploy compliance officers to help managers understand and fulfil that accountability and responsibility.

Of course, if you're an SME then 'numbers of compliance officers' doesn't apply. But exactly the same focus on making compliance a key part of what managers do and are accountable for certainly does.

Across the minefield: compliance and ethics meets real life

Fair treatment of bidders

A company (ABC Co) is coming to the end of a four-year supply agreement, under which it has purchased the facilities management services it requires at its various offices. It invites the incumbent supplier and four others to tender for a new four-year contract. All five suppliers submit bids.

ABC Co did not provide much detail about the tender process that it would follow. However, it was at least implied that any bidder spending time and money submitting a bid would be properly considered and stood a fair chance of winning if its bid was the lowest or best.

As is sometimes the case, the incumbent supplier had an inbuilt advantage, as ABC Co would incur significant additional costs and inconvenience if it changed provider. However, this fact was not made clear to the other bidders.

One of the bidders (XYZ Co) is about to contact ABC Co to enquire why it has heard nothing about the tender process or progress, when it discovers that the incumbent supplier is in possession of ABC Co's bid tab, showing all bidders' pricing and other confidential and commercially sensitive information.

XYZ Co contacts ABC Co's chief ethics and compliance officer and asks: 'Can this really be consistent with the commitment in ABC Co's code of conduct for suppliers to comply with the law, to act honestly and with integrity at all times, and to treat its suppliers fairly and with respect?'

Is this how ABC Co would expect to be treated by its clients?

This is quite a common scenario. Did ABC Co merely run the tender process to comply with its own procedures and to 'keep the incumbent supplier honest'? Did ABC Co provide details of the other bidders' prices to the incumbent supplier, to ensure the latter's bid was the cheapest?

A company that is not required to conduct its tenders in accordance with public procurement laws may, in principle, be able to define and follow any process it chooses, or indeed no process at all, when inviting tenders and awarding contracts to suppliers. Likewise, a bidder may feel at liberty to ask the company to tell it what price it needs to match or beat to win the award.

However, when you think about it, when you invite someone to bid for work, you are requesting that they spend time, effort and money putting their best foot forward, and they very likely do so in good faith and in reliance upon your express or implied representation that they will win the work if their bid is the lowest or best; that you will run a reasonably fair and orderly process; and that, by the way, you will not disclose their competitive or other confidential information to their competitors.

If you breach this representation, there is a strong case for saying you have committed a fraud against the losing bidders.

And if you are a company that has published an express commitment to do business honestly and with integrity, and to treat suppliers and others fairly and with respect, how do you square that statement with this conduct? And how do you expect to earn people's trust and enhance your good reputation?

'It's up to you'

Your manager is bullying one of your colleagues. She's a really popular manager, has just received a company award, and your colleague has pleaded that you don't say anything.
Just do nothing?

You've lost a memory stick. You placed some confidential information on it so you could work at home, though you knew you shouldn't have done that. You're going to be in real trouble if you report it – and you know the stick was encrypted.
Just keep quiet?

At an event you meet a local politician. They have started a wonderful charity that supports the local community in which your company is working. The politician asks if we'd like to give a contribution.
How would you reply?

He's been such a great manager. But now he's different. Shouting, impatient, aggressive. This week he actually made someone cry. You've discussed it with some colleague, and they think it's best to do nothing.

Do you agree?

14

Implementation

The Compliance and Ethics function – and everyone else

In this chapter we look at what will make the implementation and structure of compliance effective in an organization: how you can put the right structure into place, the position and role of the Compliance and Ethics function, centralized versus decentralized policies and procedures, the role of management – and the role of everyone else. We also look briefly at implementation in a joint venture or other company not wholly owned or controlled by your organization.

Hammers and nails

THE SIEMENS SCANDAL

In 2006 a massive corruption scandal erupted involving the electrical engineering giant, Siemens. As a result, the company suffered huge fines, penalties and reputational damage for breach of anti-corruption laws. Yet, at the time of the scandal, it was alleged by some people that 700 compliance officers were in position across the company.

As the American psychologist, Abraham Maslow, famously pointed out, 'If the only tool you have is a hammer, you tend to see every problem as a nail.'[1] Many organizations still believe that the only way to ensure compliance is to have a large, powerful, independent Compliance function operating as policemen and auditors. A central purpose of this book is to make it clear that the solution lies in a very different approach.

Just having policies and procedures, no matter how nailed down they are, doesn't result in compliance. Nor does counting the number of hammers. What matters is that your Compliance and Ethics function structure, headcount and expertise reflect your organization and are suited to the effective implementation of the programme, and that the code of conduct and the culture of the organization create a common purpose and culture of compliance and ethics every day and for the long term. Moreover, for your programme to be effectively implemented and embedded, accountability, responsibility and ownership also need to radiate outwards and reach everyone.

The position of the Compliance and Ethics function in the organization

Let's first consider structure from the perspective of the head of the Compliance and Ethics function – usually the chief ethics and compliance officer, to use our preferred terminology, regardless of the actual title used or whether the organization only has one full-time or even part-time person performing that role.

Ideally this person should:

- be as senior as possible in order to have sufficient authority and independence;
- have as direct a line as possible to the senior leadership;
- ideally be a member of the senior management team or, if not, report directly to someone who is.

In our view, if seniority, authority, independence and direct access are not all present, there is something both structurally and attitudinally wrong with compliance in the organization – and chances are everything that then follows is unlikely to succeed.

The multifaceted skills, experience and characteristics of a good chief ethics and compliance officer are also vital (something we examine in more detail when we look at the model chief ethics and compliance officer). But from the point of view of top-level commitment, the key point is that, if someone too junior and ineffectual is appointed, they will not be able to do an effective job, and senior management will have failed to fulfil a key part of the commitment expected of them.

Indeed, in some cases, one wonders if senior management of an organization have chosen someone quite junior and ineffectual *in order to* ensure that compliance does not get too powerful and does not interfere too much with the organization's work and, especially, its revenue and profitability.

Structuring the Compliance and Ethics function

Implementation is not just about the chief ethics and compliance officer and Compliance and Ethics function, as previous chapters have shown.

But it does require a chief ethics and compliance officer/Compliance and Ethics function to take responsibility to become a subject matter expert, learn about compliance and ethics programme requirements, and provide education and guidance thereon; effect the risk assessment and the design of the programme, and drive implementation (with top-level support).

Does the chief ethics and compliance officer have to be a lawyer?

No, and nor does the Compliance and Ethics function have to be staffed with lawyers.

Later in this chapter we will look at the qualities, character, skills and experience that the ideal chief ethics and compliance officer would embody, and we will see that such features are not likely to exist in one person. A lawyer is likely to embody more of them than the average professional, but the possible or likely gaps in a lawyer's make-up could be in some of the most important areas.

Yes, the person designing and implementing a compliance and ethics programme needs to understand the relevant laws or regulations, assess the risks, draft appropriate policies and procedures, provide training and be strong at verbal communication, lead or participate in investigations, and do certain other things that the typical lawyer (if there is such a thing) should be reasonably proficient at. It also helps that a qualified lawyer will usually have an overriding duty to the court to uphold the law, and a professional duty to behave honestly and with integrity.

However, the chief ethics and compliance officer also needs to:

- understand ethical and reputational risks and stakeholder expectations that go beyond and are different from legal and regulatory requirements and risks;
- be conversant in internal controls, monitoring and auditing;
- be a specialist trainer and educator;
- an organizational and cultural change manager;
- have a good understanding of the business and credibility with Sales and Operational functions and leaders.

In the examples that follow, we examine how organizations of different size and resources may design and structure the chief ethics and compliance officer role and/or the Compliance and Ethics function:

- We imagine a lawyer and a Legal function to illustrate the different options and considerations, and this approach is very common. But bear in mind that a non-lawyer may make an equally good or much better chief ethics and compliance officer.
- Also, until the Compliance and Ethics function becomes a standalone concern, other functions such as HR, Finance or Audit, and Risk, Health and Safety, or a combination of these, could conceivably be used instead of the Legal function. After all, they already perform aspects of a Compliance and Ethics function.

Using someone other than a lawyer

Let's take an example. If an organization's biggest compliance risks, or those that it is looking to address first, relate to sales and marketing practices, it may very well be that a former sales director would be the best person to create the new role and function and take the first steps (risk assessment, policy writing, training) to design and implement a compliance and ethics programme. That person's understanding of the relevant sales and marketing practices, and his or her credibility among their target audience, could trump other considerations or preconceptions about a compliance officer's ideal profile.

The ideal sales person turned compliance officer will know every trick in the book, so if they are creating a policy or control, or investigating an alleged breach, they will be able to say: 'This is how I would do it, and I know damned well that's how they would do it, so I reckon I know how to prevent it or where to look for the breach.'

As the compliance and ethics programme and function grow, they may continue to be led by that person, or they may morph into a broader compliance programme and function under the leadership of a more 'classical' compliance professional. But in some cases, that original man or woman may still be the best or uniquely equipped person in the organization to handle the role.

Indeed, there is a lot to be said for this approach of using a 'poacher turned gamekeeper' to drive a new compliance initiative, despite scepticism about sales and marketing people being involved in compliance, and mutterings about foxes and hencoops.

In most cases, however, the Legal function, even if it comprises only one lawyer in a small organization with limited resources, probably/ typically has the broadest remit and reach and is thus best placed to perform the role. For instance, the Finance function is responsible for a comprehensive set of financial controls, including policies, procedures and controls that are relevant to managing many compliance risks, and it will likely be conversant with auditing and reporting. But it will not typically have reach into, responsibility for, or access to other areas of the business and how it operates in practice.

If an organization has the scale and resources to build a large Compliance and Ethics function, it may have the luxury of staffing it with people from different functions and with very varied, complementary experience and skillsets – a policy writer, a trainer, a systems expert, a respected former salesperson with exceptional credibility, a fraud investigator, a risk manager, an auditor, a litigator, etc. This is especially true if the Compliance and Ethics function is centralized, whereas a decentralized function will still tend to need a generalist in each location – who in the majority of cases will probably be a lawyer. We will return to this subject of centralized versus decentralized, and the pros and cons of each approach, but for some organizations the choice may be dictated by how far spread its offices and operations are.

But wait a minute: some people have told me that Compliance and Legal should be separate

Good point. We have talked about whether the typical lawyer is likely to have the best skillset to perform the chief ethics and compliance officer role, especially in a small organization or in the early days of a compliance and ethics programme, when the role may be part-time. But there are other factors to consider, chiefly regarding independence.

Many experts, especially in the United States, say that the Compliance function should not report into the Legal function but should report into the chief executive or an independent Board Committee or committee chair.

Even if the chief ethics and compliance officer is a lawyer, they and their function do not need to report into the Legal function, but they will effectively do so if they are also performing a legal role (such as a general counsel or regional legal director). The goal is to ensure the Compliance and Ethics function has direct, unfettered access to the governing authority of the organization, and that it is as independent as possible. A good General Counsel and Legal function should act as the 'conscience of the company', as well as legal risk managers and wise counsellors. Properly qualified and licensed in-house lawyers should (depending on jurisdiction) have an overriding duty to the courts and to their professional body, which in theory should mean they act ethically and in compliance with the law.

The above factors should ensure that a CECO's independence is not compromised by reporting into Legal, in most cases. In our experience, the right general counsel and Legal function can make a good home for compliance most of the time, especially if the Legal function is well regarded by the senior executive and the organization as a whole.

But issues can arise if and when the general counsel's responsibility to protect the company's backside conflicts with the chief ethics and compliance officer's desire to get to the truth. This conflict can normally be managed, provided the CECO has that direct access to, and preferably an independent reporting line to, the chief executive, an Executive Ethics Committee and/or, preferably, to an independent non-executive director or Board Committee.

Two examples of conflicts that can occur

- The CECO believes people working for the company may have committed a serious offence for which the company could have some exposure, and that the company should investigate thoroughly and get to the bottom of it. The general counsel points out that there is currently no evidence, and if the company digs too much it could find out something it would prefer not to know and might have to disclose.

- The general counsel maintains that the directors and officers of the company have a duty to shareholders to maximize returns whilst complying with the law, and that they would be in breach of that duty if they complied with some higher, ethical standard that the CECO is advocating (this is the same example we used in Chapter 1).

The above examples are very significant, but most are smaller and subtler, often derived from one or more of the following truisms identified by a very old friend of Andrew's, Keith Korenchuk:

- Legal tend to like to control the flow of information; Compliance often like to disseminate.
- Legal look to defend conduct; Compliance look for root cause and how to improve.
- Regulators view Legal as advocates and Compliance as having an 'independent' responsibly to 'do the right thing'. To put it another way, lawyers take the facts and present them in the light most favourable to the organization; Compliance focus less defensively and tries to take them as they are, saying: 'OK, if that happened, what do we do with that in terms of process or reaction.'
- Practically, the role of lawyers is episodic, whereas the Compliance and Ethics role is systematic. That sets up differing expectations and priorities as well as work styles.

So, the potential for conflicts is real, even if they may occur relatively rarely. In practice, the CECO's view will in any case only prevail if the CEO can be persuaded of it, and the reporting line is usually not the main barrier to this. And, in any case, most organizations below a certain size do not have the resources for a standalone Compliance and Ethics function reporting into the CEO.

The other main factor to consider about Compliance sitting under and reporting into the Legal function, or into any function or person other than the CEO, is this: ultimately, there is a limit to what the chief compliance and ethics officer can achieve, if their authority and mandate do not flow directly from the CEO. The role is a classic example of an 'influence without authority role', and as we have said elsewhere, the CECO's ability to influence ultimately relies upon people believing that they speak with the CEO's voice and are carrying out the CEO's wishes. A CECO can achieve a great deal reporting into Legal, but eventually they and their function will reach a glass ceiling if they do not become one of the CEO's direct reports.

Using 'compliance and ethics champions'

We also talk about 'compliance and ethics champions' in the examples below, but we are not necessarily advocating their use.

The MD of an organization, or of a business unit that forms part of it, is the compliance and ethics champion, and if the role of championing compliance and ethics is given to someone else – perhaps to someone who does not even have the gravitas and skills to be a chief ethics and compliance officer – that risks undermining the importance of the programme and the message. It calls to mind the story about the vessel whose safety performance deteriorated when the management team, which had been jointly responsible for safety, appointed a safety manager!

On the other hand, depending how large the organization is, how limited its resources, and how geographically dispersed its people and operations, compliance and ethics champions may be the only way to put at least some hands-on responsibility for compliance and ethics in the hands of someone locally. Everyone is responsible for compliance, including (most importantly) the leader, but someone needs time to get things implemented, provide training and guidance, and respond to questions and concerns.

That means:

- local compliance officers, if the organization can afford to hire someone or spare at least part of an existing functional manager's capacity;

- or part-time compliance and ethics champions, if it cannot.

And, of course, a 'poacher turned gamekeeper' can make an excellent compliance and ethics champion, so if you can persuade a sales and marketing person to help champion the cause, why wouldn't you?

Champions are an optional help, but officers are what you should have, even if part-time. So, in the examples that follow, we assume the chief ethics and compliance officer is likely to be a lawyer, and that the Compliance and Ethics function may sit under Legal and be staffed with lawyers.

Although this might be quite realistic for many organizations, it is intended to be illustrative, not prescriptive, and it should be read in the context of what we say above, especially for:

- small and medium-sized organizations that may be very resource-constrained, or in which the role and status of the in-house lawyer may not be a given;

- very large organizations, which may have the luxury of creating a standalone function led by a chief ethics and compliance officer who could have no legal background at all. (We have known CECOs who are or were professional risk managers, auditors, people with a finance background, HSEQ specialists, even IT specialists.)

As in many places throughout the book, we have also assumed that the organization is a company with a board of directors and, especially if the company is listed on a stock exchange, Board Committees and a separate executive management team. Again, this structure is illustrative, and private or family-owned or small or medium-sized companies or organizations with a very different structure should adapt this guidance to their equivalent ownership, governance and management structures.

Identifying 'compliance and ethics champions'

Where there are separate divisions, business units, or country or site operations, the organization may wish to identify people who are as senior as possible within those operations whose job title, skills and personality make them a good fit to become local 'compliance and ethics champions' – helping to promote an understanding of, and adherence to the compliance and ethics programme and obligations of the organization.

Compliance champions will have a full-time role independently from their additional compliance responsibilities, such as finance, HR, procurement or perhaps even sales and marketing. In addition to their functional or managerial reporting lines, they will have a separate (dotted) reporting line into the compliance and ethics officer.

Separate from their day-to-day responsibilities, local compliance and ethics champions will engage directly with other local management and stakeholders (such as employees, suppliers, customers, partners etc.) on matters concerning the promotion of, and adherence to the compliance and ethics programme.

Examples of how compliance and ethics might be structured

Regulators recognize that organizations will adopt different structures for their 'Compliance function', and recognize this even in its simplest form, so long as it has functional responsibility for the compliance programme.

Accordingly, depending on the size, business model and risk profile of the organization, any one of the following structures is potentially able to fulfil the necessary responsibilities of a chief ethics and compliance officer or Compliance function and, more broadly, deliver the effective compliance and ethics programme required by applicable law and best practice.

Example 1: The simplest, 'non-specialist Compliance and Ethics function'

Even if the organization does not have the resources, size or risks to justify a full-time legal counsel, less still a compliance officer, someone must have the accountability and responsibility for understanding and assessing the risks and designing and implementing an appropriate programme.

Typically, one of the senior officers or managers will be designated as responsible for developing and implementing a fit-for-purpose compliance and ethics programme. For compliance and ethics subject-matter expertise, this person will lean on any in-house legal advisors and risk managers, outside counsel or other outside help.

In practice, who the compliance officer or function reports to will depend on a number of factors, including the size, structure and maturity of the organization, the sector in which it operates, whether it is local, domestic or international and the compliance and ethics risks it faces

It is worth noting that where the organization is a small or medium-sized enterprise, the most senior officers are likely to be involved in almost every decision of any materiality. As such, they will be responsible and liable in the eyes of the law and the public/media for any non-compliant or unethical event. If they are directors, they will likely have responsibilities under statute.

Example 2: Legal counsel/function with compliance responsibilities

Often a natural development of Example 1, here the organization is of a size, maturity and/or risk profile to justify employing one or two legal counsel in-house. Where this is the case, it will make sense to give the responsibility for the compliance and ethics programme to the Legal function.

In small to medium-sized organizations, the legal counsel may not have an executive position, instead reporting into one of the executive officers, such as the head of Finance or Risk.

While this executive may not have day-to-day responsibility for compliance and ethics (having delegated such responsibility to the legal counsel), from the perspective of the management and interested parties externally, this executive officer will be the point of contact and the person they will engage with at first instance for compliance-related discussions.

As with Example 1, the compliance officer will be resource-constrained and will rely on external expertise and, possibly, compliance and ethics champions within the business units.

Example 3: General counsel either alone or with support assuming compliance responsibility

In this situation, the organization is of sufficient size, maturity or risk profile to justify employing a senior lawyer with enough experience and gravitas to be general counsel and who is part of the executive management.

In such situations, the general counsel will typically perform the role of chief ethics and compliance officer, and the Legal function will also be the Compliance and Ethics function.

The general counsel will almost certainly have one or more lawyers working for them. Such lawyer(s) will also assume compliance responsibilities. In either case, a network of 'compliance and ethics champions' may also be desirable, to ensure the programme is embedded within the organization and there is a means of gathering feedback. Indeed, in some organizations compliance and ethics may struggle to take root without such a network.

Examples 4 and 5: Subject-matter expert chief ethics and compliance officer and dedicated Compliance and Ethics function

The next two examples illustrate a situation where the organization has taken the step to invest in a compliance and ethics subject matter expert dedicated to the development, implementation, promotion, monitoring, enforcement and continuous improvement of the compliance and ethics programme.

EXAMPLE 4

The chief ethics and compliance officer reports into the general counsel and relies on the Legal function for compliance officers. The CECO may also create a network of 'compliance and ethics champions' where there is inadequate legal cover and no other suitable managers to act as compliance officers.

The CECO should ideally, but may not, have a reporting line into the chief executive to facilitate direct communication between them, but they should have a clear and unencumbered reporting line to the chair of the Audit or Compliance Committee of the board to create a degree of independence from immediate line management control and influence.

EXAMPLE 5

The chief ethics and compliance officer is a member of the executive and has a dedicated, fully resourced Compliance and Ethics function of experts with managerial, operational and compliance-risk-specific subject matter expertise (for example, anti-bribery/anti-corruption, export controls, anti-money-laundering or data privacy).

Such structures are typical in highly regulated sectors such as the financial, insurance, pharmaceutical and telecoms sectors. However, they may also be seen in very large organizations in other sectors (including oil and gas, extractives, defence and possibly construction) with a global footprint that have exposure to countries and/or operational strategies with a significant risk profile.

The CECO will have a reporting line into the chief executive and a clear and unencumbered reporting line to the chair of the Audit or Compliance Committee of the board.

Centralized versus decentralized Compliance and Ethics function

How and where the resources are deployed will be influenced by the size, shape, risk profile and culture of the organization.

Some organizations choose to have a centralized function in which the compliance officers have a solid reporting line directly or indirectly to the chief ethics and compliance officer. Some choose to have a decentralized function in which most of the compliance officers have a 'solid' reporting line to a member of the senior management team of a region, country, business unit or function (preferably to the managing director or equivalent), while retaining an independent, 'dotted' reporting line directly or indirectly to the CECO.

We believe the decentralized approach is the better option. It allows the function to spread across the organization rather than sitting at a central fixed point. After all, compliance is a management responsibility and a compliance and ethics programme will not be effective if it simply relies on lots of independent, centrally located compliance officers to police it, who do not share the goals and challenges of the business unit or division. Moreover, the independence of compliance officers, even if they do not have a solid reporting line to the chief ethics and compliance officer, can be assured by different means, not least through their professional independence.

Conversely, if the managing director or equivalent of a particular part of the business is unethical or otherwise determined to break the law or breach policies, the problem will not be solved by having an independent police or audit function.

Centralized versus decentralized compliance and ethics programme

Compliance implementation is also about the structure of the programme:

* whether the policies and procedures can or should be centralized or decentralized;
* whether the organization has one business management system or, instead, a set of minimum expectations that apply across the group but can be implemented locally with a degree of flexibility;
* or a combination of both approaches.

In principle, at the very least there should be one code of conduct, and preferably there should be one organization-wide set of policies and procedures, including not only the financial control framework and procurement process, but also one sales and marketing policy, one anti-bribery policy, one sanctions screening procedure, etc. But this may not be possible in view of the geographic and organizational structure that the new chief ethics and compliance officer inherits.

Effective and efficient implementation of a compliance and ethics programme requires integration of compliance policies, procedures and controls into the existing policy, procedure and control framework as far as possible, rather than adding on bureaucracy and duplication. However, many organizations are federated, and more still will have geographic or cultural silos where one can find a determination to do things 'our way'. The organization may actually, and by design, be a conglomerate, which cannot or does not wish to adopt many – or any – centralized policies and controls, or even common values and a single code of conduct.

Some leaders of large organizations are convinced that creativity will be stifled, accountability will not be accepted and take root at the right level, and performance will not be adequately incentivized, if the organization is too centralized.

All of these things may or may not be true, or relevant to a particular organization, but the designer of a compliance and ethics programme will need to balance these considerations against the benefits of one, clear centralized set of policies, procedures and controls.

One centralized set of policies, procedures and controls is ideal from the purist's perspective and from the selfish perspective of the chief ethics and compliance officer and other Compliance function heads. Among other things, it can:

- be made clearer, simpler and less open to misinterpretation;
- benefit from one message and one 'brand';
- avoid all the little – often unintentional – differences that gradually undermine the effectiveness of the programme (for example, one business unit referring to 'whistle-blowing' when the organization as a whole has decided the term 'speak up' is more likely to encourage people to come forward; another business unit having an opaque FCPA compliance policy, when the organization as a whole prefers a more inspiring, less legalistic, more values- and principles-based ethics and anti-corruption policy, etc);
- be easier to measure, monitor, audit and report on.

Implementing a compliance programme in JVs, fiercely autonomous subsidiaries and conglomerates

We are adding some remarks on this here, as it is an important and often problematic area. However, it should be noted that the subject can often be a complex one, and this section is in no way meant to be comprehensive.

Many of the issues discussed in this chapter – about how to structure a Compliance and Ethics function, centralized versus decentralized policy and procedure frameworks, and compliance and ethics champions – are often accentuated when an organization or its chief ethics and compliance officer are faced with structuring a Compliance and Ethics function and/or implementing a compliance and ethics programme in:

- a wholly- or majority-owned subsidiary, or a standalone division or other business unit that likes to plough its own furrow, keep head office at arm's length and remain fiercely independent. We have all seen them...;
- a conglomerate of wholly-owned but deliberately autonomous companies, with partly or wholly different internal control frameworks, branding, values and thus, quite possibly, even a separate code of conduct;
- a joint venture company (with at least one other significant shareholder).

Joint ventures present a familiar issue often discussed by practitioners and mentioned in the International Anti-Bribery Standard (ISO 37001). Depending on a range of factors, including the extent of ownership or control exercised over a JV company, an organization may well be legally or reputationally liable for non-compliance by that JV company. Yet it may not have sufficient influence to require the JV company to implement a compliance and ethics programme, or over the design of any such programme.

In all three cases outlined above, it is likely that:

- the relevant company will not participate in one centralized system of policies, procedures and controls that the organization and, potentially, its other subsidiaries and associated companies use;
- the organization's chief ethics and compliance officer will have little or no authority, and will struggle to have enough influence, to persuade the relevant company to implement a compliance and ethics programme identical to, or acceptably consistent with, the organization's programme, or at all; and
- in terms of functional structure, any compliance officer or even compliance champion within the relevant company may not be

part of, or in any practical sense answerable to, the organization's chief ethics and compliance officer or Compliance and Ethics function.

Yet the organization must ensure a fully appropriate compliance and ethics programme is being implemented in each of those entities, so that it can:

- provide assurance that the relevant business unit, subsidiary or joint venture company is committed to – and has a reasonable chance of preventing – non-compliance; and
- prevent its own compliance and ethics programme from being deemed ineffective by prosecutors and other stakeholders.

Deploying the right skills and resources

In an ideal world, and with relatively unconstrained budgets, the chief ethics and compliance officer charged with designing and implementing a new or completely refreshed compliance and ethics programme needs to hire staff or pay for external providers with the following skills and to be responsible for the following areas:

- Subject matter expertise. If you're developing an anti-bribery programme or a sanctions and export control programme, you need to hire people or pay for service providers who have expertise in those risk areas.
- Policy development. The appropriate expertise may be found, at least in part, in the previous bullet, but the subject matter expert is not necessarily expert at writing clear, engaging and effective policies.
- Training and education, whether in person or by e-learning, which may or may not require external providers or a learning management system and the capability to develop and deliver appropriate content.
- IT systems, as so much of a compliance and ethics programme can and should be systematized and leverage existing systems and information.

- Investigations skills and procedures – suspicions and allegations of non-compliant conduct, whether reported via whistle-blowing or reported or detected via another channel need to be investigated to ascertain whether the non-compliant conduct took place, and to find control failures and control weaknesses.

The (very) ideal model of a chief ethics and compliance officer

I'm very good at integral and differential calculus
I know the scientific names of beings animalculous
In short, in matters vegetable, animal and mineral
I am the very model of a modern Major-General.
GILBERT AND SULLIVAN, THE PIRATES OF PENZANCE

If you're not a chief ethics and compliance officer or planning to become one, this may look like one section you can definitely skip. But if you think you can leave compliance and ethics to the chief ethics and compliance officer, who will go riding like the Lone Ranger over the compliant hills and ethical plains, you've been watching too many movies.

Everyone has a role in helping compliance and ethics to make a real difference to their culture and their bottom line. Spending just a bit of time here seeing things from the peculiar perspective of the CECO will help you to understand what your role is.

Want to be a chief ethics and compliance officer?

Then here's your job description.
You are required to be:

A salesperson. With operational experience and understanding. And credibility. A talker. A trainer. A policy writer. A process engineer. An investigator. A litigator. A risk manager. A psychologist. A motivator. An influencer without authority. Part of the local management team, sharing their goals and incentives. Independent. Ethical. A lawyer (but not too legalistic). Likeable, but willing to be unpopular. A business partner. A police officer (but also not a police officer). An auditor. A negotiator. An idealist, but also a pragmatist. With a streak of evangelism – but not too much. Who realizes that nobody can be fully whiter than white. Who can relate to others – a chameleon. With strong personal integrity and values.

(Still want the job?)

A significant percentage of chief ethics and compliance officers are lawyers but, as can be seen from the above list, you will not find all the ideal skills and personal qualities in one person, and lawyers are not necessarily the people who have most of the above skills.

If you have the resources, structure and good fortune to have a centralized Compliance and Ethics function with two or more full-time compliance officers, then you can seek to cover all of the above qualities by combining the different skills and experience of different people from different roles.

Whether or not a CECO happens to be a lawyer, the fact is that they have to be multi-skilled. A whole range of approaches and tactics may also help, and below we take a brief look at what three random examples of approaches that often get overlooked but which might benefit every compliance and ethics officer.

Reaching out, and building a network

Compliance and ethics are fundamentally social – they are the common wealth shared by a community of people who work together. And yet the Compliance and Ethics function is all too often placed down an isolated cul de sac seldom visited by anyone else because, for most people, it is off the business map.

This is very largely the result of an organizational mind-set, and it can and does change wherever people begin to understand the business relevance of effective compliance and ethics. However, the chief ethics and compliance officer often has a great deal of 'socialising' work to do to begin getting everyone to see that relevance.

This is very largely about building trust with everyone you interact with.

- For effective implementation, the Compliance and Ethics function needs to reach out and speak to the business functions and explain what they do, how they do it and why it's important. But just as importantly the Compliance and Ethics function needs to ask what the business functions do, how they do it and why it's important.

- Listening – being curious, inquisitive and interested – generates mutual respect and understanding, which is a vital currency to build the support-and-influence network that effective compliance needs across all the functions and departments.

- Engagement outside of formal compliance and ethics communications results in a much more open discussion. It helps you and the business get to know each other, creating confidence and trust, which will be vital when each requires the support of the other.

- Embedding a culture of compliance and ethics throughout the organization relies on a network of supporters and influencers willing to repeat and reinforce the messages and behaviours. The same network is needed to give direct, honest and constructive feedback: what is working, what is not; potential issues; actual issues. While formal lines of communication exist, the informal ones often provide the most timely and valuable information.

Making what you do relevant

It's very often a challenge for others in the organization to see the chief ethics and compliance officer as 'on their side' – an asset to the business rather than an impediment. Shifting an ingrained perspective like this takes time, but it can be helped by extending the compliance role more directly into the business agenda. For example, the chief ethics and compliance officer might choose to champion at least one of the organization's values – not just the things that are closest to the 'compliance role' like integrity, ethics, fairness, respect, but those which are perceived as driving the business, such as teamwork, innovation, excellence or performance.

Of even greater appeal to the business will be your ability to do things like:

- using stories and anecdotes to make what you have to say relevant, interesting and memorable;
- inviting business leaders and managers to your functional meetings and away-days to contribute their perspectives and challenges.

Developing your style

What you are trying to do is create visibility across the business through marketing and networking in order to develop the active vigilance of a community. Having a presence across the organization is part and parcel of an effective programme.

However your style develops, a common trait must be proactive engagement. The aim is to be invited into discussions rather than being left behind, and that starts with simple things, like these:

- giving a short presentation at management away-days on a hot topic or potential area of opportunity in which compliance and ethics subject matter expertise can help create a competitive advantage;
- engaging with HR to include compliance and ethics training in all management and leadership training, whatever the level at which it applies.

Role description for a chief ethics and compliance officer

If you are trying to write down the chief ethics and compliance officer's job responsibilities, the following non-exhaustive lists may help.

General responsibilities

The CECO should be responsible for the following:

- Design, implement, oversee and monitor a best practice ethical compliance and ethics programme appropriate to the size of, and risks faced by the organization.

- Help the organization to assess and manage compliance risks.
- Help to embed a culture of ethics and integrity.
- Act as a business partner to help ensure that line management understand and accept their accountability for compliance.
- Perform a second line assurance monitoring role consistent with the above.
- Create and working closely with a network of suitably competent compliance officers.
- Work closely with any Internal Audit and Risk Management functions and, potentially, with external independent assurance providers.
- Help to enhance the organization's reputation for compliance and ethics through:
  - external reporting;
  - stakeholder engagement;
  - profile raising at external seminars;
  - thought leadership;
  - fostering and participating in collective action.

Specific duties

- Help identify and assess compliance risks.
- Promote and raise awareness of compliance risks, procedures, issues and initiatives.
- Review the extent and effectiveness of compliance policies and procedures.
- Recommend necessary improvements to compliance policies and procedures, and ensure that they are implemented.
- Identify compliance training needs and audiences and deliver or oversee the delivery of appropriate training.
- Provide expertise and guidance on compliance to the organization's business units or functions and collaborate and share best practice with other compliance officers.

- Answer questions from employees about the code of conduct and other compliance procedures and generally be a subject matter expert on compliance and the code of conduct.
- Play an appropriate, agreed role in compliance approval procedures.
- Act as the main communication channel regarding reporting of incidents and allegations of non-compliance.
- Oversee or quality-assure compliance investigations.
- Participate in, oversee and/or help to design and coordinate compliance monitoring, auditing and other assurance activities.
- Provide reports and data on compliance risks and issues, and compliance and ethics programme implementation.
- Act as an ambassador for compliance, ethics and integrity at the organization, both internally and externally.

'Mind the gap'

We've all seen it: the ball is passed. Then there's a mix up. One member of the team thinks it is meant for another. So neither takes it. Instead, the opposition do. The game is lost.

So who's actually in charge of compliance and ethics? Is it the chief ethics and compliance officer? After all, they're responsible for implementing an effective programme.

But compliant and ethical behaviour are a requirement and responsibility of everyone in every business function engaged in any activity that has the potential to create a compliance and ethics risk.

However, overlapping responsibilities create confusion, inaction or contradictory actions – or all three at the same time. Where there are gaps there is the potential for risk to fester and materialize into a real issue. And if it does materialize, there is potential for significant consequences to the organization and individuals.

That's why identifying where there are overlaps or gaps in responsibilities involving compliance and ethics risks is crucial to an effective compliance and ethics programme. Each player needs to know what their role is in helping the team to stay compliant and competitive.

Other specialist functional responsibilities

For some subject matter areas, the Compliance and Ethics function will assume primary responsibility. But there are particular areas that may be allocated to other functions such as Finance, Tax, Environment Health and Safety, Human Resources, Information Technology, Company Secretarial, or Corporate Social Responsibility.

Figure 14.1 identifies the typical compliance responsibilities assumed by other functions.

However, depending on the nature of the organization, its product and service lines, its size and geographical spread, and its risk profile there may be other specialist compliance functions with important legal or ethical compliance responsibilities. Figure 14.2 illustrates some of the possible interactions.

The reality is that all functions within an organization have some compliance-related responsibilities for reasons of operational efficiency and subject matter familiarity and expertise. For example, HR is better placed to develop, implement, monitor, enforce and improve working practices within the employee workforce. Likewise, Finance is better placed to manage financial controls and reporting.

From Figure 14.2 you can see that a number of functions appear more than once, and the Compliance and Ethics function often performs an unofficial role acting as a liaison officer between them. You may also notice that 'Legal' appears as a collaborative function in every case. This is not unsurprising. Compliance is often derived from a statutory, regulatory or other legal construct – ie 'hard law'. Where it is not, the interpretation of the 'soft law' and consequences of non-compliance or non-application by the organization often require or benefit from legal input. For this reason, compliance responsibilities are often assumed by the Legal function either in their entirety or in part.

FIGURE 14.1 Compliance responsibilities assumed by other functions

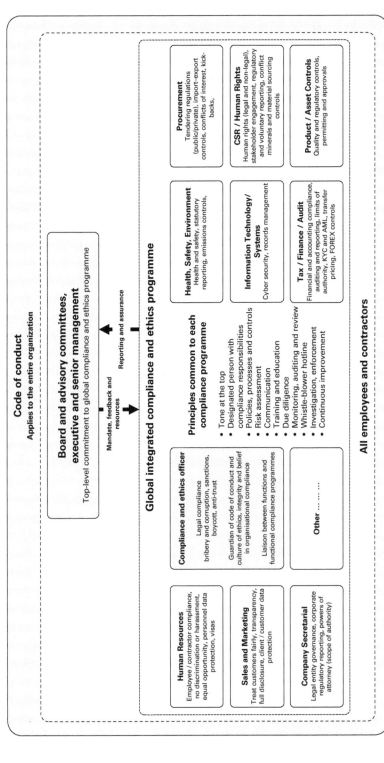

FIGURE 14.2 An integrated global compliance and ethics programme

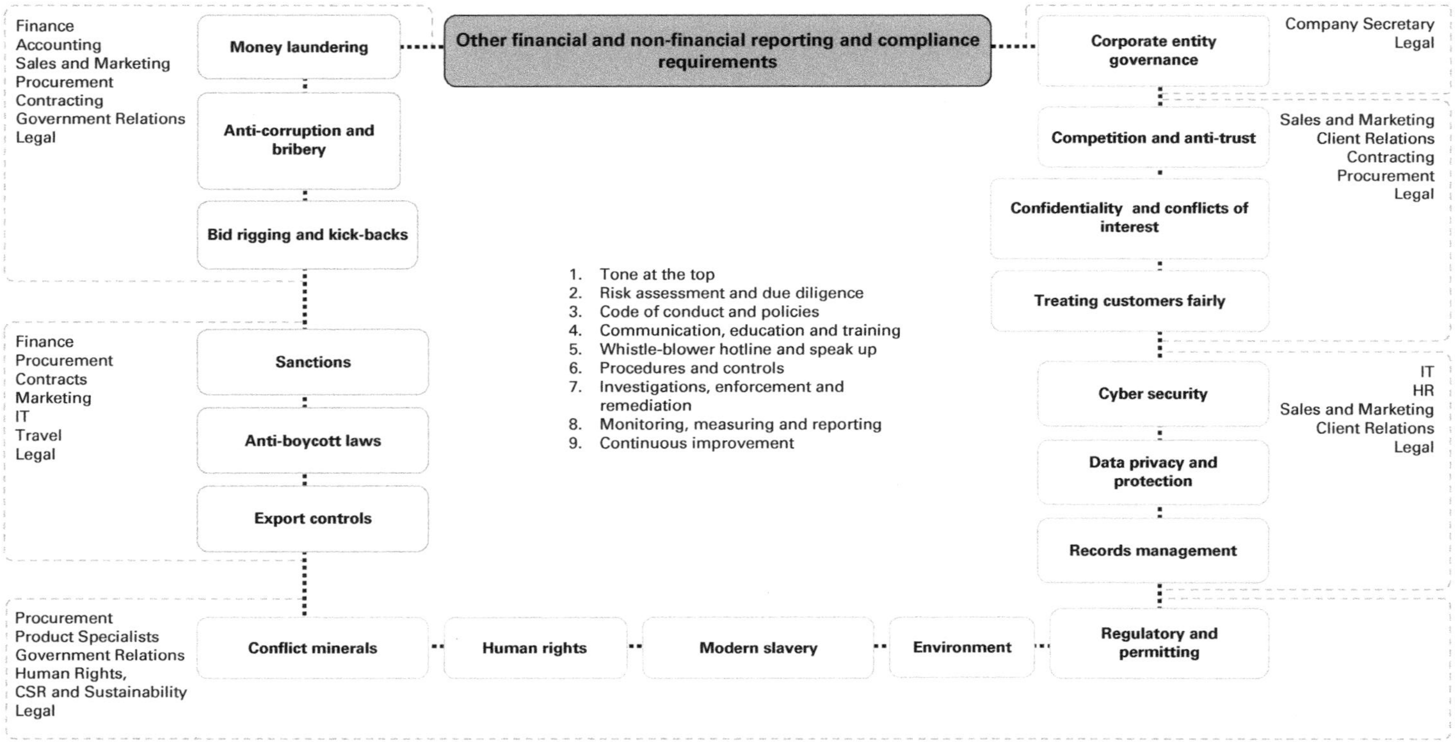

The role of management

Managers and, in larger organizations, the management team of any separate region or business unit, are responsible and accountable for ensuring:

- they conduct their business ethically and with integrity;
- that legal and reputational risks are identified and managed;
- and that their employees and third parties are complying with the organization's code of conduct and all applicable laws.

So they must:

- take all reasonable steps to ensure compliance;
- know that their compliance procedures are in accordance with the organization's expectations and requirements, and comply with the code of conduct and all relevant laws;
- and check that their compliance procedures are being effectively implemented.

The role of employees

When it comes to compliance, most organizations tend to think of their employees much as a shepherd thinks of his sheep – liable at any moment to wander off and cause all sorts of trouble unless watched over all the time. We hope this book has made it very clear that compliance does need to be systematic and programmatic. It needs to make rules – based wherever possible on shared values – and enforce them. But on its own that's not enough.

Effective compliance only happens when its ownership is shared by all the members of the community that it exists to protect. Yes, that means employees seeing that compliance and ethics are what shape the world they want to live in and the rules they want to live by. But it also means that they must be its willing and accountable champions.

This doesn't just ask organizations to re-imagine what compliance can be and can do for business performance. It asks employees themselves to take on the management of compliance too – all the way to the front line.

This is the cultural side of compliance and ethics that this book argues must be an equal part of the equation:

> If employees are trusted in a way that gives them room to exercise responsibility and own the values and rules that their compliance and ethics programme and code of conduct enshrine...
>
> and if they trust that they will be heard, supported and protected if they stand up to defend or improve those values and rules...
>
> that then provides fertile ground for a culture of willing compliance to take root.

It may be your business, but in the end it's their ship.

So in the end, who is responsible for effective compliance?

- The chief ethics and compliance officer? Yes.
- The CEO? Yes.
- The executive board? Yes.
- Managers? Yes.
- Employees? Yes.

Compliance doesn't play alone or in isolation. It's a team game. It's the business of everyone.

Across the minefield: compliance and ethics meets real life

Out of sight, out of mind

You propose a review of your compliance programme to ensure you have the most up to date information on what regulators expect and an external view on where there may be room for improvement. Your request is turned down. 'Why give the answer to the regulators?' and 'Out of sight, out of mind. We'll deal with it if anything comes up.'

Changing the system that lines pockets

You are new to the company and you notice that meetings with the regulator always seem to take place at one of several five-star hotels outside of the city. The meeting agenda is structured such that it requires at least one night, but more typically two. The company has to cover the immediate costs of travel, a per diem for each regulatory attendee, and hotel expenses.

You ask yourself why such meetings can't use the company meeting facilities and board room, the costs of which are already borne by the taxpayer. You also learn that the government officials will double up in their hotel rooms, and have arrangements with the hotels to receive the monies the company has paid for the unused hotel rooms.

The response given is that this is the way it is done – they're the regulator and they will make it difficult.

'It's up to you'

They're investigating an incident. Someone got so badly injured that they'll never be able to work again – and they've got three young children. The company will provide a generous compensation package. There's just one problem – you saw what happened and you know it was entirely the fault of the injured person.
Speak up or say nothing?

You only have only competitor. You know the price they're offering. If you undercut them, you'll push them out of the market and you'll then be able to charge whatever you want. So you go ahead and undercut them, though your price is a temporary loss-maker for your company.
Fair enough?

Someone on your team has weight problems. There are lots of jokes about it, and you know it's really upsetting them. But when you ask, they say they don't want to complain because then everyone would think they're not a team player.
Leave well alone?

One of the designers keeps leaving the drawings for a new engineering concept lying on his desk overnight. There are valuable new innovations involved. You've already suggested that they put the designs away but have been told to mind your own business. *Should you?*

Note

1 A Maslow (1966) *The Psychology of Science: A reconnaissance*, Harper & Row.

A final word

So what's the future of compliance and ethics?

One of us worked for someone who would say, 'Never mind a values-based compliance programme – I would settle for people just following the damn rules.' But as we have shown in this book, it is hard to communicate copious rules and make sure they are understood. People don't have the bandwidth anyway. Most importantly, they don't have the motivation.

So, what's the future of compliance and ethics?

Will it go the way we have argued it should? To be effective rather than merely defensible? To rely far more on culture, values and trust than rules and monitoring?

Maybe it has to. Compliance requirements and expectations are growing at a rate that shows no sign of slowing; they are increasingly informed by stakeholders' ethical demands; and organizations and their staff will not have the capacity to manage these risks and meet these expectations through the old, failed approach.

Or, much more to the point, does this mean we see a way in which organizations will become less prone to scandal and more in tune with their role as a positive and positively influential part of society?

And do we think that aberrant individuals are more likely to be stopped or exposed by those around them before they do too much harm?

The honest answer is... it depends whether the approach we advocate is the one that wins the argument. Will it? Yes. And no – but perhaps the nos have it right now by a margin.

Why do we say that? Well, it's in part because the agenda we have set out in this book is still misunderstood or resisted by many in business who continue to see compliance and ethics as the enemy of enterprise culture.

And it's in part because compliance and ethics is still not recognized or registered by the majority of people as their friend – a defender and protector of what they value and the world they wish to live in, one they in turn must defend and protect.

But there are other currents and forces in play that offer both hope and threats.

The biggest is what we have just mentioned at the top: ever-growing compliance requirements and expectations are increasingly informed and fuelled by stakeholders' ethical demands and organizations' recognition that they need to be socially responsible. This is potentially very positive – unless, that is, the response is to erect vast thickets of rules and enforcement, and ignore the critical importance of getting the crew to understand it's their ship.

Another major factor will clearly be the ascendancy of technology and artificial intelligence. As we've already stated in this book, technology is very much a two-edged sword. It is already changing the way in which organizations – and regulators – approach compliance. The reasons are, on the surface, good ones: accessibility, user-friendliness, much greater control at much less cost, the ability to monitor, analyse and extrapolate information that can help to shape policy and strategy.

Technology can also help by making it easy to disseminate and gather information, to identify training needs and create and deliver content, and by improving risk assessment and approval workflows. It fact it can be used to systematize and improve most procedures, and to generate data that makes measurement potentially more meaningful. And AI will increase the power and adaptability of technology exponentially.

But technology does not lend itself to culture change, embedding accountability and a values-based approach. Instead, it tempts organizations, regulators and champions of defensible compliance towards more procedures and controls, and more monitoring. Moreover, regulators and prosecutors will expect organizations to use technology: 'You could have controlled or monitored that activity more, but you chose not to.' So it can be risky for organizations to ignore it.

There is a very real potential downside here if, as a result, compliance and ethics becomes a mechanical, non-human tick-box exercise that simply takes place in the virtual world. In such a scenario, defensible compliance is likely to continue to predominate, along with reasons to reduce investment, time and resources.

What's more, as AI technologies are used to gather increasing amounts of information about individuals, their use can be increasingly viewed as intrusive.

This is already happening, and in certain areas of the world the consequences are becoming all too apparent. Employees come to see the company they work for not as something whose mission, purpose and values they believe in, and not as a culture they share and own, but as a remote and prying Big Brother bent on control. When that happens, then compliance, and the means organizations use to engage their employees in it, is likely to be resented and resisted by default.

Possibly one can look at this as a positive opportunity: equip and encourage staff to take a values-based approach, cut down on the rules and procedures, and monitor how they do. Then again, who wants to work for an organization that is going to monitor your every move?

But none of this needs to be the future, and it will not be if organizations recognize compliance and ethics as a vital resource in building a sense of shared purpose, and a shared mission to succeed within a working environment that people value and cherish together.

A values- and ethics-based compliance programme can provide clarity and advice around what the right decisions and actions are, but it is only when that programme is brought to life within a culture everyone cares about and endorses that an organization will become self-compliant.

In such an organization, people will ask or check when they are not sure; challenge when they see something that appears to go against what their community and culture value and report it when they believe something is not right, knowing they will be supported and action will be taken.

To return to the place we began, *really effective compliance* is the voice of the community it belongs to, and can only be achieved when the Sun and the Wind are working together.

INDEX

Abrashoff, Michael 12–13
accountability 75–77
across the minefield *see* real-life situations
Age of Damage 11
aid sector, consequences of compliance
   failure 5–6
artificial intelligence (AI) 79, 344–45
assurance 99, 289–305
   auditing 290
   components of 290
   functional assurance 291, 292–93,
      295–96
   implementing a compliance and ethics
      assurance network 291–99
   independent assurance (internal and
      external) 291, 292–93, 296–99
   independent compliance monitor 302–03
   management assurance 291–94
   measurement and reporting 303–05
   measurement of compliance 289–90
   measuring ethical targets 304–05
   monitoring 290
   need for 289–90
   quantitative versus qualitative
      assurance 299–302
   SMART objectives 304
   visible commitment from the top 301–02
   whistle-blowing statistics 303–04
auditing *see* assurance
authentic pursuit of compliance and
   ethics 2–3
authentic storytelling 69–70
authority, unquestioning obedience to 55–56

balanced scorecard approach to bonuses 51
barriers to success 41–60
   battle for hearts and minds 42–44
   burden of effective compliance
      implementation 56–58
   charismatic leadership 55–56
   complacency 47–48
   corruption 54–55
   culture 51–56
   doubt 42–44
   human psychology 45–47
   ineffective compliance officer 59

ineffective ethics champions 43–44
knee-jerk reaction to compliance
   issues 47–48
lack of management time and
   attention 58–59
lack of resources for compliance 56–58
need for awareness of 41
negative perceptions of compliance 59
power distance 54–55
scepticism 42, 43
short-termism 59–60
silence in the face of unethical
   conduct 48–50
unclear responsibility for compliance 45
uncommitted people 44
unquestioning obedience to
   authority 55–56
see also compliance failure
best practice in compliance, development
   of 26–27
Big Data 79
bonuses, balanced scorecard approach 51
bribery 22, 25, 26, 135, 141–42, 144–46,
   175–77, 181–94, 220–22
bureaucracy, compliance and 73–74
burning platforms, knee-jerk reaction to
   compliance 47–48
business, role in society 2–3
business ethics, definitions 32–33
business mission, compliance viewed as
   irrelevant to 19
business values, versus personal
   values 66–68

Carillion, collapse of 33
CECO *see* chief ethics and compliance
   officer
charismatic leadership 55–56
charitable donations 193–96
chief compliance officer xxii
chief ethics and compliance officer
   (CECO) xxii, 112
   challenge of bringing about
      change 61–63
   consequences of ineffectiveness 20, 59
   developing your style 332

chief ethics and compliance officer
(CECO) (*continued*)
finding and working with
champions 121
ideal model 329–32
making what you do relevant 331–32
need for authority and resources 19
potential conflicts with the legal
function 317–18
qualifications 313–16
reaching out and building a
network 330–31
role 312–13, 332–34
see also communication, education and
training
chief executive officer (CEO) 111–12
clients, communication with 218–20
code of conduct and policies 94–95, 165–75
charitable and community
donations 193–96
commercial sponsorship 194–96
common problematic policy
areas 180–99
conflict with local culture or
laws 199–200
conflicts of interest 188–90
corporate policies 175–76
dealings and links with customers'
representatives 193
dealings and links with public
officials 190–94
dealings with business partners/third
parties 197–98
definition and function 167–68
encouraging everyone to read it
and live it 166–7, 169–70
establishing the rules 167–68
facilitation payments 184–88
gifts 180–84
hospitality 180–84
language used 166
level of detail in a code 176–77
lobbying 196–97
overarching status of the code of
conduct 169
political contributions 193–94
purpose 169
red flag checklist 191–93
supplier codes of conduct 178–80
why it is special and why it matters 169
why principles alone won't work 168
why rules alone won't work 168
code of conduct creation 171–75

construction principles 173–74
easily accessible information 172–73
interactive guide 172–73
level of detail 176–77
precision 171–72
what it should cover 174–75
collective action initiatives on
corruption 220–22
collective effort 70
commercial interests, conflict with
ethics 79–80
commercial sponsorship 194–96
communication, education and
training 95–96, 203–24
approach to communication 223
being useful and convenient 214
bringing the issues to life 207–08
communicating compliance and ethics
policies 203–04
communication in collective action
initiatives 220–22
communication versus education and
training 205
communication with consortium and JV
partners 217–18
communication with third
parties 216–17
creating awareness 205
making e-learning more effective 215–16
making time for training 214–15
making training land with your
audience 206–15
measuring effectiveness 216
positive case for training 214–15
target leaders and management first 207
training examples 208–13
training versus education 206
turn employees into communicators and
teachers 213
using real-life dilemmas and values
moments 208
with clients, investors and other
stakeholders 218–20
work with what you have 214
community donations 193–96
complacency, barrier to effective
compliance 47–48
compliance
business need for 21–22, 61
definitions 29–30
establishing ownership among everyone
involved 12–13
features of effective compliance 13

history of 22–28
integrity-based approach 23
interaction with culture 16–17
making it effective 12–13
power of business to circumvent the
    law 21–22
principles-based approach 23
scale of the task 61–63
social need for 23–25
use of alternative terms for 81
compliance and ethics
avoiding gaps in responsibility 334–35
continuous evolution of practice 35–36
definition 16
ever-growing requirements and
    expectations 343–45
evolution from voluntary to
    mandatory 35–36
future of 343–46
future role of technology 344–45
other specialist functional
    responsibilities 335–36
in practice 35–36
responsibilities assumed by other
    functions 335–36
responsibility for 45, 334–39
compliance and ethics champions 318–21
Compliance and Ethics Committees 100–01
compliance and ethics function
centralized versus decentralized 324–25
example structures 321–24
position within the organization 312–13
positive influence on business 72–73
potential conflicts with the legal
    function 317–18
quantity over quality approach 9
role as a business partner 72–73
separation from the legal
    function 316–18
size of 311–12
structuring 313–25
viewed as a hindrance to the
    business 72–73
compliance and ethics programme
appropriate for the organization 65–66
assurance 99, 289–305
centralized versus decentralized 325–26
code of conduct and policies 94–95,
    165–75
communication, education and
    training 95–96, 203–24
consequences of failure 38
continuous improvement 99–100, 305–07

definition 37–38
due diligence 93–94, 135–62
factors influencing effectiveness 101–02
feedback 95–100
fitting into the organizational
    structure 101–02
getting agreement and ownership 63–65
holistic and integrated approach 88
holistic and multidimensional
    nature 65–66
implementation 311–39
integrated global programme 337
investigations, remediation and
    enforcement 98–99, 265–85
keeping it alive 81–82
key components 90–100
long-term focus 81
organizations' need for 15–16
procedures and controls 97–98, 247–61
range of applications 74–75
rewards of success 39
risk assessment 93–94, 135–62
road to compliance 87
simplifying the complexity 68–69
SMEs 88–90
speak-up culture see whistle-blowing and
    speak-up culture
starting points 88
storytelling 69–70
top-level commitment 90–93, 111–31
values-based approach 345–46
whistle-blowing and speak-up
    culture 96–97, 227–44
compliance clause, length and
    complexity 254–57
compliance failure
caused by deliberate scepticism 19
caused by wilful dishonesty 20
compliance viewed as an
    impediment 10–11
consequences of 5–6, 38
culture and 7
defensible compliance view 9–10
doing the legal minimum 10–11, 17
human factor 6–7
incentives and compliance objectives not
    aligned 18
ineffective approach to compliance 7–9
ineffective compliance leaders and
    officers 20
lack of incentive to follow the rules 7–9
lack of leadership 17
lack of management accountability 18

compliance failure (*continued*)
  lack of relevance to the business
    mission 19
  no sense of ownership of the
    programme 18–19
  programme is not driven by ethics and
    values 18
  rules- and obedience-based
    programme 18–19
  viewed as policing the business 19
  see also barriers to success
compliance officer *see* chief ethics and
  compliance officer (CECO)
conduct risk 135
conflicts of interest 188–90, 260–61
consumers, demands for responsible
  business 10–11
continuous improvement 99–100, 305–07
controls *see* procedures and controls
corporate culture *see* culture
corporate policies 175–76
corporate scandals 2–3, 21–22, 54
corporate social responsibility (CSR) 33
corruption 21–22, 135, 220–22
Corruption Perceptions Index (CPI) 54–55
country risk assessment 149
cultism 56
culture
  creating a compliance culture 14–15
  definitions of corporate culture 51–53
  ethical culture 71
  ethics-based organization culture 16–17
  influence from the top of the
    organization 130
  interaction with compliance 16–17
  local culture 53–55
  potential barrier to compliance 7, 51–56
  role in effective compliance 13, 14, 63
culture of responsible accountability 75–76

decision-making, ethics versus commercial
  interests 79–80
defensible compliance view 9–10
dishonesty, threat to compliance 20
donations, charitable and community
  donations 193–96
doubt, barrier to compliance success
  42–44
Drucker, Peter 51
due diligence 93–94, 135–62, 257–58

education *see* communication, education
  and training
emotional competence 92

employees
  expectations of organizations 84
  need for a sense of ownership of the
    programme 18–19
  need to see the relevance of compliance 19
  response to rules and regulations 18–19
  role in compliance
    implementation 338–39
enforcement *see* investigations, remediation
  and enforcement
ethical culture 71
ethical dilemmas 32–33
ethical origins of compliance 22–23
ethical targets, measurement 304–05
ethical values 32
ethics 18, 30–33, 34–35, 79–80 *see also*
  compliance and ethics
ethics-based competencies of job
  candidates 71
ethics-based organization culture 16–17
ethics champions, challenge to be
  effective 43–44
Ethics Committees 100–01

facilitation payments 184–88
fake news 2
feedback 95–100, 243–44, 265
Fink, Lawrence 33

gagging orders 49
gifts 180–84, 258–60
Giono, Jean 61–62
Global Infrastructure Anti-Corruption
  Centre (GIACC) 107, 222
governance procedure for investigations 276
guidance sources and standards 102–07
  for SMEs 88–90

head of ethics and compliance xxii
health and safety culture, lessons from 14,
  27, 50, 67, 257
Health and Safety Executive (UK) 24–25
history of compliance 22–28
Hofstede's Cultural Dimensions 54–55
hospitality 180–84, 258–60
human factor in compliance failure 6–7
human psychology, nudge theory 45–47
Human Rights and Business Dilemmas
  Forum 32

implementation of a compliance and ethics
  programme 311–39
  burden of effective compliance
    implementation 56–58

deploying the right skills and resources 328–29
examples of compliance and ethics structures 321–24
influence of the size of the compliance function 311–12
in JVs, subsidiaries and conglomerates 326–28
position of the compliance and ethics function within the organization 312–23
qualifications of the CECO 313–16
responsibility for 334–39
role of employees 338–39
role of management 338
role of the CECO 312–13, 329–34
structuring the compliance and ethics function 313–25
using 'compliance and ethics champions' 318–21
in-betweeners, barrier to compliance success 44
incentives, alignment with compliance and ethics 50–51
incentivizing accountability 76–77
independent compliance monitor 57
Institute of Business Ethics (UK) 222
integrity 23, 34–35, 53, 81, 207
investigations, remediation and enforcement 98–99, 265–85
assessing the significance of the case 277–78
basic principles 272–73
being fair, consistent and even-handed 269–70
disciplinary proceedings 276
ensuring the investigation is independent 275
ensuring the process is just 279–80
external resources 281
good practice guidance 271–82
governance procedure 276
handling whistle-blowing and other reports 277–78
having the right skills and guidance 270–71
importance of enforcement 266–69
investigator's perspective 282–85
making decisions based on the evidence 280–81
pitfalls to beware 282–85
preparing an investigation plan 278–79
remedial action and sanctions 98–99, 281–82
reporting an employee to the police 273

reporting the findings of fact 275
role of HR 274
when an organization should self-report 267–69
when the need for investigation arises 265–66
who should be involved in internal investigations 273–74
ISO 37001 (Anti-Bribery Management Systems) 89, 104, 176, 232, 237, 327

joint-stock corporations, risk to society 24–25
joint venture (JV) partners, communication with 217–18
Jones, David 66

Korenchuk, Keith 317–18

laws, ethical and non-ethical origins 22–23
leaders
charismatic leadership 55–56
commitment to the compliance and ethics programme 15, 90–93
emotional competence 92
influence on compliance behaviour 14
lack of commitment to compliance 17
personal leadership culture 55–56
problem of ineffective leaders 20
see also top-level commitment
legal function, separation from the compliance function 316–18
libertarian paternalism theory 46–47
limited liability corporations, risk to society 24–25
Lincoln, Abraham 21–22
lobbying 196–97
local culture 53–55
local management, influence of 118–20
long-term focus 81

management
commitment to the compliance and ethics programme 15, 58–59, 90–93
influence on compliance behaviour 14
lack of accountability for compliance 18
role in compliance implementation 338
see also top-level commitment
Mandelstam, Nadezhda 50
Maslow, Abraham 311
Me Too movement 22
measurement see assurance
middle management, influence on compliance behaviour 14

Milgram, Stanley 55
Mill, John Stuart 48
money laundering, anti-money laundering
    compliance 141–42
monitoring *see* assurance
moral compass 32
moral dilemmas 32–33
morals 30–31
motivating compliance 77–78

NGO scandals 2–3, 5–6
non-disclosure agreements 49
non-ethics-based compliance 23
nudge theory 45–47, 78

organizational culture *see* culture
organizational structure, position
    of the compliance and ethics
    function 312–13
organizations
    Age of Damage 11
    appropriate compliance and ethics
        programme 65–66
    compliance viewed as an
        impediment 10–11
    compliance viewed as policing the
        business 19
    defensible compliance view 9–10
    doing the legal minimum on
        compliance 10–11
    exposure of abuses of power 22
    holding to account 28
    incentives aligned with compliance and
        ethics 50–51
    incentives and compliance objectives not
        aligned 18
    incentivizing accountability 76–77
    integrated compliance and ethics 74–75
    need for a compliance programme 15–16
    power to circumvent the law 21–22
    reasons for compliance failure 17–20
    shareholder and stakeholder
        demands 10–11
    stories told about 69–70
    when commercial interest conflicts with
        ethics 79–80

performance appraisal 76–77
personal leadership culture 55–56
personal values, versus business
    values 66–68
persuasion, art of 64
political contributions 193–94

power distance, tolerance of corruption
    and 54–55
principles-based approach to compliance 23
procedures and controls 97–98, 247–61
    compliance clause 254–57
    compliance risk assessment 252
    conflicts of interest 260–61
    contracting 253–54
    definition and purpose 247–48
    due diligence 257–58
    financial controls 251–52
    gift and hospitality procedures 258–60
    high-risk third party approval and
        monitoring 253
    HR procedures 251
    identifying where procedures are
        necessary 248–49
    procurement/supply chain
        management 252–53
    specific to compliance and ethics 257–61
    tendering/client/commercial controls 252
    types of 251–54
    ways that procedures can help 249–51
procedures-based compliance 247–48
project/transaction risk assessment 150–51
propaganda, versus authentic
    storytelling 69–70
psychology
    nudge theory 45–47
    of risk 136–37
public officials, dealings and links
    with 190–94

RACI matrix 276
real-life situations
    accessing a colleague's computer in their
        absence 224
    allegations against a supplier 108
    allegations of incriminating activities in
        your supply chain team 223–24
    avoiding scrutiny of expenses claims 245
    awareness of bullying by a manager 309
    bribe required to gain access to
        healthcare 286
    business trip expenses 162
    carelessness with commercially sensitive
        material 341
    cash-in-hand ex-VAT quotations from
        contractors 245
    colleague makes homophobic comments
        on social media about team
        members 246
    colleague selling drugs 109

colleague under mental stress 132
colleague with an alcohol problem 201
colleague with insider knowledge of a
    government department 224
contract kick-backs 201
contract offer conditional on removal of
    your environmental programme 262
contractor attempts to circumvent gifts
    and hospitality policies 223
customs bribes 109
discovery a tradition of payments to local
    government officials 246
discovery that a client has been
    overcharged on a contract 286
discovery that a colleague has falsified
    expenses 224
discovery that a contractor practices
    religious discrimination 286
discovery that another company
    routinely overcharges your JV
    partner 286–87
double standards of support for
    staff 108
expensive gift from a supplier 109
gifts to customers 132–33
highly confidential email sent to the
    wrong person 262
inadvertent access to commercially
    sensitive information 201, 263
jokes made about a team member's
    weight problem 340
kick-back to an estate agent 108
loss of confidential information 309
manager prevents disabled employee
    from applying for a certain job 286
manager's behaviour has become
    unreasonable and aggressive 310
offer of sensitive information on
    competitors 133
person badly injured and you know it
    was their own fault 340
personalities and promotions 163
policy on business lunch expenses 200
political manoeuvring 162
pressure to provide excessive hospitality
    to the regulator 340
price fixing by a business partner 163
pricing at a loss to push a competitor out
    of the market 340
psychology of being challenged 131–32
recommending a relative for a post 163
reluctance to review the compliance
    programme 340

request for a contribution to a
    politician's charity 309
request to submit a bid with no intention
    of winning 246
share buying on insider information 133
stopping the rot 132
supplier found to be mistreating their
    employees 201
supplier hospitality offer near to contract
    renewal 201
suspected improper payments instructed
    by a majority shareholder 261–62
team member 'bad-mouthing' colleagues
    and managers on social media 287
temptation to side-step import
    regulations 163
uncool to remind other employees of
    company code of conduct 286
unfair contract tendering
    procedures 308–09
unfairness of price-match offers 262
variable environmental standards across
    the company's operations 245
when the team is willing to take
    risks 263
recruitment, ethics- and values-based
    competencies of candidates 71
remediation see investigations, remediation
    and enforcement
reputation, harm caused by corporate
    scandals 54
resources, requirements for effective
    compliance 56–58
responsible accountability, culture of 75–76
risk assessment 93–94, 135–62
    bribery risk assessment 144, 145–46
    conduct risk 135
    continuous improvement 148
    country risk assessment 149
    defining reasonable risk
        management 139–40
    general tips 146–47
    getting a clear understanding of the
        risks 144–46
    grading the risks 147
    managing the risks 148
    methodical approach 143–44
    planning and design 142–56
    problem with assessing risk 137–38
    project/transaction risk
        assessment 150–51
    psychology of risk 136–37
    reasons for assessing risk 138–39

risk assessment (*continued*)
  red flags 153, 159–60
  repeating and refreshing the risk
    assessment 148
  third-party risk assessment 152–53
  timing of 140
  understanding the relevant risks 138–39
  versus due diligence 140–42
risk management
  compliance as a form of 29–30
  integrated compliance and ethics 74–75
  third parties' compliance
    programmes 156–60
Robinson, Crawford 282–85
rules and regulations
  enhancing compliance with 12–13
  reliance on obedience to 18–19
  understanding the sense and importance
    of 12–13
rules-based compliance 247

sanctions *see* investigations, remediation and
    enforcement
scepticism, barrier to compliance success 19,
    42, 43
shareholder returns, influence of
    compliance 10–11
short-termism, barrier to compliance
    success 59–60
Siemens scandal (2006) 311
silence over unethical conduct, barrier to
    compliance 48–50
Sills, Beverly 87
Simon, Herbert A. 46
small and medium-sized enterprises
    (SMEs) xx-xxi, 74, 88–90, 320
SMART objectives 304
social media 22
social need for compliance 23–25
society, risk from limited liability
    corporations 24–25
speak-up culture *see* whistle-blowing and
    speak-up culture
stakeholders
  communication with 218–20
  demands for responsible business
    10–11
standards *see* guidance sources and
    standards
Steare, Roger 66
storytelling, versus propaganda 69–70
Sunstein, Cass 46
suppliers *see* third parties

tax havens 22
technology, influence on compliance and
    ethics 78–79, 344–45
terminology xxi–xxii
Thaler, Richard 46
third parties
  approval and monitoring procedures 253
  communication with 216–17
  compliance programmes 156–60
  risk assessment 152–53
  supplier codes of conduct 178–80
tone at the top 90–93, 112
top-level commitment 90–93, 111–31
  allocation of budget and resources 129
  consequences of inaction from the
    top 124–25
  elements of 122–26
  enabling perspective 126–30, 131
  enforcement perspective 130–31
  finding and working with
    champions 121
  fostering culture 130
  identifying the organizational 'top'
    115–20
  identifying the people at the top 114
  importance of consistent visible
    action 125–26
  influence of local management 118–20
  management time and attention 129
  positioning compliance and
    ethics 128–29
  spheres of influence 112
  spoken words 123–24
  tone at the top 90–93, 112
  what it looks like 113–20
  why it is critical 126
  written words 122–23
training *see* communication, education and
    training
Transparency International 54–55, 89, 221,
    222
trust 13, 81

United Kingdom
  Bribery Act (2010) 25, 26, 102–03, 106,
    180–81, 255, 256–57
  Corporate Manslaughter and Corporate
    Homicide Act (2007) 24–25
  Health and Safety Executive 24–25
  Ministry of Justice guidance 89, 102–03,
    106, 111
  Public Interest Disclosure Act 237
  Serious Fraud Office 267

United States
    Department of Justice 267
    Department of Justice Federal Sentencing
        Guidelines 25–26, 88–89, 102,
        104–05, 113
    Foreign Corrupt Practices Act (1977) 25,
        184–85, 254–55, 256
    origins of the modern compliance
        programme 25–26
    preamble to the Constitution 165, 166
    Securities and Exchange Commission 26

values 18, 31, 32
    personal versus business values 66–68
values-based approach to compliance 16–17,
    247, 345–46
values-based competencies of job
    candidates 71

Weinstein, Harvey 49
whistle-blowing and speak-up culture 22,
    49–50, 227–44
    anonymity issues 233–36
    branding 240–41
    characteristics of a speak-up
        culture 244
    culture and 53

designating cases as whistle-
    blowing 237–38
external whistle-blowing
    helpline 238–40
handling investigations 277–78
hotline 96–97
importance of 227–28
importance of communicating
    success 241–44
importance of creating a process people
    can trust 230–31
investigation and remediation
    procedures 236–37
making it live and work 240–44
part of a feedback process 243–44
problem with whistle-blowing 228–30
regional and cultural differences
    231–33
speak-up line 243–44
what it takes for someone to speak
    up 229–30
what to call the policy and
    helpline 240–41
whistle-blowing statistics 303–04
Wikileaks 22

zero-tolerance policies 14, 182

CPSIA information can be obtained
at www.ICGtesting.com
Printed in the USA
BVHW022132060122
625649BV00013B/750

9 780749 4829